D0228638

RACING IN THE DOCK

RACING IN THE DOCK

The Inside Story of the Biggest Scandal in Horseracing History

Richard Griffiths

ACKNOWLEDGMENTS

While this is not a situation to wallow in, huge thanks are needed all the same: to Brough Scott, Julian Brown, Adam Ward and Graham Dench for their invaluable help with this book, and longer term to James Underwood for a place at his academy!

Lots of love to my family and above all to Dawn for – how did she want this put? – her "love and support during journalism's darkest hours".

You also think of everyone in racing who played things by the book. No way should their achievements be overshadowed.

Extract from poem *Death of a Naturalist* by Seamus Heaney reproduced with kind permission of Seamus Heaney and the publishers Faber and Faber Ltd.

Published in 2002 by Highdown
An imprint of Raceform Ltd
Compton, Newbury, Berkshire, RG20 6NL
Raceform Ltd is a wholly owned subsidiary of MGN Ltd

A catalogue record for this book is available from the British Library.

ISBN 1-904317-09-X

Designed by Sam Pentin
Printed and bound in Great Britain by Biddles Ltd, Guildford and King's Lynn

CONTENTS

FOREWORD

Brough Scott

This is the story of the worst scandal ever to hit the British Racing scene, a nightmare scenario of mafia style corruption beyond our worst imaginings. This is a book that is needed when the fall out is still fresh. And Richard Griffiths is the only writer who could have set about the task.

For he is not only a first rate journalist, but is as independent minded as he is well-briefed on the racing scene. He neither indulges in the easy outsider "all racing is bent" innuendo nor retreats into the "it's all a load of rubbish" defensive corral. Richard Griffiths is someone who ended his eight years of sterling news and feature work with us at the *Racing Post* precisely because he wanted a bigger and wider challenge than we could offer. In this book he has found it.

Here I have to declare a responsibility. For it was my phone call in June 2002 that launched our author on his quest. For the previous 18 months he had been covering the trial of the Brian Wright gang as a freelance and on its conclusion wrote a summary of quite breathtaking completeness. Reading it was to finally realise how serious this particular cancer had been, and how important it was that its extent should be laid out for racing and the wider world to see. I have not had many good ideas. But this was one of them.

For this was a scandal which needed exposing with understanding as well as anger. Merely trumpeting the Dick Francis plus dimensions of the wrong doing would not be lesson enough. It required putting into context by a writer who knew how the racing pieces fitted, who could appreciate that a story sensational enough already would not need sensationalism in the telling. The result is often most shocking when the pages are at their coolest, when you begin to realise just how far the cat's cradle of connections had spread, when old jockeys like me have to reflect "there but for the grace of god would I...."

Because racing, and in particular jockeys, bit the apple of corruption the moment the first bet was struck all those years ago. Suddenly your every move or lack of it in sporting competition has the potential for someone else to win or lose. No other group of sportsmen have such an intensity of pressure, of hangers-on wondering "what chance yours tomorrow", of what first appears to be a wealthy admirer developing into something more sinister once the bets go wrong.

Over the years the vast majority of riders have handled that pressure with the same style and sense that got them to handle the galloping racehorse in the first place. But every now and then a problem begins to build and if the snake is not scotched early it can get a whole bench of riders under its sway. In my time the worst ever was in France which ended with jail sentences for more than half of the local top ten. I remember the charm of the "jock" who turned out to be the Mafia contact man. Somehow neither I nor my horse were apparently worth the serpent's kiss. But it could have happened. And this book is the most glaring proof ever printed as to how, for others, it has happened since.

Richard Griffiths remains a racing fan and in this book he has done his game a notable service. He has written a thriller with a purpose – that it should never, ever, happen again.

INTRODUCTION

THE END OF INNOCENCE

"Then one hot day when fields were rank
With cowdung in the grass the angry frogs
Invaded the flax-dam; I ducked through hedges
To a coarse croaking that I had not heard
Before. The air was thick with a bass chorus."

Seamus Heaney, *Death of a Naturalist*

I love horseracing.

It's been that way since I was 13 and watched agog as my older brother Ben swapped his 50-pence pocket money with a bookmaker, who gave him £16 in return. You couldn't help but be curious.

"Tell me more," I said. So he did. He told me to back two horses. Both losers. And it was fabulous. My first bets, and both, like another significant induction that springs to mind, were over in less than two minutes.

But for that short space of time those horses were mine. Mine to pick out amid the harlequin scramble of each race. Mine to cheer, to coax, urge and despair of. Mine to remember, with thanks, forever.

Take a bow, Le Moss. You fucked up at Newmarket, but indelibly shaped my life. It was the same with the other horse, Troy. I can still see him, taut and focused down at the start, waiting to be loaded for the Prix de l'Arc de

Triomphe. Even through the wires and cathode rays of our crappy TV, the occasion overwhelmed me.

There was something magnificent about the challenge that he faced. Troy had gone all the way to France, to Paris, to the golden glories of Longchamp in the autumn, to try to win his final race. It just all seemed so glamourous, worth knowing.

I can still remember the flash of colour as Troy pounded towards the finish, all heaving effort and stretched out legs, trying to get past the remaining two horses in front of him and shatteringly failing to do so.

Le Moss's entirely unpredictable defeat – at least that's what Ben said – meant that it mattered little whether Troy won from a betting point of view, but I wasn't thinking of grubby yellow dockets with faint signs of your handwriting on them. I was thinking: "How can I get more of this?"

The *Belfast Telegraph* gave me more. Every night I would come back from school and grab it. Turn to the back pages and there they were: Tomorrow's runners. No form, just names and races and numerals. I'd blindly try to work out which horses were coming into form and pick out the likely winners and then switch on the radio for the results to see if I'd got it right the night before.

This is what horseracing can do. It consumes you, blinds you to the humdrum. Let's you forget about homework and your adolescent woes. You keep scrapbooks, you draw diagrams of racecourses, you play racing board games, substituting the names of fictional horses for those you know, imagining that you are on them, competing against real life rivals.

Don't you?

And you bet. You dash into your local bookies, stake your five-pence yankee and run out again, before anyone asks what you're doing there. You go home, and you watch with untold excitement as your bet unfolds. Always a yankee. It took me 12 years to land one and only then after ruling out any horse that started higher than 1-3.

The bookies and the *Belfast Telegraph* weren't quite enough. I had to see things for myself. So my dad Bill (Bill and Ben? It's all a bit weird) would whiz me off to Down Royal racecourse, usually ending up at Downpatrick by mistake on the way.

There, at this pastoral course that neighboured the Maze prison and its infamous H-Blocks and even more infamous prisoners, I found peace. The thrill of seeing my first top-class horse – Monksfield! – cannot be shifted from memory.

Soon family holidays were being spent at York, where we would flock like pilgrims to the three-day Ebor meeting. We got to see Lester Piggott, wearing the Queen's colours, too, as a result of a horrible fall Willie Carson had there on Silken Knot. We backed him blindly, and gazed at his leathery contoured face as he cantered past us on his way to the start. York was where I wore my first suit. I looked a joke, but it didn't matter as I pretended to look knowingly at my racecard while absorbing the heady effects of an alien drink called Black Velvet.

Some of my mates sniffed glue. I never got that. What better than racing – with a little Black Velvet to provide your teenage kicks.

Compared to the small, tipping sheets I would devour each break, school mattered little. It was there to be 'mitched', certainly on the first Wednesday of June and without question for three fond days of March. They could not be spoiled. Afternoon registration, I was told, took on a resigned familiarity. My name was called out, no answer came, and the teacher would say: "Of course, it's Cheltenham." Detention was handed out and it was all very amicable.

York, Down Royal, the impossibly hilly inclines and fat, hairy athletes of Downpatrick, Cheltenham and the Derby on TV, how do you improve on that? Can you indeed?

Maybe.

All this time I had been thinking: "Imagine if you could make your living from horseracing, if somehow you could inveigle your way into that unspeakably intoxicating and seductive world. How great would that be?"

Very great is the answer. A horseracing journalist. Cor!

No one really has the right to be so lucky. To go to Ascot, Newmarket, Cheltenham, Epsom, the Prix de l'Arc de Triomphe, Breeders' Cup, Japan Cup. And be paid to do so.

Pinch me now.

I say all this to make clear that I never wanted to hear about the bad bits; never could I have imagined how awful things were; never could I have imagined that I'd be writing, as I am now, about the most sustained, systematic attack on the sport's integrity that there has ever been.

Never could I have foreseen the end of my adolescent idyll.

That's why I keep thinking of Seamus Heaney's naturalist and how without warning he obliviously came of age, of how his "nimble-swimming tadpoles" turned into noisy, threatening frogs, "Poised like mud grenades; their blunt heads farting.

I sickened, turned, and ran."

Running is no good. Ultimately, no one in racing can hide from the sport's own "great slime kings . . . gathered there for vengeance."

Nor should they. The issues are too Brobdingnagian to be ignored. Everything horseracing has dreaded has turned out to be going on right under its collective nose. Doping, bent jockeys, fixed races, drugs barons washing their money through racecourse betting rings. It's a dreaded litany, and it's one that's true.

Please don't think that racing is endemically crooked. That simply isn't the case. Nearly every race, nearly every day, takes place without cause for disquiet. The heroic moments and pulsating outcomes that we have all admired are unblemished by the tale that's about to be told.

Neither is this a tale without levity. As well as the wrongdoing and deception, the harrowing abuse of a magnificent pursuit, there's colour and character, even humour. There's sadness, too. Regret, hubris and that most common condition of all; human weakness.

Horseracing, in all its aspects, is never colourless. That's why I love it.

HEROIN FOR HORSES

Where there's betting, there's trouble. Always has been, always will be. Floodlights in football mysteriously go on the blink. Cricketers are wooed by sub-continental schemers. Racing is no different. People want to use it to make money by cheating.

Betting is about winning, as is any sport. No one should be surprised that people will bend the rules to do it. We have seen what lengths a procession of bionic-lunged, chemically hardened super-athletes are prepared to go to just so they can come out on top.

People will do the strangest things to do the same in horseracing. That's part of its charm, that it likes to flirt with the odd and outrageous. From its earliest days as an organised sport in the 18th century, racing has carried with it a scent of scandal.

Daniel Dawson did his best to enhance that image and ended up paying with his life. In 1812 he was convicted of fatally poisoning three horses with arsenic. He never meant to kill the horses, he said, just stop them from winning races. Dawson was hanged for his over-exuberance.

"If gentleman condescend to race with blackguards, they must condescend to be cheated." These were the wise, prophetic words of judge Baron Alderson after he had presided over a scandal that plagued the heart of British racing – the Derby itself, which was won in 1844 by a horse called 'Running Rein'. However, 'Running Rein' was in fact the four-year-old Maccabaeus.

At the start of the 20th century, one trainer, George Lambton, became so appalled at the level of doping in the game that he personally set out to expose it. Lambton knew of the antics of an American-born trainer, Enoch Wishard, who was based in Newmarket and had been yielding terrifically improved performances from his horses by giving them cocaine. Wishard and his associates were thought to have made up to £2 million between 1897 and 1901 by backing their own drugged horses.

(Incidentally, did you know that the slang term for heroin, 'horse', derives from its frequent use in nobbling favourites in America?)

To prove what was going on, and the incredible effects it was having, Lambton doped five moderate horses of his own and publicly declared his altruistic experiment after four had won and the other finished second, all showing vastly improved form.

Lambton achieved his aim of forcing racing's rulers, the Jockey Club, to recognise and be more alert to the perils of doping. The mischief continued, though. Inevitably. A former Australian soldier, Peter Barrie, was sentenced to three years hard labour at the Old Bailey in 1920 after he was found to have dyed brown the white facial markings of a talented hurdler called Shining More and backed her to win under a different name at Cheltenham.

Once more, in 1958, the Derby was desecrated. The pre-race favourite, Alcide, had to be scratched a week before the race following the effective but unsophisticated ploy of smashing his ribs.

Pinturischio, the ante-post favourite for the 1961 Derby and the expected mount of Lester Piggott, was 'got at' in the stable of his trainer, Sir Noel Murless. Pinturischio was given a purgative called croton oil, which was used on constipated elephants and rhinos. The mind boggles, especially when you consider that the late professional punter Alex Bird believed it may also have been used on a hugely promising two-year-old called Gorytus as recently as 1982.

In the same year as Pinturischio, the Ascot Gold Cup winner Pandofell was also doped at his trainer's yard, while suspicions surrounded the run of Pas Seul in the 1962 Cheltenham Gold Cup. His trainer, Bob Turnell, described the symptoms displayed by Pas Seul to Murless, who likened them to those suffered by Pinturischio.

Ribofilio's appalling run in the 2,000 Guineas at Newmarket in 1969 was never effectively explained either. Alex Bird was one of many onlookers convinced he had been nobbled. "Spectators watched in amazement as Ribofilio (ridden by Lester Piggott) walked past the post like he was drunk," wrote Bird. "Ribofilio was a great horse, ruined by the dirty deeds of the dopers. And that is what Lester thought too."

STUN GUNS

So we can see that modern day racing has hardly been pure. The problem, sadly, was not confined to the D'Arcy days of cads and breeches.

In 1982 owner Ken Richardson was handed a suspended jail sentence, fined and warned off by the Jockey Club for 25 years for his role in the Flockton Grey scandal. It emerged that he had run a three-year-old, Good Hand, in the guise of Flockton Grey to win a race for two-year-olds only at Leicester.

A car dealer from Peckham, James Laming, was involved in an ingenious exploitation of racing's reputation for hanky panky when, in 1989, he claimed that he had devised an ultrasonic gun, concealed in a pair of binoculars, to nobble a horse at Royal Ascot the previous year. That horse, Ile de Chypre, had jinked and unseated his rider, Greville Starkey, close to the finish line with the race at his mercy. Laming claimed that Ile de Chypre had been spooked by the sound of a high pitch wailing noise from his stun gun.

It's worth pointing out that Laming made this claim during a drugs trial in which he was asked to explain the presence of a large amount of cash in his car. That trial hit the front pages but soon became regarded as a bit of a joke. The same cannot be said of what's about to follow.

These tales – of fact, not fantasy, and all the nastier for it – also feature men in the dock who seek to cover-up their wrongdoing through claims of racing and betting derring-do. Sure, racing has always had its scandals. But none have proved as enduring, as devastating and shocking as this one.

FROM DICK FRANCIS TO FRANZ KAFKA

Brian Wright. Remember the name? You won't be able to forget it.

He is the man suspected not only of being in charge of one of Britain's biggest ever drug smuggling gangs, but also the man who has brought racing to its knees through his corrupt involvement in the sport for a period of at least 15 years.

That's a long time to wreak havoc.

Brian Brendan Wright had been involved in racing as a hard-hitting punter since around 1985, when the Jockey Club first received a tip-off warning of his alleged criminal links.

More serious news came in 1996 when the Jockey Club was told that Wright and his associates were conspiring with a group of jockeys – not many, but enough, probably less than 10 – to fix races. Chances are this had been going on for some time before. Dermot Browne, a former jockey and trainer, alleges that he helped fix races on Wright's behalf when he was a jockey in the late 1980s. Browne, a dashing character with a troublesome edge, says he was by no means alone.

Even more dramatically, we will hear how Browne's claim that he doped, on Wright's behalf, an astonishing 23 horses in a two-month burst in 1990. The Jockey Club detected only three of those dopings and remained ignorant of the vast majority until some years after, when their records no longer remained to cross-check whether Browne was telling the truth.

Browne pops in and out of this story like a pantomime villain. His tales of skulduggery are unarguably shocking and take us through a door to a place no one involved in horseracing truly ever expected to go. It's a dark place, corrupt, full of drama, intrigue and omnipresent uncertainty. The further you go through this door, the more inhospitable the landscape becomes, and the less confident you feel of escaping from it.

Some people dismiss Dermot Browne as a wild man with little respect for the truth. That would be convenient – and almost certainly wrong. He's no angel, for sure, but for his own reasons – reasons he will tell us about – he has probably done us all a favour. He has opened up our eyes to the dirty side of racing.

Racing's reputation has been badly soiled, no doubt about it, but remember the context: we can never be certain how many of Britain's 7,500 races each year have been, are being, and will be fixed. Bar actual admissions from trainers and jockeys that they have conspired to prevent a horse from running on its merits – and the chances of that are not good – the necessary level of proof will always be missing.

Suspicions are commonplace; intelligence, in a world that thrives on gossip, is less so. But proof? When it comes to fixing races, we hardly ever get a smoking gun.

Doping is, of course, a form of race-fixing, although it is a rarer phenomenon than that of a jockey not trying. It should, in theory, be easier to prove, as horses can be tested for illegal substances if they run inexplicably badly.

Have dopings gone unnoticed because dozy racecourse stewards have not ordered a horse to be tested? Chances are that they probably have. Dermot Browne's doping spree was off the scale. So bad, you'd like to think it could never happen again. Lessons have surely been learnt.

Not entirely. How many dopings have there been since 1990? We can't be certain, although you can count the number of confirmed cases on both hands. The most significant ones, two jumpers called Avanti Express and Lively Knight, came in 1997, just as the Jockey Club was preparing to hand over a dossier on alleged corruption in horseracing to the police.

Its intelligence was based largely on Brian Wright and suggestions that he had a group of jockeys on his payroll who provided him with privileged and bang up-to-date punting information – which is against the rules of racing – and even helped him fix races. Wright is thought to have become heavily involved in horseracing in the mid-1980s, when he was regarded as a fearless gambler, and only scaled down his illicit involvement in the sport between 1998 and 1999, when he was named as the man suspected of being at the helm of a massive cocaine smuggling gang. He did a lot of damage in between.

The Jockey Club's decision to call in the police had unimaginable consequences, starting with the out-of-the-blue arrest of three jockeys – Leighton Aspell, Dean Gallagher and Jamie Osborne – in January 1998.

Osborne was one of the very best of his profession. His arrest was hard to comprehend. It would be like a Manchester United player being lifted for match fixing.

Two other jockeys were arrested as part of the same investigation a year later, and these were even bigger names. One, Ray Cochrane, had won the Derby; the other, Graham Bradley, was one of the most charismatic and talented Jumps jockeys of his generation.

All were subsequently cleared from the investigation. Bradley was the only one of the quintet to be charged, although the allegations of race fixing against him were dropped within weeks.

In all, 15 people were arrested, the majority of whom did not operate directly within the sport. Five of them were charged and brought to trial, accused of engineering the dopings of Avanti Express and Lively Knight. The case collapsed on the grounds of insufficient evidence, making a mockery of a lengthy and expensive investigation that left horseracing's integrity stranded in a sea of highly damaging intrigue and rumour.

At the time it was widely assumed that the Jockey Club, in particular its security chief Roger Buffham, was as culpable as the police for the bungling of the case. We'll see about that.

Turn each page, absorb each chapter, and you won't be blamed for feeling that the tales of Dick Francis have come to life. A somewhat surreal case at the Old Bailey in February 2000 will only heighten that sense. It features Jamie Osborne, a former detective called Bob Harrington and the accusation that Harrington had told Osborne he could help him bribe his way out of the race-fixing investigations. Harrington was not only claiming to be working on Osborne's behalf, he had also been recruited as a well-regarded police informant.

It's not just Dick Francis that's coming to life. It's Roald Dahl, Joseph Conrad, even Franz Kafka. "Someone must have been telling lies about Joseph K, for without having done anything wrong he was arrested one fine morning."

Both Osborne and Harrington know what it's like to be arrested. Both, like Joseph K, the central figure in Kafka's menacing book *The Trial*, insist on their innocence. It's unlikely that they can both be right.

The jury decided that Harrington was the liar and he spent time in prison as a result. He is still around, though, and as befits someone with a career in undercover work, remains impressively 'in the mix'. Harrington, for example, led me to Dermot Browne when all other attempts were failing. I hadn't even been aware they knew each other.

Dermot Browne pops up in this trial. Not in person but with head-shaking suggestions that Osborne – who from the witness box strongly denied Browne's allegations – had been a naughty boy and accepted £20,000 to stop two horses on behalf of Brian Wright.

How did Browne inveigle his way into a case that outwardly had nothing at all to do with him? Read on.

In the meantime, let's consider Roger Buffham, a man who if he was given 10 pence by each of his friends in racing would struggle to buy a newspaper. Buffham lost his job in 2001, in circumstances that had nothing to do with his ability to do it. As part of a £50,000 settlement with the Jockey Club, he signed a confidentiality agreement that prevented him from disclosing details of any investigation he had been involved in.

That didn't stop him. To the undisguised fury of the Jockey Club – its normally restrained Senior Steward Christopher Spence described him as "a snake" – Buffham was found to be acting as an advisor to BBC's *Panorama* programme, which was compiling an investigation into racing's links with corruption. In particular, it would focus on the Jockey Club's ability to do its job, questioning whether it was as committed as it should have been to policing racing.

Things got ugly. Like cornered rats, the Jockey Club spent fortunes in the courts trying to prevent details of its security investigations entering the public arena. It successfully gagged Roger Buffham, with a strict injunction, which is why we won't be hearing too much from him.

Yet Buffham was *Panorama*'s chief witness, its 'whistleblower'. Much of its information came from documents he had retained – the Jockey Club say stolen – after leaving his job.

So back to the High Court, it was, this time for an attempt by the Jockey Club to stop *Panorama* using Buffham as a source. Bad move. It lost, just as the leading bookmaker Victor Chandler had done in a separate legal challenge against *Panorama*. The message from the judge's bench both times was that racing had some serious, ongoing integrity issues that a public, which wagers £5 billion of its money each year on the sport, had every right to hear about.

It also has every right to hear about the extent of Brian Wright's racing involvements. In shocking detail, the evidence of two trials at Woolwich and Southampton Crown Courts, concerning alleged drug smuggling, tell us the truth.

These trials, along with three others, concluded a massive Customs and Excise operation known as 'Extend', which featured the seizure of 494kgs, or £61 million worth, of cocaine. Brian Wright's cocaine.

Operation Extend resulted in the conviction of 16 people worldwide, who were between them handed sentences of more than 215 years. Among them was Wright's son, also known as Brian, who was one of seven men tried at Woolwich in a case that lasted 14 months, easily one of the longest in English legal history. Wright junior was found guilty of conspiracy to import and supply cocaine between 1996 and 1999 and sentenced to 16 years.

During his trial, which required you to go through heavy searches and police officers armed with machine-guns in order to attend, Wright gave a vivid portrayal of his father's racing empire. He did so in denial of accusations of cocaine smuggling. He was simply an employee of his father's racing empire, which earned fortunes through betting, not drugs smuggling, he said.

That wasn't all. He told how his father would bet in huge amounts, regardless of whether it was with legal or illegal bookmakers, would entertain some of the best jockeys British racing had ever seen, and had a contacts book that contained, in the words of one Jockey Club source, "almost every name in racing".

Remember one thing: as that source added, "it doesn't mean they were all 'at it'". Equally, as the senior steward Christopher Spence remarked: "It is perfectly fair to ask why they were in those books."

Here's the answer: at the very least, many – although very possibly not all – of the jockeys in the contacts books of both Brian Wright senior and junior were providing cherished, punting information. Exclusive, privileged information that the betting public had no clue about. That is most definitely against Jockey Club rules, especially when it's in exchange for financial or other rewards. Which was very often the case.

That was made abundantly clear during the Southampton trial of a former jockey, Barrie Wright, who is no relation to Brian. Barrie was accused – and acquitted – of conspiracy to import cocaine.

The trial further lifted the wraps of Brian Wright and his racing methods, through not only Barrie's own testimony but also that of his close friend Graham Bradley. It is astonishing stuff.

During both trials, the question of whether jockeys were helping to fix races was notably missing from the agenda. In no way should that mean that it doesn't occur. Brian Wright himself stepped out of the sunny shadows of exile to be quoted, in somewhat strange circumstances, in a newspaper interview in September 2002.

"I ran a huge operation and had a string of jockeys giving me vital information," the 57-year-old, who left Britain when his son was arrested in 1999, said. "If I needed a rider to win or lose a race, he did. If I wanted to fix a race, I could."

Brian Brendan Wright, we don't doubt you. Not for one moment.

Let's consider the evidence.

1

THE NEEDLEMAN AND THE DAMAGE DONE

In May 2000, Dermot Browne voluntarily gave an interview under caution, and using an alias, to police in a hotel in Ireland. Over three evenings and a total of seven-and-a-half hours, he provided a graphic, detailed and above all disturbing account of the part he had played in horseracing corruption. Browne told police officers from both sides of the Irish Sea of the names and races of the 23 horses he claims to have doped in a two-month period between August and September 1990 on behalf of Brian Wright.

It is an absorbing account that illustrates the ease with which the life of a man with troubles can freewheel out of control.

Should we believe him? Everyone will have their own view, although it is perhaps significant that this was the second interview Browne had given to police within the space of a few months. The two interviews are said to be consistent in their allegations and detail. Browne also took a probity test, with the conclusions favourable as to the veracity of his words. Such an assessment may amuse those who have known Browne; a man would be extremely rich if paid on every occasion he was described as "a loose cannon".

By his own admission, Browne was beginning to drink too much during this period, he had money worries and his career as a trainer was going nowhere fast. He was ripe for wrongdoing.

According to Browne, there are only two other people in the world who knew at the time what he was up to. One of them was an accomplice who was with Browne on every occasion that a horse was doped. We are going to call him Alfred. I know this man. He's alright. He doesn't deny the substance of what Browne has told the police. But he does question the exact detail. Browne, he says, would think nothing of dropping a mate in it, would not always take on board the consequences, would have no difficulty in changing what really happened to suit his own needs, and then "turn up 10 years later as if nothing was wrong".

Much of this chapter is based on Browne's own words, using the transcripts of his police interviews. Those words can't be dismissed out of hand. Too many times, too many things stack up. But it is also part of the deal with Dermot Browne that some of his tales will unravel.

That is the dilemma of the man. He makes claims that astound you, that grip you, but also frustrate and confuse you. As with so many of the incidents that have put racing in the dock, nothing comes with a complete guarantee.

There is one thing, though, that can't be disputed about what he says. More than anything, it's a hell of a story.

LEAVING GOODWOOD AT GUNPOINT

Having a gun put against your head is one reason for agreeing to dope racehorses. It happened to Dermot Browne at Glorious Goodwood, one of the highlights of the Flat racing calendar, on 2 August 1990, and it's not the sort of thing you forget.

Browne had recently fallen out with an owner who took away 11 horses from his Lambourn yard, with an obvious effect on income. At the time he had only two employees and not many more equine inmates. "So we were gradually trying to build up my yard again," he said in his police interview.

Needing to attract new owners, Browne had decided that picking up straw and gazing at empty boxes was no way of improving the situation, so he set out to schmooze. That is what he had been doing at Goodwood on the day he felt the cold, threatening heat of a pistol on his temple. And he had been doing it rather well. Using his contacts within the weighing room, Browne had found out the latest on which of the day's runners were fancied or not.

"I could go to the races, amble into the jockeys' changing room, speak to the riders about their chances on horses, and then go out and meet actual owners. I would say I had spoken to such and such a jockey earlier this morning or down in the sauna or in the jockeys' weighing room and he says he's got a good chance of winning, back this horse," he said.

"So they'd go off and back the horse and they might give you a hundred quid or a couple of hundred quid, so at least each day I went racing I would earn a few bob. The more times you give people a winner the more they'd gain confidence in your ability so that one or two people agreed to buy a horse and I started to work that way."

At Goodwood, Browne was entertaining a group that he said included George Michael, the pop singer, and his racing-mad father. Michael, a racehorse owner was not then the global superstar that he is now. The public inconvenience of his Los Angeles arrest was distant in the future. Nonetheless, Browne had clearly impressed some members of his group, who were talking about having horses with him. The yearling sales were coming up and one of them had dangled the carrot of a £10,000 to £12,000 commission to be pursued over dinner that night. Browne couldn't refuse. He was on a roll and needed new owners badly.

There was just one problem. "At this particular time I had a phone call from a gentleman in Newmarket wanting to send his son up to me for about six weeks for the holidays period for experience. He didn't want paying and that suited me fine. He said he was a good kid and he wanted to work in a yard and because of the fact that my father (Liam, a successful trainer on The Curragh in Ireland) had a good reputation for producing apprentice jockeys, he knew I'd look after him."

Browne arranged to meet the man's son that day at Goodwood, but "I decided that I couldn't really go and bring this young fella back to Lambourn now, I would stay and try and get me bit of business done and I was enjoying myself as well because there were a couple of nice women there."

The solution was to try and get the young man a lift back to Browne's house in Lambourn, so the trainer headed down to the Goodwood stables complex in search of one of Peter Walwyn's staff, who he knew well, to give him a lift in the trainer's horsebox. "They could drop him off at my house and I would sort him out myself in the morning," Browne said, without mentioning whether the young man ever made it to Lambourn. Hope he's not still waiting.

Browne walked across to the area where Walwyn's horses were stabled. Because he was a trainer, the security staff knew him well. No questions were asked. He saw people busy around a horse in one of the Walwyn boxes and walked straight in. "As I went into the stable, I looked first and thought I was in the right stable but I saw a few faces that I didn't recognise," he said, "and so I turned back. Then I looked again and it was the right number (on the box). So I made a comment like 'who are you, what are you doing here?'"

Few answers, just a needle and a gun. "I could see one guy stood to the side of the horse and put something into his pocket, which I obviously know now was a syringe, a needle and a syringe, and the other guy stood at the horse's head and as I walked in a fella came from left behind me and walked over and more or less said to me 'it's none of your business' and swore in a London accent. He basically produced a handgun, a small handgun. I wasn't used to seeing things like that. I knew these were the wrong people in the wrong place, type of thing. They didn't fit in with Peter Walwyn's stable lads, I knew that.

"They told me to turn around and follow them out and keep me mouth shut. The fella that stood at the horse's head came over and grabbed me by the arm and told me to walk out and said to me that I would have to go out through the doors into open space and not to walk across the grass, to go around the footpath, walk around and out through the gate and say nothing because he would be behind me. So I just did as I was told."

Browne was marched out of the archway of the racecourse stables to where the horseboxes were stationed. Browne's white jeep was already parked there. "I got there and they told me: give them the keys and they were on the phone a few times. I didn't know who they were talking to at the time (he soon would). I didn't hear much of the conversation, just more or less acknowledgement of one or two things.

"The fella that had the gun sat in the back beside me and the other fella, the taller fella, drove and the smaller fella that had the syringe sat in the passenger side." There were a lot of fellas and just as much confusion. The car headed to London. "I didn't say a word. There were plenty of things going on in my head," said Browne.

Bet there were, namely: "what the fuck is going on, what the fuck is going to happen to me?" As the jeep hit the summer streets of the city, Browne recognised the area he was in. It was Holland Park, a swanky part of west London that neighbours Kensington. The car stopped and Browne was escorted into a hotel that he also knew, the Halcyon: smart, expensive, chic, discreet.

Next stop the bar, where Browne recognised a man he knew from his riding days. Brian Wright.

THE WRIGHT DEAL

Brian Wright recognised Dermot Browne, too. "I knew him straight away and he knew me," Browne said. That might have saved him his life. "I went up to him and kinda he said to the guys 'it's alright lads'; in other words he knew me and (then) they were alright. It wasn't such a bad scene. Obviously he had been on the phone to them and they had been on the phone to him, discussing (how) they got caught and they were bringing this person to London.

"I said to Brian 'what the fuck's going on' (as predicted), and he sat me down and basically tried to explain to me the situation."

The situation, according to Browne, was that Wright, well known at the time as a major gambler, was seeking an edge with his betting. He had apparently woken up one morning and decided things weren't working. According to Browne, Wright was worried he would "end up skint" if he continued to pay jockeys to stop horses and lay horses as well as backing them.

The edge Wright decided he would seek was to dope horses. He said that one of Browne's former National Hunt colleagues had been recruited to do this, but had "bottled out" when push came to inject one day at Newton Abbot.

According to Browne: "Wright just sat me down and said to me would I be interested in getting involved in it now, and I knew everything was going on. He offered me £10,000 for it.

"All he said to me was 'look, you see it happens and if it's done just say yes and if it's not done just say it is not done. There is no problem if you say it's not done."

That's not bad money: £10,000 for overseeing a doping, although Browne was soon to discover that the deal wasn't quite as straightforward as it seemed. In the meantime, he sat at the bar and waited as Brian Wright made a call. Half an hour later another man turns up. This man – Alfred – was introduced by Wright "as the man who would provide the juice".

Alfred told Browne his juice was guaranteed to work and would knock 15 lengths off a horse on the Flat. He had used it "many times" before.

Browne had a decision to make: whether or not to join a doping gang. He was handed a few bob for his troubles and the return of his car keys. He drove back to Lambourn knowing there was some serious thinking to do.

THE THREE MUSKETEERS

Yes, was the answer. Browne rang back "a day or so later" and told Brian Wright he would do it. Wright moved quickly and sent him back to Goodwood that same day.

The deal, Browne thought, was straightforward. "He offered me money to basically oversee that other individuals were, you know, physically doping the horses. Or I had the option of doing it myself, depending on what way it was going to go.

"Basically, it involved meeting (with Alfred) before each race meeting. He would give me a syringe with about 2ccs of a substance in it, which I didn't know at the time what it was. I just called it the jungle juice.

"(Alfred) had indicated that he could get this stuff that would slow a horse down but he also mixed it with something else that wouldn't show up if the horse was dope tested.

"Whether he mixed something in with it or not I don't know. But I do know I have seen horses that I physically doped myself . . . and saw them run moderately and I saw them being brought into the veterinary box for examination afterwards. Yet nothing was ever said about it in the papers or by the Jockey Club."

The doping team had a masterplan, albeit a flexible one. They were looking almost exclusively at races with three or four runners, especially if there were two fancied horses, another with an outside chance and one with no chance. "Therefore Brian Wright could lay money on either the favourite or second favourite, whichever was doped, and then back the other one," Browne explained.

"Brian Wright would ring me having spoken to (Alfred). At the time, Brian Wright had people in a lot of major stables, all the Flat stables in Newmarket, maybe a travelling lad. Or he would have a senior stable lad, or work riders, guys who would have a jockey's licence but don't ride many races but they did ride regular race work at home so they would have a good indication as to whether a horse is galloping well or not. There is no point in going to a race and we will say: 'right, we will dope that' . . . then find out that horse has been galloping terribly. You know, we had to have that information as well."

Browne was told that only he Wright, and Alfred were in on the act, but he later believed that Wright was sharing the information with certain bookmakers, probably by laying bets as well as staking them.

Call them the Three Musketeers, if you like. But each of the trio had an important role to play. Wright would choose the race and do the punting, Browne, obviously, did the doping, although it became a source of frustration that he earned little money through betting. And Alfred? Alfred was key.

"He was a main core of it as well because he would turn up and have it (the drug, which we now know was ACP) measured out . . . already wrapped in their syringes in a damp cloth to hand to me," Browne said. "He would watch the horsebox arrive, noting the horse they wanted to dope as it came off the horsebox."

So not only did Alfred supply the juice, he also identified the target. Sometimes he would even ask to see the stable lad or lass of the horse concerned knowing it would provide a window for Browne to dope. "He used to say there were certain security men at certain racecourses he knew a bit better than others," Browne said. "He would see them on different days and they figured he was just a punter. He was there trying to chat to some of the stable lads and lasses trying to get some information because it is very important to find out how a horse travelled to a race. If it had been sweating up badly, that in itself can lose a race."

The needle would be administered – "same time every time, in the chest". Browne said he would always stick the needle in first – it was small and didn't have to go in intravenously. He would wait a while, attach the syringe, and slowly push the plunger to inject the ACP. "If you get the whole thing and try to stick it into him and he jumps, it will follow him around, or it would break or fall on the ground, or it would do damage to him," Browne said. "The whole idea was to do it without drawing blood or as little blood as possible. You didn't want the stable lad or lass coming back and seeing all this blood trickling down."

Each time Browne entered a horse's box he would find it tied up or wearing a muzzle, to prevent it eating or drinking too close to a race. "If a horse was head collared and tied up it was easier. If it was muzzled they could soon fly out the stable," he said.

Usually a doping would be carried out 75-90 minutes before a race – "(Alfred) reckoned that was how long you needed for the stuff to actually work properly," Browne said, so that the horse was relaxed and unfocused by the time he arrived at the start. According to Browne, a doped horse would often urinate "so whatever was in him at that point would be done (as in useless) as evidence for a Jockey Club test afterwards."

A doped horse "would run a little lethargically. A jockey would push and shake and smack and the horse would respond a bit and he would feel he was getting there and then he wouldn't. It would knock around about 15 lengths off a horse on the Flat, especially if it was a three-year-old or older over a distance of a mile upwards. The further the race the better it worked on the Flat; I wasn't interested in doing it over Jumps."

So that's the theory. Let's see what happened in practice.

BROWNE GETS BUSY

By doping an Arab-owned runner, which was in the care of a Derby-winning trainer and ridden by a champion jockey, Dermot Browne's first wave of the needle was aimed straight to the heart of racing's establishment.

The horse was Hateel, the race was the Listed Schroders Glorious Stakes, a £30,000 feature of the Glorious Goodwood meeting. The four-year-old was owned by Hamdan al-Maktoum, a member of the ruling family of Dubai that had invested on such a massive scale in British racing. Sheikh Hamdan was having a season of outrageous success, thanks largely to the staggeringly quick Dayjur, who is to feature in a later doping incident, and Salsabil, a brilliant filly who took on – and beat – the colts in the Irish Derby. His retained jockey, Willie Carson, was having an equally unbelievable season. As he took the leg up on Hateel he was also mulling over a freshly imposed careless riding ban. Carson's was the best known face of the weighing room. He was the Queen's jockey, and one of the few of his profession to break into mainstream celebrity. He even appeared as a team captain on *Question of Sport*.

Hateel's trainer Peter Walwyn was 'old school'; tall and traditional with an intimidating military air that belied the fact that he was really rather approachable, if slightly batty. Walwyn had won the previous day's big two-year-old race, the Lanson Champagne Stakes, with Mukaddamah. Like Carson, who closed the Glorious Goodwood meeting as leading jockey, Walwyn was on a roll.

Despite Carson's ban, owner, trainer and jockey all had reasons to be cheerful as Hateel made his way down to the start. What they weren't to know, of course, is that someone had been quietly upsetting their golden times and that Hateel was coming to terms with an infusion of ACP.

This had been a typical Wright gang effort; they had started as they meant to go on. Four runners, one of them a 16-1 chance, thus making it in effect a three-horse contest. "Brian Wright reckoned if he took out the second favourite or favourite he could back the winner very easily," said Browne.

Hateel was chosen because of Browne's familiarity with Walwyn's staff and where his horses were stabled at Goodwood. He and Alfred met near the toilets in the lads' canteen. "Now at that point it was when I found out that I was expected to dope the horses because they didn't have anybody else to do it," Browne recalled. "But as I was there I said I would do it. (Alfred) gave me the syringe and the needle was on top of the syringe and there was a bit of cork stuck on top of the needle and it was wrapped in a damp cloth in a plastic bag.

"I just walked in, went over, went in, and gave it (Hateel) a jab in the chest. It was no problem, it was easy."

Walwyn's lads had almost certainly gone to change into their smart gear, to be ready for leading Hateel around the parade ring. Browne wiped away any traces of his actions with some straw or horse shit, left the yard and handed the needle back to (Alfred). He then rang Brian Wright, who was chilling out by the pool at a nearby hotel, and told him that the doping had been done.

Browne believed that Wright often placed his bets underground, illegally, "so that way none of the money should reach the racecourse so there shouldn't be a big scream."

When assessing every doping, it is important to remember that Wright may have bet in a manner that meant his bets couldn't be traced. Equally, if he bet on course, Wright would have a chorus line of lieutenants ready to step up to the row of bookies and bet frequently, in small (ish) amounts, again so as not to cause a panic. Such an approach would also hit the ring hard and fast.

Although it was against the agreement, Browne couldn't resist telling one or two people that there was a good bet to be had. He had a near-empty yard to fill, after all.

Hateel's effort in the mile-and-a-half race was short-lived. "Willie Carson rode him in his typical style: push, push, push, and all that kind of thing. The horse finished third, the second favourite won, so it looked just like Hateel didn't sparkle on the day."

Hateel, the first horse Browne had doped, was tested by Walwyn the following day. "But it may have been out of his system by then as the test returned negative," Walwyn said. "It was only later that I heard from another jockey who rode in the race that his penis was hanging down at the start, which is a classic sign of a horse having being doped."

Not only was it a classic sign, it would soon become a familiar sign as the dopers started to run amok.

TESTING TIME

Dermot Browne waited little more than 24 hours before his next strike. Absaar was a three-year-old filly owned again by Hamdan al-Maktoum (surely it wasn't personal?), although trained this time in Newmarket by Alec Stewart. Absaar was the second favourite in a three-runner race at Windsor and was entering handicap company for the first time. She looked a banker.

Browne met Alfred in the lads' canteen. He was handed a plastic bag containing a needle and a syringe with a plastic cap that had a wet cloth around it.

He was told where Absaar was stabled and he found the box easily. It was a hot day and he noticed that Absaar already looked in a desperate state. She probably didn't need any dope to help her underperform, but she got it all the same. The syringe goes into the filly's chest, just as it had with Hateel. Job done, no problem. Another race had been fixed.

Browne makes a call to Brian Wright to tell him just that. "Have you met the other fella?" Wright asked him. Yes, he had. He had met Alfred and all was well – for the dopers at least.

Already hot and bothered, Absaar now has to compete in a 12-furlong handicap with a syringe full of dope inside her. The race is won by the well-backed 8-13 favourite Once Upon A Time – owned by the Queen. It's fair to say that Her Majesty was not aware of the helping hand her filly had received. Maybe Brian Wright is a Royalist? It was, after all, the Queen Mother's 90th birthday. Poor old Absaar finishes second of the three runners, beaten 15 lengths. It is the third and final race of her career, while Dermot Browne's career as a doper is only just beginning.

Four days after he had doped Absaar, Browne once more can be found skulking around the stables with a plastic bag inside his pocket. Inside that is a damp cloth. Inside that is a syringe. Inside that is ACP. It is a Russian doll full of menace. Dermot Browne is at Kempton, to dope a two-year-old maiden called Stylish Senor trained by James Fanshawe in Newmarket.

Getting into the stables was no problem this time as Browne had a runner, Total Sport, in the same race. The owners, who included the son of the former Leeds and England manager Don Revie, had told Browne they would be moving the horse to Richard Hannon. Browne had agreed, but asked if he could give Total Sport her debut run. The owners agreed, not knowing the thinking behind Browne's request.

Entry into the Kempton security complex was no problem. Browne walks across to where Fanshawe's horses are stabled. Stylish Senor is there. Unfortunately, so is his lad, keeping his horse from the needle and Browne from an expected £10,000 pay-day.

Something had to be done. Browne notices that the lad has a quarter marker outside the box. These are plastic stencils that are slapped across a horse's rump to give its coat a well-groomed, diamond-patterned appearance. Browne returned to where Total Sport was stabled and told the lad in charge of him to put some quarter marks on the colt's backside.

"Erm, how do I do that?" the lad asked, unwittingly helping Browne with his plan. "Look," Browne said. "I haven't got time to be doing this: go and get that young lad from the box to show you," pointing in the direction of Stylish Senor and his groom. While the young lad from Stylish Senor's box sportingly left his post to show a colleague how to quarter mark a horse, Dermot Browne nipped in, gave the horse an injection in the chest and walked out of the box unnoticed.

Somehow, Stylish Senor still finishes second, while Browne's runner, competing without the aid of ACP, came second last after banging her head on the stalls. As he leaves the grandstand to go down to the unsaddling area for also-rans, where he will somehow have to explain a lacklustre effort to the owners, Browne saw Stylish Senor being led away to the testing box, where horses provide urine tests after every race.

His heart stopped.

A WIDER FIELD

Nothing showed up from Stylish Senor's dope test. The fact that ACP could be used and yet go undetected raised some serious threats to racing's integrity. Yet it provided Browne and his cohorts with invaluable reassurance.

"That was the first time I saw a horse being tested after having received it (ACP) so I knew after that when I heard nothing of it and there was nothing in the papers afterwards that what (Alfred) had said, that he was putting stuff in to mask this juice as he called it, he was probably right. It wasn't detectable," he told the police during his interview in Ireland. "Whether he was mixing anything else with it, I don't know."

Browne's police interview took place 10 years after the doping spree he is meant to have orchestrated. Somehow, he remembers each incident in phenomenal detail. Could he be making it up?

Stylish Senor's trainer, James Fanshawe, was asked about the Kempton race even later than Browne, in 2001. He also remembered it well. "Stylish Senor was a decent horse and I was very disappointed with the way he ran at Kempton, even though he was second," Fanshawe said. "He'd travelled really well at Newmarket first time out but at Kempton, Wally (his jockey Walter Swinburn) said he never felt right and made really hard work of it. I definitely suspected something."

However, whereas Browne claimed that Stylish Senor was tested afterwards, Fanshawe said he wasn't, "so we couldn't prove anything".

Yet the Newmarket trainer volunteered one significant detail. "It was only later," he said, "that I found out that Jason Ward, who was looking after Stylish Senor, had left him unattended when Dermot Browne asked him to show his lad how to use the quarter marker on his filly."

That recollection is uncannily similar to Browne's. In fact, it is one small detail that appears to confirm one almighty revelation.

Browne had other good reasons to remember that race. Two years after doping Stylish Senor, he was the subject of a Jockey Club inquiry into six possible rule breaches. They included running Total Sport at Kempton when she had not been properly vaccinated and signing a false declaration that she had.

He had been fined £100 for those irregularities on the day of the race, small beer compared to the money he expected to make and the money Brian Wright had made by backing the winner, Sea Level. Money had been heading towards Sea Level like a moth to a flame – at least £70,000 had been taken out of the ring at Kempton on that one race. Someone was feeling confident.

Uncharacteristically, Wright had targeted a 15-runner race instead of his usual small field, so his information for Sea Level must have been strong and trusted.

PINK BELLS AND GREEN LIQUID

Paddock watchers at Bath on 14 August would not have noticed that Pink Bells had been doped, but someone was there, watching the filly in the paddock, seeking reassurance. It was Alfred.

All he was looking for was a glazed eye to tell him that the dope was working. The signals with fillies tended to be a lot more subtle than with colts who had been doped.

A trip to Bath had suited Browne. He was there to try and claim a horse from one of the races. It gave him a legitimate reason to be in the stables. If anyone asked, all he was doing was window shopping, being professional.

Once more he had taken hold of a syringe full of a yellowy green liquid, handed to him in a plastic bag, with a damp cloth around the syringe to keep it cool. This time the handover had been at a nearby pub. Browne walked through the main gate of the racecourse stables. He waited a while in a gap between two boxes. He had already been given the stable number for Pink Bells, but she wasn't difficult to find because of her coat colour – roan, a greyish strawberry

He only needed 20 seconds to make the hit. No need to find a vein and make it pop up. All he needed to do was stab the needle in the chest. He put the call in to Brian Wright to say that all was well before walking across the road to the racecourse proper, ready to watch a race that he knew had been fixed. Pink Bells loses, Sandford Springs, Brian Wright's choice, wins. Pink Bells, trained by another Derby-winning trainer in Paul Cole, was in fact last of four, more than 25 lengths behind the winner. That's suspicious. So Alfred did a bit of eavesdropping on the post-race conversations of the horse's connections. No mumbles of concern this time. They'll come later.

Browne was at ease with his situation. Having seen Stylish Senor being taken away at Kempton to be tested – although it is not clear if the horse actually was – Browne had faith in the efficacy of the dope, whether or not it had been mixed with a masking agent. He had also been lifted by a meeting with Brian Wright at a service station near Lambourn. Wright had produced £9,000 in readies from the back of his car with the promise of more to come.

Browne and the gang were enjoying a rich harvest. The time of year suited them. Firm ground meant small fields. Small fields meant easier pickings.

Wright would ring around his contacts to find out who fancied what. There was a lot of talking done. Chances are that in a race of five runners or less, Wright would know at least two of the jockeys; he would also have contacts in nearly all of the top yards.

He would have made a great newspaper tipster, what with his own deep knowledge of form and his impeccable sources. That's why he was a tasty gambler: he didn't take chances. It is all very well to fancy a horse, but Wright knew just how much could go wrong when you had half tonnes of horseflesh colliding with each other and jockeys who might have left their brains in the sauna or whatever bar and bed they had been in the night before. Brian Wright couldn't take any risks. He liked to close each deal with a needle.

Well armed with the latest information on who was fancied, who had been going well on the gallops, who would like the ground, who had missed some work through injury, Wright would make his choices. Sometimes he would ask Browne to dope a specific horse; sometimes it didn't matter if it was the first or second favourite. As long as he knew one of them couldn't win.

It was usually on the day of the race that Browne would receive a call from Wright to discuss who should be doped. The race in question had already been identified. The London *Evening Standard*, with its overnight declaration of runners, was an invaluable guide for the dopers. Once they had chosen a race, all Browne needed was to know where the horse was stabled – which Alfred would tell him, he had everything in hand – and 90 minutes for the juice to kick in.

DOPERS ON A ROLL

Newbury was Dermot Browne's local course so he knew his way around it. On Saturday 18 August, he had been given the nod to dope Ijtihaad, a strongly fancied horse from local trainer Dick Hern's yard. Willie Carson was the rider.

Hern's staff were well known, so again his horses were easy to pinpoint at the racecourse stables. Browne parked around the back of the stable yard, having skipped the main route in to come through a housing estate and through the back gates. Here, the syringe, as usual in a plastic bag, was handed over to him.

Browne went upstairs to the stable lads' canteen and opened a round glass case with a key in it for the fire door. Through there, he was given access to a metal stairway down into the stable yard itself. He found an empty box and waited until a stable lass turned up with a horse that was due to be stabled there. Browne pretended to be having a pee before leaving.

He walked past the row of Dick Hern horses, drugs in pocket, and found a converted stable where the racecourse maintenance man kept his tools. They chatted while Browne peeked his head out occasionally to see if the chance was there to get at Ijtihaad. His chance came, the needle went in and Browne returned from whence he came, back up the steel steps, closing the fire door and returning the key to its case. Then it was back to the canteen to return the used needle. Brian Wright took a call soon after, telling him that Ijtihaad had been doped.

Ijtihaad duly finished last of five, 20 lengths behind the fourth horse. Again Browne claimed the colt was dope tested. If he was, nothing showed up. The race was over a mile and five furlongs and the dopers reckoned the longer the race the more effective the ACP. Ijtihaad's performance certainly endorsed that view.

The doping of Ijtihaad provided further confirmation that no race was untouchable. He was doped in a Group 2 contest, the Geoffrey Freer Stakes, he was doped at a Grade 1 racecourse, and he was doped under the noses of some of the most experienced, most loyal stable staff in the business.

Whether Brian Wright benefited from this doping is hard to weigh up. The winner was Charmer, ridden by an up-and-coming jockey by the name of Frankie Dettori. Charmer was the 4-1 third favourite; but the 13-8 favourite Assatis could finish only fourth.

It must have been tempting for Browne and his cohorts to lie low after such a daring raid on Newbury. But by now they were on a roll and just two days later they were at it again.

THREE SYRINGES EMPTIED

Berillon was doped at Windsor and according to Dermot Browne "it all went to plan on the day". He had been handed the syringe at some outside tables and chairs near the lads' canteen, but entered the stables area through a gap in a wire fence. A spot of blood appeared on the doping victim, which Browne wiped away to avoid the suspicion of his lad.

Berillon was a three-year-old trained by Guy Harwood, who had made a winning reappearance the time before at Ascot. The dopers had targeted an unusually large field, but Brian Wright appears to have been putting in the calls beforehand, doing his homework. Berillon was the one he wanted out of the reckoning. At 7-4, he was much the most serious rival to the 13-8 favourite and subsequent winner Baylis. The third horse in the betting was sent off at 7-1. By doping Berillon, Baylis's chances had been helped enormously.

Over nearly 12 furlongs the ACP had clearly done its job. Berillon finished 10th of 13, leaving his jockey, Pat Eddery, to reflect more than a decade after the race: "I remember saying to Guy that something was drastically wrong, as he'd won on a tight rein at Ascot. I couldn't believe how badly he'd run, and we couldn't understand it." Until now.

And until now, Browne's dopings had been pretty straightforward. The next one wasn't.

Tyrone Bridge, a four-year-old running the following day in the two-mile Lonsdale Stakes at York's prestigious and extremely popular Ebor meeting, certainly got the needle. "He went bananas, he was trying to eat me, to bite me, it took me ages to get him. I had to grab hold of him, and give him a good slapping . . . he was a right bastard," Browne said.

No doubt Tyrone Bridge spoke highly of Dermot Browne, too. He was a tough horse, who even in normal circumstances needed pushing along almost from the start. Even with ACP inside him, he somehow managed to finish second of five, beaten six lengths by the winner, Chelsea Girl.

This was another doping that you would struggle to call a success because Chelsea Girl was a 12-1 shot, with Tyrone Bridge only third favourite at 100-30. Wright's obvious betting options were: the 5-4 favourite Teamster and 2-1 shot Wajna. But Teamster was pulled up and Wajna was a well-beaten third.

Browne, in the meantime, was becoming restless. His payments hadn't been coming through with the weight and regularity he had expected. Rather than receiving the £10,000 he was expecting per doping, Browne was unhappy about being paid in dribs and drabs, if you can call it that, of £2,000, £3,000 or £4,000.

In his police interviews he admitted he might have miscalculated the £10,000 payment – it was, in fact, to be shared between him and Alfred – although Browne still reckoned he was owed between £25,000 and £30,000. Whatever the true state of his account with Wright, it emerged that Browne was involved in a lucrative little sideline.

The day after Tyrone Bridge's never-say-doped second in the Lonsdale, Mujadil was sent off the 5-4 favourite for another Listed race, the Roses Stakes for two-year-olds. He won like the good thing he was, by two-and-a-half lengths. Good thing? Well, the second favourite had been doped.

Only seven lined up for the Roses, so Silken Sailed's introduction to what Browne termed "the jungle juice" was a shrewd move. Brian Wright had news from Newmarket that Mujadil was working well, so Browne, armed as usual with the ACP, was given the stable number for Mujadil, he in turn gave Mujadil a jab in the chest, gave back the syringe and rang Brian Wright to say "mission accomplished". On his way back to the racecourse, Browne – breaking the code of conduct he had agreed with Wright – mentioned to a local bookmaker that he thought the favourite was a certainty.

Silken Sailed finished a tailed-off last, endorsing Browne's view that the dope had a bigger effect on juveniles. "He only went for about 50 yards and I thought he'd broken a leg or something," the colt's trainer Bill O'Gorman recalled. "Something was wrong with him and I wanted him checked, but I don't think they had the facility there to scope him. He never got over that, and although I ran him once more, at Ayr, he ran horribly again."

Again, it is not just that Browne doped two horses in two days that is so alarming. It is that he did it at one of the top meetings in the racing calendar. And he did it again on the third and final day. This time it wasn't in a supporting race, either. He doped a horse in the Group 1 Nunthorpe Stakes, one of Europe's premier races for sprinters.

Where was the racecourse security? You might well ask.

Argentum was the horse the dopers wanted out. Not surprisingly really as, at 11-4, he was easily the biggest rival to the odds-on favourite, Dayjur. To illustrate just how much of a two-horse race this looked to be, the next best of the nine runners in the betting was Statoblest at 14-1. Argentum had returned to form at Goodwood on his previous start, having run disappointingly at Royal Ascot on ground that was considered too soft for him. There was no chance of that happening again at York; the ground was good to firm after a baking hot summer.

Yet he never stood a chance. He was edgy and sweating in the paddock and ran too freely for his own good on the way down to the start. Regardless of the heat, his behaviour was conspicuous.

Away from Argentum's discomfort, Dermot Browne was in his element. "I was at the races on that day in the champagne bar," he recalled in his police interview. "There were people talking about it (the race) and I said to them that Argentum wouldn't win. They were listening to me after the previous two days because I had mentioned things to them. I said 'no, I didn't think that fella would win' and made up some excuses to them. They thought I was doing very well at the advice stakes so they were backing winners and buying drinks. I remember distinctly saying to them that Argentum wouldn't win."

And he didn't. Argentum was soon outpaced and having to be ridden along. He made late ground at the finish to come in a hugely credible fourth, but that was still seven-and-a-half lengths behind Dayjur. In the betting ring Argentum had attracted plenty enough money – although less, predictably, than Dayjur, a flurry of bets on whom included nine at £2,000 to win £3,000. The doping of Argentum shows just how little was left to chance. The way Dayjur won, setting a track record in the process, suggests he was a total good thing anyway. Sure, 8-11 is not an attractive price. But when you bet in the amounts that Brian Wright did, you can end up making at least £50,000 in the 56 seconds it took Dayjur to win. That's a better rate than any building society.

Browne's assurances that Argentum wouldn't win earned him a gift from his local bookie: £400 quid out of the boot of his car.

That was York done and dusted. Three syringes had been filled and emptied as Brian Wright's betting wadge grew even bigger. Browne travelled to London to meet him and he and Albert were given £5,000 between them.

Three days later, on a Sunday, Browne took a call from Wright. He'd spotted an ideal race at Ripon. Would he mind if he headed back to Yorkshire? Browne didn't seem to mind.

BAD DAY AT THE OFFICE

Despite its Listed status, the Bonusprint Champion Trophy for two-year-olds had attracted only three runners. One of them was the 4-6 favourite Anjiz. It was Brian Wright's kind of race. Two horses with strong chances and then an outsider, an absolute rag at 12-1.

This time the needle went to Timeless Times, a horse who provided one of the highlights of the 1990 season by achieving a record-equalling total of 16 wins as a two-year-old.

Timeless Times was easy to find, stabled as he was near the entrance to the stables. He finished last of three, although only two-and-a-half lengths and a head behind Anjiz. His trainer Bill O'Gorman did not view this as a "mystery defeat" and Timeless Times was back in action a week later and won. "I wasn't suspicious, but one thing I would say is that the lad who looked after him was so proud of him he'd have shown him to anyone," O'Gorman said.

Perhaps he did.

Browne remembers that two-day Ripon meeting well – for a start he had enjoyed himself on a night out with the cast of Emmerdale in Harrogate. But that's not the only reason. The next day Brian Wright had given him a multiple order and Browne ended up doping the wrong horse.

One of Wright's targets seemed a surprising one, coming as it did in a 19-runner handicap. Yet dutifully, Lothian, the 9-4 favourite, was doped, and finished well down the field in 14th.

The race was won by the 15-2 second favourite, Highflying. If Wright had calculated that Highflying was a good thing without Lothian, trained by Barry Hills, then all you can really do is applaud.

After that doping, things got a bit muddled. Browne also had an order for a stablemate of Lothian's later on the same day. That horse was called Laxey Bay, who was the 8-15 winner of a three-year-old conditions race, despite Browne's attempts to dope him.

As he walked into Laxey Bay's box, Browne noticed a bucket of water in the stable. That was strange. So close to a race a horse would usually be muzzled or tied up to stop it from eating or drinking.

All the same he doped the horse and then got chatting to Barry Hills' stable staff. It was only then, that it emerged that the Hills team had picked up another runner from Newcastle the night before and were stabling her at Ripon prior to a return south to Hills' Manton base. That horse is thought to have been the filly Cameo Performance, who had won the Listed Virginia Stakes. And that was who Browne had doped, not Laxey Bay.

Problem was: he'd already told Brian Wright that all was ok. And as it turned out it wasn't. Once he realised his error, Browne attempted again to dope Laxey Bay, but the stable lad who looked after him just couldn't be lured away.

Perhaps to make amends, Browne said he was then asked to dope another horse by Wright – the name and trainer of which he can't remember – and in his panic and his confusion doped four horses from the same yard. Just to be sure. Four horses doped, and even the man who nobbled them can't remember who they were.

"It wasn't a good day, you know," was Browne's assessment. "It was a bad day at the office."

Things were getting out of hand for Browne. For the rest of us, it was just becoming more and more mind-boggling. All this could be true, you know.

WAKI GOLD FLATTERED

Undeterred by his Ripon cock-up and the fact that the juice was running low due to his anonymous four-horse blitz, Browne moved on to the following day's meeting at Redcar.

A more conformist race had been identified, a nine-furlong maiden for three-year-olds. Five runners. Not what you would call a quality contest.

Still, no chances were being taken. A white Mercedes, up from London, arrived at the course to deliver a new supply of ACP. Brian Wright's plan was to back either Waki Gold, the 4-6 favourite, or Kisu Kali, next best at 2-1, in the race.

Two of the five runners had absolutely no chance, so Browne doped Kisu Kali, and just to be safe, the third favourite Taj Victory as well. The path was clear for Waki Gold to skate up, which he did.

Browne had phoned Brian Wright to explain what he'd done – "straight up?" was apparently the response – and also try to get a bet for himself on Waki Gold. He reckoned he was owed £30,000 by Wright and wanted all of that bet on Waki Gold. "I knew myself it couldn't get beat unless the ground opened up". Whether the money went on or not, Browne said he never received it.

"When I went into the stables I went in disguise. I hid on the far side of a horse who was a bit frisky . . . as he approached the gate I gave him a flick in the arse with the bucket so he jumped and kicked and the security man ducked in the door and I slipped in behind and I held the horse for her (the lass in charge) as she washed it down and scraped it." He could see the stables and decided he would go for Waki Gold, but he was disturbed while he was in there. Browne used a familiar excuse: he pretended he was having a pee.

Waki Gold's trainer, the late Paul Kelleway, was not a man to underplay the merits of his horses. So when his horse won by five lengths, Kelleway started planning with typical ambition.

Unfortunately, Kelleway was not to know just how much Waki Gold had been flattered by his Redcar win, running as he did against two doped horses. So from a tinpot race at Redcar worth £2,394 to the winner, Waki Gold found himself shipped to Italy for his next start, a Group 1 race offering £150,000. Not since Rocky Balboa was plucked from the streets of Hell's Kitchen to fight Apollo Creed had there been such a dramatic tilt at a windmill. Unlike Rocky, though, Waki Gold was never a real contender again.

Browne remained in Yorkshire to dope a horse at Thirsk two days later. He went on a recce to check out the layout of the course, and particularly the stables, the night before.

The Bill Watts Graduation Stakes was perfect for the dopers' needs. Three runners, one of which was a clear outsider. Wright wanted to back Pipitina, an 11-8 shot, meaning the 10-11 favourite Kasayid drew the short needle.

Browne and Alfred had checked in to a nearby bed and breakfast so there was no need to meet up before racing and hand over the syringes. Browne's view that the longer the race the more effective the ACP, gained further credence, as over two miles Kasayid finished 21 lengths behind the winner. Had enough yet? The dopers hadn't.

FAMILY AT WAR

Rat-a-tat-tat, the dopings went on. Browne and Alfred once more stayed locally for a meeting at Ripon the following day. It was a decent race they hit on, the five-furlong Horn Blower Stakes featuring some smart if not quite top-drawer two-year-olds.

Browne identified the filly he was after, Family At War, by the rug bearing its trainer's initials outside the box.

Family At War had looked the most dangerous of the five rivals to the favourite Vintage Only, who was returned the 4-7 favourite although he only won by a head. That was enough though, to allow Brian Wright to collect, and the colt had been the subject of some heavy on-course money. Family At War, meanwhile, laboured, unsurprisingly, to finish fifth of six without ever troubling the leaders.

"She was one of our better two-year-olds and she disappointed us that day. Looking back, I suppose that's why," Family At War's trainer Jimmy Etherington reflected wryly.

The doping roadshow was to head south after Ripon, to resurface after a 10-day break at Leicester.

Still Browne was pestering Brian Wright for more money, believing he was owed significant amount for his efforts. He met Wright in a London snooker club and was handed £5,000. "He said he was still trying to sort out the Ripon mess (when the wrong horse was doped) but I figured he still owed me £35,000," Browne said.

Ever resourceful, Browne suggested to Wright that he purchased around 20 cheap horses, at as little as £1,000 a time. They could be trained by Browne and run at every meeting they planned to do a doping, thus providing Browne with easier and more legitimate access to the stables.

Quite how long it would have taken the Jockey Club's security team to spot that Browne always seemed to have a runner whenever a doping took place is a moot point. On the evidence of everything they appear to have missed so far, you couldn't have banked on it ever happening.

But there was almost certainly another reason for Browne's enterprising suggestions. The number of horses in his stable was dwindling. Soon the

Jockey Club would be keeping a close eye on the situation.

To Leicester, the course at which two months later Lester Piggott would make an astonishing return to the saddle at the age of 49.

Word had filtered through that the Henry Cecil-trained Peter Davies should not be opposed on his debut in division two of the EBF Kegworth Stakes, despite the presence in the line-up of the eventual 4-7 favourite Claret, who was also making his debut. "I had no problems at Leicester. I walked straight in and the horse was on his own," Browne said. "I administered the ACP to him and came out with no problem. Again, he was one of Dick Hern's so I was very au fait with their kit and caboodle. You can spot it a mile off."

Peter Davies was 5-1, a tempting price if you knew the favourite had been doped. Something wasn't right, though. Browne noticed that Peter Davies had drifted from 7-4, hardly a sign that he was being heavily backed. "I figured it had something to do with what happened at Ripon, the horses that went wrong," Browne said. "Wright was maybe changing his pattern of betting."

One way of doing this would have been to bet underground, with unlicensed bookmakers, as he had done before. Certainly the recorded bets on course hardly suggested a typical Brian Wright gamble: one bet of £600 to win £3,000 and one of £500 to win £2,500. He wouldn't have got out of bed for that.

Peter Davies won, nonetheless; Claret ran surprisingly well to finish third. "I just remember being very disappointed because he was way above average and we thought he would win any ordinary maiden. He was one of those that we would have expected to win," his jockey Willie Carson said more than 10 years on.

NORWICH DOPING RAISES SUSPICIONS

The date is now 13 September 1990. It's a Thursday, two days after the decanting of Claret. The focus has switched to Doncaster's St Leger meeting, the defining moment of Browne's career as a doper. It was a busy time. He had his own runners at the meeting and, with the traditional yearling sales taking place across the road, the place was buzzing.

A three-year-old colt by the name of Norwich had been lined up for the next hit. Trained by Barry Hills – again – Norwich had already won five times that season, most recently in the Group 3 Hungerford Stakes at Newbury.

Once more the dopers were fixing a prestigious race; this time it was the Group 3 Kiveton Park Stakes over seven furlongs. Norwich was sent off the 11-4 joint favourite along with the horse that went on to win, Green Line Express. Wright had studied closely the likely tactics of the race and figured that Green Line Express would make the running while holding off his challengers at the finish. And that is exactly what happened.

Browne had little trouble picking out the Barry Hills team; he had worked with one of Hills' staff while an amateur rider with Michael Dickinson. Once more, Browne earned a bit on the side by selling information about Norwich – not that it was doped, but by saying it wouldn't win. "He (the recipient) just thought that I was giving him information I was receiving from the stable lads about the horse travelling badly and stuff like that," Browne said.

Barry Hills had been watching Norwich in the paddock and was a man content. Norwich was relaxed, whereas usually he would have been edgy and on his toes. It was good to be calm. But the more Hills observed Norwich, the less sanguine he became. Norwich was clearly too subdued; like, as his trainer noted, "someone being drunk, a horse not with the world at all."

Not long after Hills' son Michael was given the leg up on Norwich, he started to share his father's unease. Norwich slumbered his way down to the start and once there just stood around with a distant look. No hooves a prancing, no tugging at his bit, no signs whatsoever of his usual uppity edge.

Normally the starting stalls handlers have to get behind Norwich's recalcitrant backside and heave him into the gates. There he was wandering into the stalls as if he is at home. Michael Hills thought to himself: "It's as if he's been given a pill to quieten him down."

Norwich finished fourth, which sounds commendable given the circumstances but Barry Hills soon started to think the worst, so he called in the Jockey Club's security department to investigate the lacklustre performance. "It is at my request that the Jockey Club are looking into Norwich's Doncaster performance," the trainer said, although you wonder why he had to make that request in the first place.

Norwich's doping was of huge significance. It was the first one to cause serious suspicion and the first one to be detected. Looking at the result of the race in the 1990 formbook, you are struck by the small bold words below it. "Norwich subsequently found to have been administered with the sedative Acetylpromazine." A statement of such stunning baldness obviously doesn't begin to describe the drama of that hot, late summer. What it does do is remind you that the wheels were starting to spin off Browne's doping machine and that soon – very soon – the game would be up.

"THE WHOLE THING SMELLS ..."

The names start getting familiar now. Bravefoot. He's next. Just a day after Norwich, viewers of *Channel 4 Racing* see for themselves just what happens when a horse is doped.

Bravefoot was made the favourite for the Group 2 Laurent-Perrier Champagne Stakes on the strength of two wins in his two previous starts. You would have thought people would be keen to back him, but there was an uneasy mood among the on-course bookmakers prior to the race. It was picked up by betting expert John McCririck, who, live on TV, said: "The whole thing smells down here."

It was one of McCririck's best calls as a betting ring pundit. "It really was bad," he said. "I can't remember ever going on air and saying something like that. Looking back we all now know that Bravefoot was doped, like Norwich the day before him. It is horrific to think that was going on, but at the time we didn't know what was happening other than whatever it was, it was something fishy."

Bravefoot opened at evens and despite £70,000 being staked in recorded bets, he still drifted to 11-8. Strange, the morning papers had him at odds-on.

His nearest market rival Arokat, meanwhile, opened up at 7-1 in the betting but came in to 15-8.

"Bravefoot was particularly alarming but Norwich wasn't so bad," McCririck recalled. "I wasn't surprised to see him drift (9-4 to 3-1, before settling at 11-4) because there were three others in the race who were being backed. Norwich's race seemed a much more natural fluctuation. The betting didn't give a clue that anything was wrong with Norwich. The winner Green Line Express also drifted."

What McCririck didn't know, as Bravefoot sloped his way around the parade ring was not just that he had been doped, but the farcical circumstances in which it had taken place. According to Browne, who had originally agreed to oversee the dopings, rather than actually administer the ACP himself, Brian Wright had sent up "some cronies" from London to do the dirty deed.

Quite why he did this now isn't made clear, although it is apparent from the transcripts that there was a distance, even a distrust, developing between the two men.

Browne met these cronies – "cockney lads", he said almost dismissively – in the car park close to the stable yard. Because of the neighbouring sales, there would have been a lot of activity, a lot of new faces. It was a good time to do a spot of doping.

The cronies were dressed in shirt and tie to fit in with the smart but hard-working image of stable lads. Browne, still a trainer, signed them in himself to the racecourse stables and took them to one of his own horses and carried out a mock demonstration of how to dope a horse before pointing them in the direction of poor old Bravefoot.

The lesson wasn't learned. The cronies met up with Browne in the lads' canteen to explain, no doubt sheepishly, that it was mission unaccomplished. Inexplicably, Bravefoot had objected to having a needle popped amateurishly into his chest. "They said the horse was a bit of a nutcase and tried to bite them and kick them and everything," Browne recalled.

Brian Wright, who had backed Arokat, didn't like this news. Finish the job off, he said. And do it properly. Browne watched while the cronies topped up Bravefoot with a fresh squirt of ACP.

It's no surprise he was detected as well. This two-year-old of high expectations, on only his third trip to the racecourse, had been given at least 50 per cent more than the recommended dose. Browne kept a close eye on Bravefoot and noted that his lad had reported his concern about the colt's condition to other members of Dick Hern's staff. They took his temperature – fine. They trotted him up and down the stable complex to check if he was sound – he was.

But the lad, Peter West, was insistent. Bravefoot was not himself. Browne rang Brian Wright to tell him the good news. Not that Wright really needed telling. He only had to switch on his TV for confirmation that Bravefoot would not be winning.

Bravefoot was in the parade ring and his penis was visible for all to see. This is not that unusual. Some entire horses – those who haven't been gelded and thus had their assets seized by a surgeon's knife – often like to 'draw', which is the racing euphemism for waving their cock around with playful pride.

But Bravefoot was no macho man. His tackle hung limply to the ground, like an equine case of brewer's droop. This state of affairs was used with hindsight by many experts as, erm, hard evidence that Bravefoot had been doped. But despite the doubts of Hern's staff, Bravefoot was allowed to run.

His jockey, Walter Swinburn, had to give him three slaps of the whip just to get him to go down to the start. That just doesn't happen with a two-year-old. As you might expect, Bravefoot finished last of five having needed to be driven along almost from the start. Still, this was a plan that didn't work out, as Arokat was beaten easily by the 8-1 shot Bog Trotter. A stewards' inquiry into Bravefoot's running proved inconclusive. But finally the Jockey Club decided to hold its own, fuller, inquiry.

In what was proving, a busy, lively day, Browne dispatched the cronies and took it upon himself to carry out a second act of bespoke nobbling. The word had come to give Findon the needle before the closing conditions race. This seemed a bit harsh as it was Findon's racecourse debut. Yet word of her talent had clearly got out as she started the 9-4 favourite. Thanks to Dermot Browne's help she finished last of five, although how anyone benefited from her doping isn't clear. Findon was the best backed horse in the race. In comparison, there was relatively little money bet on the winner Narwala, one of two third favourites at 7-2.

Findon was one of the unlucky ones, but there were others who got away.

THE NEEDLE RUNS DRY

One of the most popular horses two compete during the 1990 Flat season was Distinctly North, whose equally popular trainer Jack Berry became the first northern-based trainer in nearly 60 years to saddle 100 winners.

Distinctly North, who ran in the colours of one of the world's most successful owners, Robert Sangster, had achieved some top-class juvenile form by the time he lined up for the Group 2 Flying Childers Stakes at Doncaster on St Leger day, less than 24 hours since the needle had gone into Bravefoot and Findon.

He won the Flying Childers, to give Berry only the second Group winner in a career that had been notable for his honesty and hard graft. In doing so, Distinctly North secured himself a pleasurable second career as a stallion, a privilege conferred on only the very best horses.

Things could have been so different. Brian Wright had it in mind to dope Distinctly North – on the day Britain's fifth and final Classic race of the season was due to be run – and told Browne to start preparing for it. "For some reason we changed our minds," Browne said.

That was the end of Doncaster, and while not quite the end of the doping, the needle was beginning to run dry.

For their next race, Browne and Brian Wright lowered their sights somewhat to a three-year-old handicap for horses rated 0 to 90 at Sandown. If it was class they were looking for, they should have waited for two more races, when the following year's Derby and King George winner, Generous, was seen in action. Instead, the target was Ambrose, trained by Fulke Johnson Houghton, who started the 15-8 favourite for the LMS Handicap.

Because of the attention that Norwich and Bravefoot's runs had created, Browne chose to make a surreptitious entrance to the racecourse stables, jumping down from a wall and landing between a stable box and the toilets, an appropriate location for someone who was soon to find himself in real shit.

Browne started chatting up the lass looking after Ambrose, actually holding the horse at one point while she groomed him. As the lass stood on one side of the gelding, Browne stood on the other, quietly slipping the needle in.

It may have been a minor race but Sandown is a major racecourse; one of the best in the country. That Browne made a concealed entrance so easily can only be described as alarming. He also claims that when he returned to the course 10 years later in the company of two police officers, he found that the gaps under gates and sneaky entrances were still there. Now that really is alarming.

"The method for getting in was still the same and I know the two officers were quite shocked to see that," Browne said. "They showed their nimbleness by gaining access as well with me on that same day that I showed them."

Brian Wright, by the way, returned to form by backing the 9-4 winner Usaylah. Ambrose managed to finish second. His jockey, Willie Carson, could have ridden the winner. "It looked as if I'd just picked wrong again, but maybe there was more to it," he said.

To close his interview with the police, Browne is asked about a handful of dopings at Yarmouth, the final dopings he claims he ever did. He tells them: "I am getting a pain in me head" and after three nights and 10 tapes of interviews, tearing through the form book and racking his brains you can hardly blame him. But at least he knew he was in the final telling of his doping odyssey, and let's face it, it's been some journey.

Nearly there now, and Dermot is preparing to end with a bang. For at Yarmouth, the council-owned seaside track, Dermot Browne got stuck into not one but three unwitting racehorses. Two of them were in the same race. A three-runner race at that. So anyone who thought the winner Cum Laude was a rotten price at 8-15 might be inclined to revise that view.

Wright had wanted to back Cum Laude in the first place, and Browne, not that surprisingly, told him to "get stuck in". That's because Browne had found it so easy to dope the first one – whether it was Flying Diva or Spode's Blue – that he went back in again and did the other.

Flying Diva was ridden by Michael Hills, the same man who rode Norwich. "I didn't notice it as much as I had with Norwich, as she was a different type. She didn't run a race, but fillies can be like that so I didn't think too much of it at the time," he recalled.

Neither did anybody else. It was not until Flying Diva became the third confirmed ACP doping that people began to look at the race. Yet while the performance of Flying Diva, last of the trio, came under inevitable scrutiny, no one had a look at Spode's Blue, the filly who finished only three lengths in front of her, having also come under the syringe.

A decade later, when Browne returned to the course with the police, he noted how little the access to Yarmouth's stables had changed. "The stables nearly back on to a road but I had easy access," he said.

Get this: one of the senior staff of Henry Cecil, the top trainer in the country at the time, had reported an incident to Yarmouth's clerk of the course, Nick Lees, on the day that Flying Diva, and Spode's Blue, were doped.

George Winsor, Cecil's travelling head lad, had noticed a large bin on the inside of the perimeter fence surrounding the stables – and a chair on the other side. Where is Inspector Clouseau when you need him.

Even worse, the fence had been squashed down. "It looked as if somebody had used this as a way of climbing in or out," Winsor said.

The response of Lees and a security guard, according to Winsor, was that "they thought at the time a lad had set it up as a short cut to get in and out of the yard." Yes, but why? "In all my years I have never seen it done before," Winsor said.

He added: "It would be very easy for someone to come over the fence and walk out the front gate of the yard, as no one ever gets checked when leaving the yard." Frightening, fucking frightening, especially when you consider that the course played host to another doping in August 1992.

With no one paying any attention to a chair on one side of a security fence and a bin on the other, it is not that surprising that nobody noticed the below-par run of a filly called Alwathba in the next race, trained by Luca Cumani. She was also doped. Browne said it had been a spur of the moment thing, having been encouraged by the ease of the previous two.

Alwathba, who was ridden by Frankie Dettori, came under pressure with two furlongs to go and could not find the finishing surge with which to win the race. She finished last of three, a 1-2 favourite turned over. These things happen in racing.

Questions were being asked, though. Geoff Snook had worked for Barry Hills for more than 20 years by the time Browne and Alfred were said to be running amok. He remembers seeing Alfred hanging around racecourse stables a lot during that period. He had noticed him at Newbury one day and again at York in August 1990. "He was not speaking to anyone or doing anything. I wondered what he was doing there, but continued about my business," Snook said, in a statement he made to the Jockey Club in February 1999. The details of that statement have never before been made public.

At York, Snook had been asked by an elderly gentleman whose role it was to hand out the keys for the racecourse stable boxes if he knew anything about Alfred, who had told the elderly gentleman that he was with "the Barry Hills lads". Snook, of course, knew this not to be true.

Snook didn't see Alfred again until 20 September 1990, at Yarmouth, when one of the horses he was supervising at the course was Flying Diva.

"I had been staying at the races hostel since the previous Monday, 17th September, 1990," Snook said. "The hostel consists of a series of cubicles, with bunk beds. I had been allocated a cubicle at the far end of the hostel. At around 3pm that date, I had occasion to go to the hostel in order to get changed. As I approached the cubicle, the same man as mentioned earlier (Alfred) emerged from my particular cubicle. He never said anything and casually warmed his hands on the gas heater as he left the building. I was aware that there had been a series of thefts from racing hostels throughout the country and wondered if this person was responsible (there is no absolutely no reason to suggest he was). I checked my case which was still locked and intact."

When he had seen Alfred at Newbury, Snook got the impression that he wanted to talk to him – this wasn't unusual – "people often do this to get 'inside' information" – although Alfred never said a word.

Snook had reason to remember the two-day Newbury meeting on 17 and 18

August. On the Friday, Norwich, in his pre-ACP days, had confirmed his ascendancy by winning the Group 3 Hungerford Stakes in style.

Interestingly, at the end of racing, Snook was packing up all the stable's equipment. Hills' staff shared a tack room at Newbury with Dick Hern's lads and had done so for many years. In that tack room Snook noticed a smartly dressed man he didn't recognise. Two of Hills' stable staff were also there. The smartly dressed man kept popping out of the tack room and talking on a portable phone – they didn't quite qualify for the term 'mobile' in those days. Snook also noticed Alfred standing by the stable gates. After about five minutes the smartly dressed man left. Snook asked one of his colleagues who he was. Dermot Browne, he was told. Snook knew the name, he knew Browne was a trainer in Lambourn and knew "there had been a lot of talk in racing circles of him being in financial difficulties."

Could Browne have been on reconnaissance at Newbury that day? For 24 hours later he says he doped Ijtihaad in the Geoffrey Freer Stakes.

Snook got to know Browne a little, although not by choice. At Chepstow, a course we have not mentioned before, on Monday 27 August 1990, Browne approached Snook and asked him about the form of a runner the stable had that day, Oriental Mystique, who finished second in a three-runner race for fillies. She started at 11-10 and was beaten a length by the 5-6 favourite, Line Of Thunder. "A brief conversation took place and I saw no more of him on that date," said Snook.

"Erm", as Dermot might say, there's a problem here. Monday 27 August was a busy Bank Holiday racing day, with six meetings in all. One of them was at Ripon, where the feature race was the Bonusprint Champion Trophy, in which the 6-4 second favourite, Timeless Times, who finished last of three, was supposed to have been doped by Browne. He was also supposed to have been out with the cast of Emmerdale that night and cocked up the doping of Laxey Bay the following day at Ripon.

Something doesn't add up, and perhaps this is a timely reminder that we should not treat everything Browne has claimed as fact. Many of his allegations do add up. Others leave you perplexed and thinking: "What a little sod."

Straw-clutchers might conclude that Browne simply got muddled up; that he knew he had nobbled one in a three-runner race on 27 August, but flicking through the form book in search of recall had hit upon the wrong one – and, of course, the wrong meeting. Perhaps!

Still, on Thursday 20 September, the day Flying Diva was doped, Snook was approached by Browne again, asking if he thought the filly would win. "I explained that I was unhappy with her form on her previous outing at Sandown, and that we might have to take the appropriate action to improve her form (such as blinkers)," Snook said.

Five days later at Kempton, when Browne had a runner, he was loading equipment into his distinctive white jeep when he saw Snook and asked him: "Did you find anything wrong with that filly at Yarmouth", prompting a short conversation between the two men. It was the last time Snook saw Browne.

By that point Browne's doping blitz – the alleged 23 in the space of two months – was over. We can't be sure how many he actually did. We can't be sure which races, which horses. What we can be sure of is that they highlight the sleepy bliss in which racing operated at the time, a time when its integrity was being bored into like a maggot making its way through an apple.

Even now, it seems impossible even to think that it happened. Let alone accept that it did.

Equipped with little more than a needle, his quick wits, his bullshit and his charm Dermot Browne and his doping cohorts became the iconoclasts that racing never wanted to entertain. With embarrassing ease they ran amok, shattering any myths that racing was clean, that the sport was somehow safe.

On one hand, you can only marvel at their anarchy. On the other, you can only shudder at the complacency and incompetence that let them cause such havoc. No longer could anyone smile patronisingly and say of horseracing: "It's not like Dick Francis, you know. This is the real world."

As I write this, there's an evening meeting from Sandown on the TV; a six-runner two-year-old race for debut horses featuring a Godolphin hotpot and a highflier from Sir Michael Stoute's yard. Information is king of the betting ring, and the information from the Newmarket gallops is dictating that this is a two-horse race.

The unavoidable thought seeps into your head. What if Dermot Browne and Brian Wright were still a team? This race would have been perfect for them.

Which one would they have gone for?

2

THE INQUISITION BEGINS

"THEY WERE DOPED!" screamed the headline of the *Racing Post* on Monday, 24 September 1990. "Bravefoot and Norwich tested positive after Doncaster flops."

For those who follow horseracing, this was a Kennedy moment: where were you when you heard the news? Jaws dropped. Clocks stopped. It was that shocking.

There had been much speculation about Bravefoot, less so Norwich, but none of it proved as heady as the truth. Quite simply, no one was prepared for the eye-popping proof that materialised just over a week after the Doncaster meeting. It needs saying again:

Bravefoot and Norwich were doped.

Go into any betting shop, listen out at any racecourse, and you will hear all sorts of slanders uttered whenever a horse runs below expectations. People will always have their suspicions.

Take Dick Hern. He knew already that sometimes when horses run badly, all you are left with are question marks that linger tauntingly in the air. Hern had an absolute flyer of a two-year-old in 1982 called Gorytus. He was due to claim Champion Two-Year-Old honours in his final race of the season, the Dewhurst Stakes. Everybody knew it was simply a case of "how far?"

That's "how far?" as in how far he would win; not how far he'd be beaten. No one could quite believe what happened at Newmarket that day. Gorytus was vanquished out of sight. He *had* to have been doped. Yet nothing showed up, and if dope didn't show up for Gorytus it wouldn't show up for any horse. That's what we thought. Nothing could ever be proved.

So Bravefoot and Norwich gave us the unexpected truth, the chilling confirmation that dopings could be detected. Sometimes.

I remember it well. Somehow I was the first one in on the *Racing Post* newsdesk – an event as rare as confirmed dopings – when the news was announced on a fateful Sunday morning. The phone rang and it was David Pipe, the Jockey Club's director of public affairs, sounding less matey and jolly than usual. He read out a simple statement that revealed that the two horses had been doped with a tranquilliser.

Christ!

Don't forget, no one knew then the full extent of Browne's doping spree, no one had any grasp of the scale or the detail until 10 years later. But the doping of two horses, let alone 23, caused an absolute sensation.

One of my tasks in the manic aftermath of Pipe's call was to get reactions, even if it was well into Sunday afternoon. Racing folk usually react to a phone call from a journalist at that time of the week about as well as they would a tramp urinating on their Gucci slip-ons. And true enough, the response each time was one of fury at being disturbed. Until you told them why you were calling. "Sorry for waking you up . . . I just wanted your reaction to the news that Bravefoot and Norwich were doped . . . Hello? . . ."

"You're not serious . . . Really? . . . Good grief! . . . They weren't were they?"

Yes they were, and all around the racing and betting industries everybody started blaming someone else; it was an inside job, a bent lad, the bookies must have known about it, a sneaky punter is on the loose, racecourse security was a joke.

One of the early theories was that Bravefoot and Norwich were the victims of the same drug used on that year's Swedish Derby favourite, Becam Badge. He had been given a tranquilliser called Plegasil, a syrup that was administered to a horse via a syringe into the mouth. It had the generic name ACP or acetyl-promazine.

We got to know a lot about ACP, even if its use was not confirmed until two weeks after Norwich had been doped. According to a leading vet, Brian Eagles, a horse could be given ACP about an hour before a race and could be expected to run badly without there being any long-lasting effects. Don't forget Norwich went on to finish second in a Group 1 race in France on his next start after Doncaster, although others such as Absaar, the second horse doped by Browne, never ran again.

The *Racing Post* ran a story claiming that the Jockey Club's chief suspect was a bookmaker; a man who has since quit the betting ring but is still involved in racing. There is no hard evidence to suggest that this man – who was never named by the paper – was involved.

Nearly a month after Browne's final burst at Yarmouth, the doping of Flying Diva was confirmed, although not that of Spode's Blue, the other horse who was allegedly 'got at' in the race. Pipe of the Jockey Club stressed that no other samples had tested positive to ACP. Were none of Browne's other victims tested, or was it simply the case that the ACP didn't show up?

Racing's pungent grapevine was beginning to ferment a suspect. The name being bounced around was Dermot Browne. He was arrested by police from South Yorkshire CID on 17 October "in connection with the interference (sounds nasty) of racehorses at the Doncaster St Leger race meeting on September 13 and 14."

Browne was held at Doncaster police station, although the three charges he subsequently faced – deception linked to dishonest cheques totalling £4,100 and driving while disqualified and without insurance – had nothing to do with horseracing.

He appeared at Doncaster Magistrates Court on 19 September and was remanded in custody at first. Later, he was bailed until the end of November on condition that he surrendered his passport, did not return to his house at Lambourn and stayed within England and Wales. His father Liam also had to provide a £20,000 surety.

Browne's arrest had taken place at 11.00am at his home in Lambourn. He had been expecting a visit and not just because of the numerous messages the police had left. Brian Wright had told Browne what was about to happen. Browne reckoned that Wright had contacts within the police, although there is no suggestion that they included those investigating Browne.

According to Browne, Wright offered him a safe passage to America if he wanted it. Browne in custody was not good news. No one knew what he would say. Wright told him "he had it from the inside" that the police were not exactly armed to the teeth with evidence against Browne.

"And they never would be," Browne said. "The only people who knew about it going on was myself and himself (Alfred)."

Wright, Browne continued, "was afraid I would implicate him as being the big man and the main man behind it and the man who was paying for it, the man who was making the most money out of it and obviously because he had a criminal record he would be in more trouble than I was because I had never had any problems before."

Browne had a visitor while he was being kept at Doncaster police station. "They bought my father in to see me and he was telling me to say my bit and once I told them what was going on they'd help me and it would make life easier for me."

He didn't do that. Instead he opted for Wright's 'say nothing' approach. Why? "Well basically because I have never been afraid of my father, my father didn't really know what was going on at the time." But Browne said he was not so much afraid of Wright but, "I believed what he was telling me was true."

Incredible as it now seems, security cameras were not in place at Doncaster's racecourse stables so there was no video footage of Browne in action. Nor was there much guilt at what he had done. Browne was asked during his police interview if he thought he had been breaking the law. He was ambiguous. It was more a case of "getting one over the bookies basically and earning money. I didn't see any horses in distress and they were eating up well afterwards. They didn't seem too bothered about it so from that point of view I wasn't too bothered and the jockeys weren't in any danger.

"I knew it wasn't legally right but I didn't think it was serious. Yeah, I suppose I knew it was a crime but I didn't think it was a serious crime. In actual fact, Doncaster CID didn't know what kind of crime it was at the time either."

The Jockey Club, meanwhile, took its own, swift action. While Browne had been waiting for the police at home, he took a call from one of his stable staff. She was in tears. A motorbike courier had arrived from London, from the Jockey Club. It was a letter saying that Browne's licence was being withdrawn due to there being insufficient horses in his yard – you needed 12 at the time. "So technically, when Doncaster police arrived to arrest me I was an ex-trainer within 10, 15 minutes. So I was never arrested as a trainer."

Losing his licence may have saved Browne money; unsuccessful trainers tend to haemorrhage the stuff. However, Dermot Browne lost more than money. His dreams of making it as a trainer, equalling if not surpassing the achievements of his father, were over after only a year.

IRELAND'S DOPING GANGS

As news of Bravefoot and Norwich's dopings and Browne's arrest sank in, it emerged that there had been strong suspicions that a doping gang had previously been on the loose in Ireland. It was thought to have made its debut at the 1982 Galway Festival and grown from there.

A nasal spray – more likely than not containing ACP – was said to have been used to nobble a series of well-fancied runners, all of whom performed badly and showed similar symptoms of lifelessness and grogginess to those doped in Britain. In the case of entires, their penises were hanging like condemned men, a la Bravefoot.

Concerns about the integrity of Irish racing deepened during the 1987/88 Jumps season. The high-class hurdler Bonalma had to be withdrawn at the start when a 6-4 favourite for his chasing debut at Tipperary. He was examined by a vet after his rider reported him "markedly off-colour". A week later, another talented hurdler, Classical Charm, trailed in last of 13 at Fairyhouse, having drifted from 5-4 to 9-2, and was found to be in a distressed condition. No trace of a prohibited substance was found in tests taken from either horse, although the Irish Turf Club did express its concern at those incidents, and another at Down Royal in Northern Ireland when the favourite Sharp Jewel was pulled up in distress.

The Turf Club's Keeper of the Match Book, Cahir O'Sullivan, said at the time: "There's no proof as yet, but we have fairly strong suspicions that a drug was used in these cases that cannot be detected at the moment . . . who is behind the so called doping ring? We have our eyes on one or two big punters, not bookmakers."

O'Sullivan, whose comments were made to Timeform's *Chasers and Hurdlers* annual, added: "We have ruled out the use of a spray-type method of administration because the particular drug we suspect would have to be used with precision to have the desired effect."

The suspicions never went away. In 1991 two horses, Dominic's Cross and Caddy, were found to have been doped with ACP at Kilbeggan. Their cases were investigated by the Gardai, whose report to the Director of Public Prosecutions was not taken any further.

But that wasn't the end of it. Actual confirmation of an ACP doping came with the positive test of a runner at Tralee on 1 June 1998. The doped horse was Tobar Na Carraige, pulled up in a two-and-a-half-mile handicap hurdle after drifting in the betting from 4-1 to 7-1. The race went to Drishouge Lad, who had been backed down to 7-2 favourite from 8-1.

Tobar Na Carraige, trained in County Cork by John Joe Walsh and ridden that day by Shay Barry, was tailed off by the time he was pulled up before the eighth hurdle. Walsh was immediately concerned and with good reason. Speaking after confirmation of the doping, Walsh said he suspected that the gelding was doped while his lad took the jockey silks to the weighing room. "I thought something was amiss with the horse very early in the race and when he came back in afterwards he was showing all the signs of having been heavily sedated," said Walsh. "He was drunk and barely able to stand."

And the point is?

Well, Dermot Browne provided a new twist to Ireland's doping issue during his police interviews. Back in 1990, when he says he met Brian Wright and Alfred in the Halcyon, on the night he had been taken there at gunpoint from Goodwood, Alfred told Browne that he had "attended races" in Ireland and that he had "doped horses in Ireland."

One of them, at Leopardstown on the fringes of Dublin, was Naevog, a mare trained by Browne's father Liam. "(Alfred) said he had to tell me now that he was party to one of my father's horses being doped at Leopardstown, that he had to tell me now because if I found out later it might mess things up," Browne told the police.

Naevog had a mixed career at Leopardstown. She won there three times, but also put in some stinkers that would have you worried. She was sixth of eight, beaten 39 lengths, when prominent in the betting for the Wessel Cable Champion Hurdle won by Nomadic Way in February 1990. Before that, she came last of 20 in a two-mile Flat handicap, for which she started an outsider.

More interestingly, the mare finished last of three in a two-mile hurdle in

January 1989 when sent off the 4-6 favourite. Naevog was examined by a Turf Club vet after that race and was found to have a heart irregularity. She soon recovered. A month later Naevog won her next start, also at Leopardstown, by eight lengths. It was a high-class contest in which she was ridden differently, from the front. That is not conclusive proof that she was doped the time before. Still, it makes you wonder, doesn't it?

Alfred had also revealed that he used to get his 'jungle juice' from "a kind of veterinary shop in Ireland, basically it was used for cattle or horses that were going to be castrated . . . to drowsy them up a bit. It was fairly easily available and it wasn't very dear but apparently whatever he mixed it with acted like a disguising or masking type of stuff to stop it showing up."

Intriguing stuff. Perhaps Eric Cantona had Dermot Browne in mind when he referred to seagulls following trawlers. Because it often feels like Browne is standing at the stern of the ship, waving some tasty looking fish in the air.

You can't help but be tempted.

JOCKEY CLUB BAN

Dermot Browne's life, meanwhile, was spiralling further and further out of control. Little more than two years after he had lost his training licence, he was warned off by the Jockey Club – which meant he was banned from any worthwhile involvement with horseracing – for 10 years.

Again, this had nothing to do with his doping of Bravefoot and Norwich, or the other unknown victims. Instead, there was a scattering of rule breaches that were forged together to ensure that Browne was a horseracing pariah. No one was shedding any tears.

On 28 October 1992, two days before his 31st birthday, Browne was found guilty by the Jockey Club's disciplinary committee of instructing a jockey not to win on one of the horses that he had trained in a race at Leicester in June 1990. Another offence was the vaccination or otherwise of Total Sport, the filly he had run at Kempton on the day Stylish Senor was doped.

The third and most eye-catching rule breach concerned selling information to a bookmaker about three horses; Argentum and Silken Sailed, at York in August 1990, and Family At War, at Ripon the following month. All three are horses that Browne said he doped, although the bookmaker concerned, David Aarons, had no knowledge at all of that.

Aarons at the time pointed out that he was not a defendant in the Jockey Club proceedings and in fact had been thanked for the evidence he provided at Browne's hearing. He denied buying information from Browne.

The Jockey Club decided that in passing the information to Aarons, while a licensed trainer, Browne had acted in "a manner prejudicial to the integrity and good reputation of horseracing". Dermot Browne did quite a lot of that. He was later to lose an appeal against his 10-year disqualification, a failure that surprised no one.

But like nagging hiccups he would not go away. In July 1993, a BBC sports investigative programme called *On The Line* ran an item about doping which featured a character in disguise called 'The Needleman'. Any guesses?

The Needleman said that he had doped over 20 horses at £5,000 a time, starting a media hunt to unmask him. It didn't take much doing. Browne's former wife Carol said that he had called her to say he would be on the programme, and although his identity and voice were obscured, she recognised his wedding ring.

At the time of the programme, Browne was wanted by police for failing to report to them over an investigation into driving offences. The following month, he also failed to appear at Oxford Crown Court to answer charges of burglary and theft of a firearm. His solicitor sheepishly explained that Browne had absconded while on bail.

Still you couldn't keep him out of the papers, although that may have been borne less out of a desire for publicity than financial necessity. Revelations mean money. So it was unsurprising that the *Sunday People* carried an interview with the man on the run.

The quotes were tabloid-tight and in stark contrast to the Bloomesque ramblings of Browne's interviews with the police. Not everything added up, either. The article referred to a "major bookmaker and his ruthless gangland contacts", who Browne had met at the Cheltenham Festival. That's not what he told the police – twice.

There were, though, references to having a gun put against his head in the article, and to the claim that he doped five horses belonging to the same trainer "because I couldn't be sure of which one I was supposed to do . . . I had to rush out for more stuff because I had only taken enough for one or two horses." That has echoes of the Ripon fiasco.

Yet there was no mention of an accomplice and Browne ridiculously claimed that Jockey Club security officials had helped him carry out some dopings. "We know the ones to go to. The ones who will accept money and let me in and out of the racecourse stables to get to the horses. It probably won't be long before we have a security guard on the payroll who'll do it all for us."

A bit like Browne's life at the time, it was hard to make much sense of the article. Browne was later tracked down to pony-trekking stables in the south of Ireland, where he had been lying low. For six years he continued to do that but when he re-emerged – as we will see later – he did so in bizarre circumstances, with real venom and equally unimaginable consequences.

JOCKEY, TRAINER AND DOPER

So what led Dermot Browne to take such a self-destructive course?

It's a typical crash and burn tale. And as you might expect, it didn't have to be that way. Browne had been born into safe, traditional racing hands. He sat on his first horse at the age of three, but then became frightened and did not go near one for six years – strange that, considering his father Liam was not only a well-established trainer, winning top-level races like the Irish Two Thousand Guineas with Dara Monarch in 1982, but also renowned for his ability to develop the careers of young apprentice jockeys.

Few of Liam Browne's graduates lacked for toughness, a prime example being Michael Kinane, who as first jockey to Aidan O'Brien has ridden some of the very best horses of recent seasons including two successive Derby winners in Galileo and High Chaparral. "We had to be up by 6.30am each day. We worked non-stop apart from 40 minutes for lunch. Often I was so tired by the end of the day that I went straight to bed. There was no such thing as a weekend off. Just a few days at Christmas and that was under duress," Kinane said in his biography, *Mick Kinane, Big Race King*. "On occasions it was murder, particularly with Liam having a go at you if you did something wrong."

Having left school at 17, Dermot rode his first winner within the year in a bumper race (a Flat race for potential Jumpers) at The Curragh. It was the first of three winners in a 10-day spell for him.

Browne then spent time in California working with a vet before returning to Ireland with a big decision ahead of him. Because of his height, he had no chance of making it as a Flat jockey, so Liam advised his son to develop his inherent skills at a Jumps stable. "He figured I would learn just as much from a good Jumps trainer as I would from a good Flat trainer."

The choice they made between them couldn't have been better. Browne arrived full of confidence and optimism at Poplar House in Harewood, Yorkshire, home to the incredible Dickinson dynasty of Tony, his wife Monica, and son Michael. Their stable jockey Tommy Carmody had learnt his trade with Liam Browne, providing an important link and contact for Dermot. "I went there (to the Dickinsons) for six months and ended up staying years," he said.

Under their guidance, Browne became an outstanding, dashing rider – "extremely good" in his own words – twice winning the amateur championship in the 1981/82 and 1982/83 seasons. He faced hot competition both times, his rivals including Jim Wilson, Tim Easterby, Tim Thomson Jones, Oliver Sherwood, and his brother Simon Sherwood who was also to turn professional and immortalised himself by guiding Desert Orchid to win the 1989 Cheltenham Gold Cup.

While he was with Dickinson, Browne was involved with the big-time. He had the thrill of riding Ashley House, the final horse of the quintet that so memorably filled the first five places in the 1983 Cheltenham Gold Cup. The following season he achieved a career-best tally of 33 winners.

He rode some good horses, too, including two Dickinson standard-bearers; Political Pop, who gave Browne his first Cheltenham Festival win in the 1982 Kim Muir Chase, and The Mighty Mac. He was a huge, bold-jumping horse whom Browne partnered to win the valuable SGB Handicap Chase at Ascot in 1983 and the 1984 Cathcart Chase, another Festival success. The Cathcart was against professionals and despite his own amateur status, Browne was anything but outclassed in that company.

It is, however, sadly appropriate that Browne is best remembered not for the races he won but one that he so dramatically lost.

The owner of Browne's Gazette was once jokingly described as "difficult" by the horse's then trainer, Michael Dickinson. He was referring to Dermot Browne, who not only owned Browne's Gazette but also worked as his groom. The gelding was one of the leading novice hurdlers of the 1983/84 Jumps season, advertising his and his rider's talents in the Waterford Supreme Novices' Hurdle at the Cheltenham Festival. For a jockey to win at that meeting is like a footballer scoring in the FA Cup final.

The gelding was made the 4-6 favourite for the 1985 Champion Hurdle, an incredibly short price for such a competitive race, on the strength of four wins on the trot. The most eye-catching of these came at Kempton in the Christmas Hurdle in which he trounced Desert Orchid – Dessie – who had yet to achieve the cult status so synonymous with the second half of his career over fences.

Cheltenham came and Dermot Browne was facing the biggest moment of his career. Victory in the Champion Hurdle takes you into the big-time. A man as assured as a young Dermot Browne would regard such a level as his automatic right.

He would have felt such future greatness rushing away from him as Browne's Gazette whipped round at the start, ruining any chance of triumph in a quick, uncontrollable moment of silliness. Just as the tapes were about to rise, he planted himself at a right angle to the direction he should have been going. Bad move. Within seconds, horse and jockey were left 20 lengths behind the rest of the field. Thirteen backsides charged into the distance just as quickly as Dermot Browne's hopes disappeared.

Browne desperately tried to make up ground, perhaps too quickly. At the first hurdle the gap had been reduced to 10 lengths, and with a circuit nearly completed they were back in there with a chance. Briefly. The effort made in reducing the deficit had left Browne's Gazette exhausted and unresponsive when the others produced their finishing kick. The gelding finished sixth, 14 lengths behind the winner, See You Then.

Monica Dickinson, Browne's Gazette's trainer, felt that the jockey had been "caught napping"; the Cheltenham stewards accepted Browne's account that his mount had simply whipped round in anticipation of the start. The stewards may have accepted the explanation. Many didn't. Even at a time when Browne was regarded as more saint than sinner, this was a ride that aroused deep suspicion.

Still, Browne continued to prosper even if you sensed that his big chance had gone. His involvement with the Dickinsons ended when Michael, so dominant in the field of Jumping, was offered the lucrative and exciting challenge of taking over Robert Sangster's string at Manton, a training centre of former glories that Dickinson had the task of transforming for the 21st century. The project was not a success and Dickinson was replaced after only a year by Barry Hills. Manton was Hills' base during the time Browne kept doping his horses.

With Michael Dickinson taking up a new calling, Browne took his cue and did the same. He moved south to the then National Hunt headquarters of Lambourn. It looked a good move.

He continued to ride valuable winners for new trainers: the 1986 Fernbank Hurdle at Ascot on King's College Boy for Nicky Vigors; the same year's Tingle Creek and Scilly Isles Novices' Chase, both at Sandown, with the Nick Gaselee-trained Berlin; in 1987 he partnered Framlington Court to win the Tote Placepot Hurdle at Kempton and Timeform Hurdle for Peter Walwyn; and he also built up a successful relationship with Mercy Rimell, for whom he rode the talented chasers Deep Moment and Golden Friend.

Browne was by now a professional and seemed set for a golden future. Yet deep down, all was not well.

Weight was a real issue. "When you are five foot eleven, it's hard to keep down to nine stone three or four. It's very hard," he said.

There were other issues to deal with, among them the biggest test of any nascent riding star. Temptation. It was not just the usual dilemma of drink, women and body-bloating nights out. You can always recover from those.

No, it was more serious. It was about being human. About being weak. About being tempted by money. About making mistakes. Again and again and again. Dermot Browne didn't do anything that different to the rest of us. He just too it took it too far.

SKULDUGGERY ABOUNDS

It's probably time for a confession. Browne was up to mischief well before he stumbled into a doping plot at Goodwood, well before he was bundled off to London at gun-point.

It all started, Browne says, when he moved away from the Dickinsons. "What I would regard as the serious corruption didn't really begin for me until

I got down to Lambourn," he told the police. "I'd had no involvement in it. Certainly, I had ridden horses for trainers and I was told not to finish in the first three or four or five but I regarded that as my job."

Don't be too shocked by this. Not every horse in British racing is run on its merits. Horses may be made to perform deliberately below their best in order to reduce the weight they carry in future handicaps and improve their odds in the betting. This issue was raised in February 2001 in an article I wrote for *Observer Sports Monthly* – under the prescient headline 'Is Racing Bent?' – in which a top Flat jockey anonymously admitted: "I think everybody accepts that a trainer doesn't always want his horse to be ridden to win. He may not say as much but he will put it in a certain way which you will recognise. That is far from uncommon."

Indeed, there is a naughty but nice side to racing in which the sport's practitioners attempt to bend the rules as far as they can without being sussed. Such ploys became the subject of BBC investigative programme *Kenyon Confronts* in June 2002, which seriously damaged the reputations of three trainers. There's more on that to come.

Horseracing is full of mischief. Browne tells of one owner, a Jockey Club member, who offered him cattle in lieu of a retainer to ride his horses. The cattle were to be kept in a field belonging to that owner's trainer. Browne was having none of it. He was convinced that the trainer would sell his cattle on the sly. Why? Because the owner used to ring Browne, also on the QT, whenever the trainer offered him a new horse for sale. He needed Browne's 'honest', independent opinion in case he was being sold a dud. Browne's assessment, however, depended on whether the trainer had offered him a percentage of a successful sale. You could hardly ask for a better example of racing's halcyon turpitude.

Unless, that is, you consider Browne's tale of a night of post-prandial reflection with another senior trainer and another, very important, Jockey Club member. "We were doing very well on the port that night," said Browne. "He (the man from the Jockey Club) just indicated to me that it would be very much in his benefit if the horse I was due to ride in a race, didn't finish in front of another particular one. But he was well pissed at the time." In *vino veritas*? You can never be too sure.

But in comparison to some of the strokes that were being pulled, this is all jolly hockey sticks material. For be in no doubt; Dermot Browne was doing things that were wrong. Very wrong. The rules weren't so much blurred as ignored.

Soon after Browne moved south, it emerged that "it was well known among jockeys that you can get yourself a few bob for not winning on certain occasions."

Equally, money could be made for passing on inside information on horses, such as a favourite that had suffered a setback – "it was common knowledge that was going on". And who would reward Browne and other jockeys for stopping horses or passing on stable secrets? You'll know the name by now. Brian Wright.

Remember how Browne had recognised Wright and Wright had recognised him in that super-smooth London hotel, and indeed how relieved Browne was at that being the case?

"I had known him before, yes," Browne said in his police interview. "I had known him from when I was riding and, you know, stopping horses and (Wright was) paying me to stop horses and giving him information and him backing horses on the strength of that information."

According to Browne, Wright would often share his inside information with bookmakers and they would split the proceeds. "If the bookmaker can get hold of that information he could take as much money as he could on the horse without shortening up the price."

Browne said he originally met Wright through two jockeys who were already close to the gambler.

The first encounter took place at an Indian restaurant in Swindon. "I went to meet him, had a chat and discussed the topic of me giving him information as regards horses that I was or wasn't riding . . . in order for him to have information to use it as tools for his betting," Browne said.

"I knew this went on a lot, common knowledge. I didn't actually know that the two boys were directly involved in it at that point but they convinced me that they had done business with him and he was fine. He always paid up and paid up well.

"It started off like that – a phone call or two, about your chances on a particular horse on a particular day, whether you thought it might win or not. Then he would ring you back and say he was speaking to some other jockeys – it could have been any number of jockeys, he knew all of them – and he would refer to their chances and he would assess other horses and then he would say to you that maybe . . . he would rather not back mine and would I be interested in putting the handbrakes on mine."

Browne would also meet Wright at the races, where the latter would entertain in private boxes. Jockeys' wives and girlfriends would spend the day there to be joined by 'the boys' at the end of racing. "You would meet other people in there who were friends of his," Browne recalled. "They were all very well dressed, plenty of Rolex watches and gold etc."

Away from the racecourse, Wright would entertain freely in London. One of his big nights out would be for an annual sports dinner, after which the jockeys would decamp to a top nightclub, Tramp. The drinks were free and the crack was good.

Browne remembers walking down the stairs to the hub of the club. He was impressed to see Michael Caine being asked to move to another table, because he was in Wright's regular one. Browne also remembers that the bill, which Wright would pick up, was in the region of £1,500. One night, drinking pink champagne, Browne decided he should buy Wright a bottle in return – but his good intentions were wiped out by the discovery that each bottle cost £150.

Fripperies aside, Tramp proved an eye-opener in more pertinent ways. "That's when I realised the extent of how well known he was to the jockeys and how many jockeys he had on his books, so to speak," Browne said. "I could see him passing money over to different people. Erm, some of the jockeys he passed money over to at the time I was quite shocked to see the names that were actually accepting money."

Browne named names. Horrifically high-profile names. There are times, despite the rush of excitement his allegations provide, when you genuinely don't want to believe what Browne is saying. This is one of those times. The names included very successful jockeys, both over Jumps and on the Flat, during the late 1980s and early 1990s.

Among the big names were some less successful jockeys, including Barrie Wright. "He was a recruitment man, you might say," said Browne. "Barrie Wright didn't ride that many horses. He had a weight problem, but he used his jockeys' licence as a tool to be able to go in and sit down and talk to jockeys, get information and go out and pass it on, no questions asked, and he would be liaising a lot."

As we know, Browne had been doing something similar. "There were other people I rang and gave them information," he said. "If I rode a horse who galloped and I thought 'this is going to win', I rang a certain few people, maybe four or five of them, because each one of them would have a bet and if it won I would collect from each of them. I wasn't having a bet myself as a jockey. No harm done basically."

He was also receiving cash gifts – some of them flamboyantly large, delivered by chauffeurs or minders to his home – from owners he had ridden winners for. There was nothing wrong with that, he felt. "I didn't see that as breaking Jockey Club rules."

Browne's association with Wright, however, was "a totally different ball game", receiving as he did between £1,500 and £2,000 for valuable information and as much as £5,000 for stopping a horse in a run-of-the-mill contest. "I never got to stop one in a very big meeting, where he could pay more," Browne said.

"Brian Wright was paying you for a business job he had asked you to do: either stopping a horse or you gave him information on the horse that you were riding and he backed it and it won and you expected your pay."

While Browne's initial visit to Tramp had caused him surprise at the extent of Wright's weighing-room network, it had also reassured him. "I felt I was doing just the same as everybody else," he said.

"Jockeys discuss things with one another, especially if a jockey is just coming onto the scene and he has recently been offered money to stop a horse. The one thing he is going to look for is basically reassurance from other people. If he thinks other jockeys that he knows have been riding for years and doing well and doing it and never got caught, he would be more inclined to go along with it.

"When you are going racing every day of the week and are involved and your whole life is racing and jockeys are like your work colleagues every day you tend to know who's involved with who and why. And they wouldn't be hanging around Brian Wright for nothing.

"I know I was in, I suppose over the years, I was in the presence and the company of a lot of jockeys and they would be on the phone and you know there were often races whereby four or five jockeys riding in the race were all on the same payroll, so you know, he didn't have to ask five lads to stop horses in the race, maybe just one or two, but the other two or three would be giving him information saying this horse isn't galloping very well or he doesn't like the ground etc, so he could narrow it down quite a lot."

When the offers from Wright started coming through, Browne felt established enough to take the risks to earn the chance to ease his troubles. "Easy money was coming in especially as it started off very gently.

"You ride horses to ride winners to begin with. You want to win the whole time. Once you have started to receive some money for not winning, and you get a bit older, winning isn't as important to you as paying your bills."

"My wife at the time was difficult any time I was drinking," Browne continued. "I was drinking champagne 'cos it's the one thing you can drink without putting weight on. Believe it or not, it dehydrates you and it's very nice when somebody else is buying it."

It may be that Browne was reaching for excuses for his wrongdoing when he made the following soliloquy. It may be that he meant it. Whatever his motives, he provides a pretty graphic, pretty desperate flow-chart of how a talented jockey goes bad.

"You are more prone to taking the money when you need the cash and if riding the winner meant paying half of it back to the tax man, and getting £300, £400 as opposed to three, four grand in cash . . . you know at a certain stage, like I said, it was jovial earlier, OK, but it is a real point: that you do have to pay a mortgage and you do have a wife who wants this and wants that and you want to provide for her and you want to get it for her so you go the extra yard to get it.

"It doesn't seem difficult because (riding) is a dangerous business, it's not like any other business, there aren't too many businesses that you go hungry in. A boxer steps into the ring but he has got one fellow to hit. When you are riding a race and there are 20 horses and you hit the ground there are horses galloping over you with steel shoes on and they are heavy and you can't get up afterwards and give them a box in the jaw – you'd get one back from them – and you break bones and it hurts and you have a short career in it. Footballers – you see them falling on the ground, even the good ones, just kicking around and lying around on the ground. It's a different ball game. You go back into the jockey changing room there and you are sitting in the sauna with other fellas night after night after night sweating and sweating and sweating and they are discussing the same thing – it's a way of life – it's . . . everybody's doing it."

While he paused for breath, Browne was asked by police if he ever considered that he was doing wrong. "At that point no," he replied. "It's just part and parcel of it. If you were to look at it from the outside, a person that wasn't brought up in the racing game and embroiled in it totally, then you could see, yeah, more obviously, that there is a crime in it."

He's not kidding.

Next he was asked if Brian Wright targeted the weak. "He wouldn't target the weak as such," Browne said, "he would have targeted people he thought he could make money from, people that were riding horses, that were going to ride horses that would be favourite. Or in other words, he was targeting people that were riding a lot of winners, who were riding good horses . . . basically, anybody that is successful.

"They won't approach you if you are not in a position to ride horses that they reckon are either worth backing or worth stopping. That's obviously because you are circulating with other riders of the same calibre."

Again Browne mentioned some celebrated weighing room names; Classic winners, Champion Hurdle winners, Gold Cup winners. "I can mention jockeys that I have seen in his company and I have seen money change hands," he insisted.

"They were doing it. I mean these people he dealt with . . . if you want to back winners you have got to be with people that are really successful. It is only rarely that you will pull off a gamble or back a winner if a lad rides a winner once every pancake Tuesday, do you know?

"Brian Wright knew what he was doing. He'd ring you up and say 'what do you reckon, any chance of winning today?' and you would say 'yeah, I think this horse will win today' or 'he won't like the ground or something like that'.

"He would invite you up to London to dinner – a nice dinner and the wife comes up for a nice evening out in London at an expensive restaurant, going home with a thousand quid in your pocket for doing nothing, basically. For just telling him you think it would win and you fancied the horse to win anyway."

Dermot Browne retired as a jockey in 1989 when he made a quick switch to the training ranks. The switch, as you might have gathered, was not a success. His biggest achievement – apart from doping – was to somehow convince the newspapers that he had a backer who wanted to set him up at Manton, at a time when it was unclear how long Barry Hills would remain there.

His on-off contact with Wright ended soon after his arrest by Doncaster CID. "I don't think he wants to speak to me," Browne said. "I certainly don't want to speak to him unless he pays me the £110,000 that he owes me."

The chances of that are not good. Wright may not even owe Dermot Browne £110,000, he might not even owe him anything. Browne's grip on his finances were nowhere near as tight as his grip on the reins of a horse he did not wish to win on.

It's his grip on the truth that counts. Some swear by it. Others question it. You decide.

3

NOT AGAIN

Even with Dermot Browne on the run, racing's landscape continued to be pockmarked with doping cases. At least their occurrence was at a less destructive rate than Browne had achieved. Indeed, there was a gap of nearly two years between Flying Diva and the next doping, although the same racecourse, Yarmouth, was involved. Not much to boast about there.

The Geoff Lewis-trained Flash Of Straw was sixth of 12 in a mile-handicap on 20 August 1992. Sent off the 4-1 favourite, Flash Of Straw could make little impression on the leaders when asked to do so at the two-furlong pole. The only obvious way of benefiting from the doping would have been to lay Flash Of Straw knowing it could not win. This was not a race that could be easily narrowed down to two horses.

Flash Of Straw tested positive to detomodine, a potent tranquilliser. The absence of ACP raised questions as to whether any of the 1990 dopers had returned to action or whether a new gang was on the loose. Only those involved know for sure.

Murkier news came in January 1993 with the first known doping of a horse over Jumps. The victim was Her Honour, at the time a candidate for one of the top races at the Cheltenham Festival, the Triumph Hurdle. Trained by Martin Pipe – whose horse Tyrone Bridge was also doped – and ridden by Peter Scudamore, Her Honour tested positive to ACP when a 6-4 favourite for the Walton Novices' Hurdle over two miles at Kempton on 22 January 1993. She finished sixth, more than 40 lengths behind the winner, having been heavily backed. The only other horse to attract serious support, the 2-1 second favourite Scrutineer, was fourth of 11.

Like other jockeys before him, and others to follow, Peter Scudamore had been pleased to notice that Her Honour was noticeably more relaxed in the parade ring than on her previous start at Warwick. "I thought the penny had dropped and she had got the hang of how to race," he said. "I was still pleased with her as she cantered to (the) post but during the race she never picked the bridle up and jumped badly. I hadn't been hard on her once her chance had gone and unsaddled to a barrage of abuse from some of the punters who had backed her as favourite."

Her Honour's doping caused a lot of anger but not at those who had committed the act itself. The anger was directed within; largely toward the Jockey Club. Trainers, in particular, were aggrieved that only once the doping of Her Honour was confirmed did the fate of Flash Of Straw emerge – seven months after his run at Yarmouth. Such a cover-up was exacerbated by the fact that the Jockey Club, under its then senior steward Lord Hartington, had tried to allay fears of a new doping outbreak, knowing full well that the problem had not gone away.

Even with a googly like detomodine, there was still some consistency between the dopings of Flash Of Straw, Her Honour and those of 1990 – mainly the fact that no one was ever charged.

Jockeys would often come muttering back to the weighing room, shaking their heads about how lifelessly their horse had run. When it came to proof, silence reigned. If doping was continuing on a regular basis, it did so undetected.

Two notable, unproven cases, involved high-class chasers, Playschool and Jodami. David Barons had strong suspicions that the in-form Playschool was 'got at' when he was sent off the 100-30 favourite for the 1988 Cheltenham Gold Cup. According to Timeform's *Chasers & Hurdlers* annual: "The reliable, usually sound-jumping Playschool was never moving or jumping with his usual fluency." The gelding's jockey, Paul Nicholls, reported "something seriously wrong", even though post-race tests and investigations showed nothing untoward.

Uncertainty also hangs over Jodami's run in the Rehearsal Chase at Chepstow on 4 December 1993, when the 2-7 favourite could only finish third, beaten 12 lengths. His trainer Peter Beaumont was as suspicious of this performance as David Barons was of Playschool's. Both thought their horses had been doped.

For all the suspicions, though, it was four years after Her Honour's doping that the next two confirmed victims emerged.

Avanti Express, trained by Charlie Egerton and ridden by Jamie Osborne, was pulled up two hurdles from the finish when the 5-4 second favourite for the HMS Exeter Novices' Hurdle at Exeter on 7 March. Lively Knight, a novice chaser in the care of Josh Gifford and partnered by Leighton Aspell, started a 1-7 favourite and had only two horses to beat in the Seeboard Novices' Chase at Plumpton on 29 March. He failed to do so, mainly because, like Avanti Express three weeks before him, Lively Knight had been injected with ACP.

The dopers were back.

THE HAPPY EATER GANG

Even if they were over Jumps, the Avanti Express and Lively Knight races carried the hallmarks of the 1990 dopings.

Avanti Express faced 10 opponents, but his Exeter contest was regarded as a two-horse showdown between him and the Martin Pipe-trained, 11-10 favourite Give And Take, who under a gallivanting, front-running ride from Tony McCoy won the race by 14 lengths.

The Jockey Club had an idea something was brewing at Exeter on the day Avanti Express was got at. Here's how that day unfolded.

There was no sign of the trouble ahead when Avanti Express was loaded into the horsebox at Egerton's stables at Chaddleworth, near Newbury. It was around 7.15am, and the intention was to arrive at the course three hours before Avanti Express's race at 2.15pm. Joe Tuite, then Egerton's travelling head lad, accompanied Avanti Express, as did the gelding's lad, Michael McCabe. McCabe was Avanti Express's soulmate; he would look after him almost every day, mornings and evenings at the stables, as well as on trips to the racecourse.

The journey was uneventful. Tuite sat up front besides the driver, McCabe slept in the back. On his arrival at Exeter, Avanti Express was unloaded from the horsebox, which was owned by an independent operator, and put in the stable box that he'd been allocated by racecourse security. McCabe and Tuite removed his travelling rug and his tail bandage and left after five minutes.

After declaring the horse to run the pair walked the course. Tuite rang Egerton to say that he was happy that the going was suitable for Avanti Express. About 50 minutes after their arrival, both men went to a Happy Eater café that neighboured the parking area for horseboxes and the entrance to the racecourse stables.

As they waited to be seated a man Tuite did not recognise approached him and said: "Hi, Joe." He asked Tuite if he had a winner for him. "We've a horse in the second race," Tuite told him. "He's a short-priced favourite, has a favourite's chance."

Once they were seated, Tuite noticed the unknown tip seeker at a table with three other men. They were frequently using mobile phones to make and take calls. Soon they were joined by another man, someone Tuite had noticed earlier sitting in a Mercedes. Tuite and McCabe were joined by some lads from Philip Hobbs' yard. The talk, as you would expect, was of horses.

The talk back at the racecourse was of a man who had on several occasions tried to gain unauthorised entry to the racecourse stables. A smallish man, balding, wearing a fading green Barbour, he had been stopped from gaining entry by the stable guard Gerald Bellew. People like Bellew had a simple task; to stop anybody who shouldn't be in the racecourse stables from being there. We already know they are not always successful. And on Friday 7 March 1997,

Bellew joined the select list of security guards who have let in a doper – whoever he was – although Bellew knew nothing of the sinister intent of the intruder.

As Bellew said himself in a statement to the Jockey Club's security team: "My principal responsibility is to preserve the integrity of racecourse stables at various racecourses on racedays."

He did this – or attempted to – by cross-checking stable passes with the names on a Stable Register of all people needing access to the stables. To aid security, closed circuit cameras were introduced after the 1990 fiascos. They are in place at the main yard entrance and when necessary at secondary entrances, too.

Bellew had been at Exeter since 8.00am that day. Sometime between 11.00am and midday the Barbour jacket man attempted to walk past Bellew and gain access to the restricted area of the stables. Bellow challenged him and told the man he was not entitled to enter the area. He left.

Not long after, the same man walked into the stable office and spoke to Bellew again. He asked if a local trainer called Gordon Edwards had arrived. He hadn't. The man left, with Bellew stating: "I did not have any suspicions about this man at the time."

Shortly before midday the trainer in question arrived, leading a horse. The Barbour man was spotted, unbeknown to the trainer, sneaking in again behind the horse's quarters. Bellew stopped him once more. The man told Bellew he had been asking Edwards to give him a job, as a box driver, having just lost his job with Martin Pipe. Bellew checked the story out with Pipe's travelling head lad, who said he had never seen the Barbour man.

Bellew then reported "the very suspicious activities which had occurred" to Malcolm Carson, the Jockey Club's Racing Intelligence officer. Carson in turn alerted the Betting Ring Inspector, Ted Biddulph, who soon observed the Barbour man in the company of four others.

Carson started taking photographs of the men – the Happy Eater men – and told Biddulph to keep a close eye on the betting patterns of the 2.15 race. That was the race in which Avanti Express ran so poorly.

One of the Happy Eaters, it seems, was already known to Malcolm Carson. He mentioned his name to Biddulph, who also knew him. "My suspicions were aroused to see him at Exeter racecourse," Biddulph said in his own statement. Biddulph monitored the betting, noting that Avanti Express opened as the 8-11 favourite, eased to evens, 6-5, before being returned the 5-4 second favourite. He attracted some bets, though: £700 at evens, three bets of £500 at evens, and one of £500 to £400.

Give And Take opened at 6-4, touched 7-4, and was then backed into 11-10 favourite, so someone fancied his chances. William Hill's on-course representative laid off money that had been placed in the firm's betting shops. Those bets included: £1,200 to £800, £1,100 to £800, and three bets of £550 to £400. There were other on-course cash bets of: £875 to £700, £1,250 to £1,100, and £500 to £400.

Talk Back, the third favourite, opened at 7-1 and stayed at that price.

The wheels were in motion. Biddulph informed the stewards' secretary, Paul Barton, of the betting patterns at a meeting. As a stewards' secretary, it was the responsibility of Barton, a former jockey, to advise the three racecourse stewards – all of them amateurs, doing the job voluntarily – of anything that might be amiss in a race. He is almost like a civil servant, offering his advice and experience while leaving the final decision to the stewards. Usually Barton's thoughts would concern incidents during the race, such as misuse of the whip, careless riding, interference, or non-triers. This time, he put forward the betting evidence at a stewards' inquiry into Avanti Express's poor show. The stewards ordered that he be routine tested.

As he noted the betting patterns, Biddulph also watched the Happy Eaters closely, spotting a man similar to the one who had tried to enter the racecourse stables. He summoned Bellew to the betting ring. Bellew confirmed it was the Barbour man.

Meanwhile, Tuite and McCabe carried on with their jobs. Taking a horse to the races can have its idle moments. After leaving the Happy Eater, Tuite had left McCabe to put plaits in Avanti Express' mane and tail while he went to the horsebox and read a book for three-quarters of an hour until it was time to change into the smarter gear he would wear when Avanti Express was being paraded. McCabe spent 45 minutes preparing his horse to look its best. During that time no one came near him.

Returning to the stable, Tuite noticed one of the men he had seen in the café. He had a distinctive appearance that reminded Tuite of someone he knew. On his way back, Tuite crossed over with McCabe, who was taking his turn to get changed. At this moment Avanti Express was unguarded.

Tuite watched the race itself in one of the racecourse bars, so he could see it close up on TV. He saw two more of the Happy Eaters in there. They were smartly dressed in a way that stood out. Too smart for Exeter on a Friday, more like Cheltenham on a Saturday, Tuite thought to himself. They looked like they had money. They would soon have even more.

Tuite knew not why Avanti Express was running so sluggishly and neither did Jamie Osborne. The start for Avanti Express's race had been delayed. This would normally have put Avanti Express on his toes, but Osborne noted what he thought was a sign of the gelding's growing maturity. He was calm and that pleased his jockey. But by the time they made it to the start, Osborne was less assured by Avanti Express's behaviour. He even started trotting him around in a bid to work the seven-year-old out of his slouch.

Watching from the bar, Tuite could see Osborne get to work on the horse distressingly early as McCoy and Give And Take started to pull further and further clear. Osborne and his mount seemed powerless to stop them, even though the jockey was desperate to keep up. He snags at the reins, digs his riding boots into the horse's ribs as an early reminder that a bit of effort is required. Nothing happens. Avanti Express remains heavy and sluggish. "Where *is* he today?" The first crack of the whip and still there is no response. "Something's up", Osborne thinks. "Something's up," Tuite thinks. They both know this isn't Avanti Express's true running.

By now, Avanti Express is practically flapping up and down on the spot. Each hurdle is an effort. He's painfully slow running into one, painfully slow moving away. The leader is outta here, the race already in his grasp. Avanti Express is all over the place. Horse and jockey don't even complete the course. Almost straight away the Happy Eaters make their way down to the betting ring, where they are seen collecting winnings. They leave the course not long after Avanti Express is led back in. Osborne, Tuite and McCabe remain clueless and confused. Concerned, too.

A hot bath and a glass of whiskey often signal the end of a bad day. But this was a bad day that wasn't going away. In less than 12 months, Jamie Osborne would be arrested in connection with the race. And Joe Tuite would pick up a letter that had been sent to him via Egerton's stables. "Be very careful Joe, you could very easily be found with the fishes," it said.

What on earth was going on?

SECOND SUCKS

Only one of the Happy Eaters is thought to have been at Plumpton on the day Lively Night was doped; and that, it should be said, could well have been a coincidence.

The case of Lively Knight could be viewed as a text book race for a doping. Once Lively Knight, 1-7 favourite, was out of the way, there were numerous ways of profiting from that knowledge, even if neither of the other two runners had a significant edge over the other. As it was, the 6-1 second favourite, Cruise Control, ended up well beaten by the 9-1 outsider of three, Stormhill Pilgrim.

One on-course bookmaker, Dave Richardson, was struck by the amount of off-course money that was being relayed to the track. Two major firms, Coral and Victor Chandler, were backing the pair of outsiders, he said.

And then, of course, there is the forecast option, backing the two outsiders to finish ahead of Lively Knight. That would make a lot of sense. A leading Irish bookmaker, Brian Graham, whose family operate as Sean Graham, subsequently passed on to the Jockey Club details of a bet someone had tried to place on the Lively Knight race.

Graham told the *Racing Post* in January 1999: "Someone asked for a £75 or £100 reverse forecast (backing them to fill the first two places in either order) on the two outsiders, Stormhill Pilgrim and Cruise Control.

"In a three-horse race, when the favourite is long odds-on, and the forecast on the other two would pay about 33-1, that is not a bet that you want to know. It is plain as day that something could be wrong." Graham said the attempted bet came from a British firm of bookmakers.

Anyone who had backed Lively Knight soon knew their fate. Just as Jamie Osborne had failed to inject some fire into Avanti Express, so Leighton Aspell was not only waving his whip at Lively Knight but drowning in the hopelessness of his plight.

Aspell had also noticed a change in Lively Knight as soon as he mounted him in the paddock. He was not his usual bouncy, bubbly self and on his toes. This time he was quiet, albeit not suspiciously so.

Aspell had been handed the ride at owner Alan Weller's insistence, in preference to his trainer Josh Gifford's stable jockey Philip Hide. Ironically, Hide had received the call up to ride the winner, Stormhill Pilgrim, instead. He was happy to take up the request, having been annoyed to lose a regular ride.

Hide had the inside track on Lively Knight. He knew he may not like the ground and he knew he may struggle to keep up over a trip that was shorter than ideal, especially if one of the others set a strong pace.

So that's what Hide did. He gave Lively Knight the slip. Aspell tried to keep the gap manageable but he and his partner never looked happy and trailed home seven lengths behind Stormhill Pilgrim. Forecast backers will have cursed the fact that he finished 12 lengths ahead of Cruise Control. That certainly wasn't the plan.

Inevitably, this was one of those races that saw the beaten horse attract more interest than the winner did. As Aspell was led back to the unsaddling enclosure, he needed no reminding that second sucks, especially on a 1-7 shot. He lacked Osborne's confidence and experience and was less equipped to deal with such a setback. He told himself that Lively Knight hadn't enjoyed the ground or was tired after a long season. Come what may, he had some explaining to do. He could see the furious face of Lively Knight's owner Alan Weller. Aspell knew that he was seconds away from a serious grilling. Some answers were needed.

Weller was indeed furious, his mood exacerbated by the fact that his horse had been beaten by a jockey he had forsaken. On the spot, Weller threatened to move his horses from Gifford's yard. He subsequently carried out that threat. "I knew something was wrong," Weller said when news of the doping emerged. "Everyone knows I went mad – I was furious about the whole thing.

"How could a horse turn around about 40lb of form in that sort of race – that's two furlongs! There's no question in my mind he should have won the race."

Inevitably, on the day the Plumpton stewards held an inquiry into Lively Knight's running, Gifford was called in and explained that the good to firm ground was, in hindsight, too lively and the two-mile, five-furlong trip too short.

Gifford, of course, had no idea of the real reason why Lively Knight ran poorly and it was not for another 22 days that tests confirmed Lively Knight had been doped. Yet it was not until October – six months later – that the Jockey Club somewhat belatedly made public the shock news that both he and Avanti Express had been doped. In comparison, it took less than two weeks to confirm the fates of Bravefoot and Norwich. It may have had its reasons for this delay.

Besides, there was something else being kept quiet. Another horse had been 'got at' at Plumpton on the same day.

BETTING EXCHANGES

The horse was Lord Rooble. Someone who really should know insists that he was also doped. Lord Rooble, a six-year-old at the time, was also trained by John Gifford, who had only two runners that day. Could it be that the doper wasn't sure which horse to dope, so he did a Dermot Browne and injected them both?

Or could it be that the gang behind Lively Knight were after a double-whammy? Lord Rooble opened up in the betting at 5-2, second favourite behind Sparkling Spring, who was sent off at 4-5. Lord Rooble drifted, touching 5-1 at one point before settling at 4-1.

Lord Rooble, ridden this time by Philip Hide, was beaten before the home turn, although there is a case for saying that the ground was too quick. That's the wonder of doping; mystery pervades every below-par run.

No tests were taken from Lord Rooble so confirmation or otherwise that he was 'got at' will never be forthcoming. Even if Lord Rooble was doped with ACP, he wasn't the last.

Two unusual cases of ACP emerged in 2002 – one of them without precedent as it involved a horse that won. Plumpton was once more the scene for scandal when the Philip Hobbs-trained Ashgar finished a lacklustre third in a novices' hurdle at the course on 30 March. The six-year-old tested positive to ACP after being beaten seven-and-a-half lengths. He was sent off the 5-6 favourite but had opened at 4-7 and had been available at evens.

Wherever the ACP came from, Hobbs insisted he had not kept it at the yard for several years. Some trainers use it to calm down temperamental horses when, for example, their coats are being clipped, but Hobbs found it unsatisfactory.

Inevitably, the Jockey Club tried to play down links between Ashgar and Avanti Express and Lively Knight, pointing to a lack of unusual betting patterns. Bookmakers don't tend to hang about in reporting suspected foul play.

The race threw the spotlight on the new gambling phenomenon of betting exchanges, the internet system that allows punters to wager against each other by laying horses to lose as well as backing them to win.

Could someone have known that Ashgar was to be doped and profited by laying the horse via a betting exchange? Nobody who places a bet through an exchange knows who they are dealing with, so in theory that could easily happen.

The market leader, Betfair, however, insists that it has strict controls that could quickly trace anyone profiting from a hooky race. That, of course, is only in hindsight and there are doubts over whether they are entitled to withhold payment. The Jockey Club's security team has inspected Betfair's facilities and were encouraged by what they saw.

Britain's high-street bookmakers have been less encouraged by the rise of betting exchanges, and in the autumn of 2002 they suggested that there were a number of races in which favourites were running unaccountably badly. They claimed that some people knew in advance that the favourites would under perform and took advantage of that knowledge by laying them on betting exchanges.

Betfair claims that its security is impeccable, but it doesn't mean its site might not unknowingly play host to a doper or a race fixer.

Equally, supporters of betting exchanges claim that complaints about their integrity are just a cynical attempt to raise doubts about the concept in punters' minds. So successful have exchanges proved that they could soon have a serious impact on traditional bookmakers' profits.

While the probity of Ashgar's race remains very much open to question, it is hard to draw positive conclusions on the case of the other horse who tested positive to ACP, Hachty Boy. Did the dopers bungle it?

You see, Hachty Boy won, and no one would ever use ACP to help a horse do that. It's a stopping drug. All the same, it was lurking in the system of the Henrietta Knight-trained chaser when it won at Wetherby on 23 May by an impressive 11 lengths. Wetherby is a Yorkshire course; not since Dermot Browne has ACP featured anywhere else but a southern track.

Again, no unusual betting patterns were reported by bookmakers, although the most significant money – not that it was much – was for the other cofavourites Be My Dream, who finished third, and fourth-placed Two For Joy. With so many horses nestled together in the betting, though, this was not a likely race for dopers to target.

Like Hobbs, Henrietta Knight was mystified as to how the positive test occurred. Yet someone, somewhere, knows the fully story of not just that case, but Ashgar as well. And even, possibly, one or two others to boot.

4

THE INSPECTORS CALL

If the dopings of Bravefoot and Norwich shook racing, then the arrest of three jockeys on 27 January 1998 was simply seismic in effect.

Equal howls of shock and anger echoed through the sport as Jamie Osborne, Dean Gallagher and Leighton Aspell were taken from their homes in dawn raids and deposited in the dark, alien cells of London's Charing Cross police station. These were the first arrests since the infamous Flockton Grey ringer scandal in 1982 that resulted in the conviction of three men.

Police from the Organised Crime Group had first been contacted by the Jockey Club in February 1997 – before even the dopings of Avanti Express and Lively Knight – following the club's own five-month investigation.

In arresting Osborne, the police could hardly have picked out a higher-profile name. He was one of the most successful jockeys of his generation and in 1992 had ridden five winners at the Cheltenham Festival. He was a glamorous, charming, popular figure. No once could quite believe what had happened to him.

Dean Gallagher lacked Osborne's profile but challenged him for talent. The son of one of Ireland's best-known senior lads, Tom Gallagher, he had celebrated the biggest win of his career in 1995 when Couldnt Be Better won the Hennessy Cognac Gold Cup at Newbury.

Aspell was the junior of the three and the least known. He was regarded at the time as one of the most promising riders in the weighing room but lacked that crucial break to take him to a higher level. This was the last thing he needed.

A fourth person, an Irishman from Cricklewood in north London, was arrested on the same day as the weighing room trio. He was later named as Ray Butler.

To widespread disgust, the three jockeys had their riding licences suspended, for at least a week, the day after their arrests, in order, the Jockey Club said, "to maintain the public's confidence in horseracing". None of the riders had been charged and their trade body, the Jockeys' Association, stressed in a statement: "The Licensing Committee (of the Jockey Club) made it quite clear that the short suspension is not a reflection on the characters of the jockeys involved."

Osborne, sidelined at the time by a serious wrist injury picked up the previous November, spoke of his "astonishment" at his arrest and loss of licence. He, Gallagher and Aspell all stressed their innocence of any wrongdoing.

Amid fevered speculation over who had profited from the doping of Avanti Express and Lively Knight, the focus turned to illegal gambling and how much of it there was. One betting expert, Ladbroke Racing's managing director Chris Bell, put the figure at 10 per cent of legal turnover – in other words £600 million. Wow.

The dust refused to settle. A fifth man was arrested in the same week. Jason Moore, 28, described as "a well-known punter" from Woodford Green, Essex, cut short a holiday in Australia and was arrested on his return to Heathrow airport on 30 January.

A heavy dollop of Sod's Law was delivered when, through sheer coincidence, an attention-grabbing libel case started in the London High Court at a time when racing was still reeling from the shock of the arrests. Champion jockey Kieren Fallon, together with trainer Lynda Ramsden and her husband Jack, successfully sued the *Sporting Life* over allegations that they had not run stable star Top Cees to the best of his ability prior to victory in the valuable Chester Cup handicap.

The involvement of Fallon and a couple as glamourous as the Ramsdens, ensured widespread interest. Indeed, the opening day of the case battled for billing with the news that Osborne, Gallagher and Aspell had had their riding licences returned.

It was a testing time for the sport, especially as the Jockey Club was coming under stinging criticism for withdrawing the licences in the first place. "Untold and possibly irreparable harm has been caused to the reputations of the riders," said Gallagher's legal rep Mark Edmondson.

Look at it from the outside: three riders were arrested in connection with police investigations into doping and race fixing; and a champion jockey was suing a newspaper for implying that he cheated on a horse. The Sport of Kings was being dragged into the gutter.

Leighton Aspell was the first of the arrested jockeys to return to action. On his first ride back he broke his collarbone, a reminder that when luck leaves town it doesn't hurry back. Two days later, Dean Gallagher's comeback ride had to be pulled up, while Jamie Osborne's hopes of returning for the

Cheltenham Festival were looking increasingly hopeless. Since falling from Space Trucker at Cheltenham, when Osborne's wrist was effectively detached from the rest of his arm, the jockey had endured an agonising and slow recovery.

By now, two more arrests had taken place. Slough-based John Matthews, who was arrested on his return from Spain, and Glen Gill, a 31-year-old from Hampshire, were known as punters who didn't mess about. Both were released on bail.

With libel cases and police investigations vying for attention, you almost forgot the pleasures racing can bring. A brilliant reminder of it came on Saturday 30 April when a 23-year-old Tony McCoy rode the fastest-ever 200 winners over Jumps. Within a month he had broken Peter Scudamore's record of 221 in a season.

And thankfully, Cheltenham was whizzing towards us. Osborne had ruled himself out, but it was still an emotional time for him as the Champion Hurdle winner, Istabraq, had been discovered as a Jumps prospect by his close friend John Durkan, whose career as a trainer was cut short by the diagnosis of leukaemia from which he never recovered. Days before his arrest, Osborne had spoken at Durkan's funeral in Ireland.

Amid the class and hurly burly of the Festival, it went almost unnoticed that, at Huntingdon, Dean Gallagher rode his first winner after 52 attempts since his arrest. Gallagher even made it to Cheltenham for the final day of the meeting, although his Gold Cup mount Couldnt Be Better was pulled up behind Cool Dawn. Aspell also had a ride in the race, finishing 10th on 100-1 shot Yorkshire Gale. He rode Lively Knight on the same day. They were sixth of eight in the Cathcart Chase.

But at least rebuilding was taking place, a process that was completed by the news on 23 April that Aspell had been cleared from the inquiry, without ever being charged. "It is a weight off my mind but there were never any doubts that this day would come," he said. "I am very annoyed that it has taken this long for it all to be sorted out."

The Jockey Club announced that it would not be taking any action of its own against Aspell, while there was a growing view that he should receive an apology, if not compensation, for his arrest. Neither came.

Despite Aspell's belated harmony, Osborne, Gallagher and the other four men arrested had their bail extended for a further two months. They had not been charged.

In June the police raided premises owned by Victor Chandler, the well-known racecourse bookmaker whose company also set up a revolutionary off-shore base in Gibraltar, which meant that punters who bet through it didn't have to pay tax. Chandler was in Gibraltar. He was interviewed on his return. "The police's action has come as a complete bolt from the blue," Chandler said at the time. "I'm always easily contactable at the end of a phone, and all the police needed to do was to arrange a meeting with me."

It had been established that Chandler had placed a bet of £6,000 to £600 on the winner Stormhill Pilgrim in the race in which Lively Knight was doped at Plumpton. The bookmaker who took the bet, Dave Richardson, stressed he did not regard the transaction as suspicious in any way and Chandler himself said: "It was just an ordinary Bank Holiday weekend hedging bet, I don't remember anything more about it. The office places hedging bets every day."

Chandler, who admitted he was worried that the incident could damage his business, was cleared of any wrongdoing the following month after a High Court hearing ruled that the Metropolitan Police had used invalid search warrants on his home and offices. They were also ordered to return all material seized.

His were not the only premises searched. Police also raided Brian Wright's property in Chelsea Harbour, Fulham, as well as one in Weybridge, Surrey. Wright was in Spain at the time although a 55-year-old man who had been looking after the London property was arrested. Another man, Matthew Parr, a 24-year-old from Fareham, Hampshire, was also arrested in June. A well-known punter, Parr also acted as a consultant to spread betting firms. He was dropped from the inquiry without charge in October.

The month ended in further frustration for Gallagher and Osborne who were bailed again until 6 October, another four months. It was the second time their bail had been extended. Osborne was on holiday, but Gallagher made clear his feelings by saying: "It just seems to be dragging on and on. The police haven't spoken to me since day one and I am as much in the dark about what's going on as anybody."

Trying to piece together what the police inquiry was all about was like trying to make a jigsaw from a crunched up box of cornflakes. Slowly, very slowly, though, details of their investigation began to emerge. As well as the dopings of Avanti Express and Lively Knight, a handful of races between 1995 and 1997 were being investigated.

One of the races the police had been briefed on by the Jockey Club was the Geoffrey Gilbey Handicap Chase at Newbury on 28 February 1997; a further indication that integrity concerns existed well before the doping of Avanti Express and Lively Knight.

Gallagher partnered High Alltitude in that race, finishing runner-up to Kings Cherry. High Alltitude opened up in the betting at 6-4 before drifting to 9-4 and came with a strong late run to take second.

Although no evidence of wrongdoing was established, bookmaker Stephen Little reported his concerns to the Jockey Club at the time, saying: "There was plenty of money for the favourite but virtually nothing for the second favourite, which worried me."

Gallagher was involved in another race that the police looked at – the four-runner Cold Ash Novices' Hurdle at Newbury two years earlier on 8 November 1995. The race was won by the 4-1 shot Yes Man, with the evens-favourite Drummond Warrior more than 25 lengths in arrears. Gallagher was on the 10-1 runner-up Romalito. There is nothing to suggest that Gallagher had not ridden the horse on its merits.

Jamie Osborne was asked by police about two winners he rode at Kempton on 21 February 1997. The first of them came on 11-2 shot Berude Not To, who finished seven lengths ahead of the runner-up Oban and a further three-quarters of a length in front of the Gallagher-ridden Aardwolf, trained by Charlie Brooks. The *Racing Post* reported that Aardwolf "jumped at least as well as the winner as they took each other on but had done his running by the time they reached the second last."

Later that day Osborne was on the 100-30 second favourite Lessons Lass when she beat High Grade by one-and-a-half lengths. Gallagher was on the 5-2 favourite Nine O Three, who finished sixth of nine. Again it should be stressed that no evidence whatsoever of wrongdoing emerged.

At a time when World Cup fever was fading, and David Beckham went into hiding following his red card against Argentina, the hunt intensified for two men photographed by the Jockey Club at Exeter on the day Avanti Express was doped. The police took the unusual step of issuing photos of them to see if anyone recognised them.

Besides the jockeys, the arrest that probably caused the biggest stir was that of Brian Wright on 16 September. He was bailed without charge until October. It was the 11th arrest the police had made.

The Observer had already named him, in June, as the 'Mr Big' at the centre of the race-fixing and doping investigations. The article also mentioned his alleged links to some of London's most notorious criminal gangs. It was said he was known by two distinctive nicknames, 'Uncle' and 'The Milkman', because he always delivered. Those who knew him in racing kept their eyes closed and ears covered to the rumours that engulfed Brian Wright's livelihood. They just liked him.

Wright was thought to have been the backer behind a golf tournament organised by Graham Bradley that was held in Spain. The tournament attracted some of Britain's best-known Jump riders and caused considerable concern to the Jockey Club.

Jamie Osborne, who was not on the golfing trip and has always maintained he has never met Brian Wright, became the second jockey to be dropped from the inquiry on 5 October. "At long last I can look forward to riding again," he said. "We have been waiting since January to have a chance to speak to the police and I told them today we were very unhappy with the slow pace of the investigation."

The day after Osborne received his good news, his name cropped up at Bow Street Magistrates. Bob Harrington, a former policeman from Reading, had been in custody since August on charges of attempting to obtain money by deception from Osborne. His arrest was the result of a surveillance operation by police that had received the jockey's full co-operation.

Reporting restrictions mean that Harrington's case – he was remanded for another month – received minimal attention. But if Jamie Osborne, even though he had been declared an innocent man, thought his troubles were over . . . well, in a tale like this, how could he?

Good news for Osborne was followed within 24 hours by despair for Dean Gallagher. He was told after 10 hours at Charing Cross police station, that his bail was being extended for a further three months. So, too, were Ray Butler, Glen Gill, Adam Hodgson, John Matthews, Jason Moore and Brian Wright, whose appearance caused something of a stir, not least because he kept his identity concealed by a scarf and a hat throughout.

On hearing his bad news, Gallagher was too drained to talk, but said a day later: "I cannot describe how frustrated and disappointed I am at this further delay as I was hoping that matters would be concluded by now. My position has not changed since the investigation started – that it has nothing to do with me – and it is not nice having this hang over me."

The number of remaining suspects was reduced to six when Brian Wright was dropped from the investigation on 30 December on the advice of the Crown Prosecution Service. He was recuperating from a triple heart bypass operation when he told *Daily Telegraph* journalist Tony Stafford: "For nine months nobody came near me. And when I was away in Spain in the summer they (the police) went to my flat. When I was bailed, my lawyer said: 'Show us one little bit of evidence.' Of course, they didn't have any evidence as there isn't any.

"As you can imagine none of this upset could have been helpful to my health. After the last bail, I remember sitting down to watch the Breeders' Cup on TV and feeling a pain in my shoulder. When I went to my doctor, he said I was sweating and clearly not right and advised me to check into hospital.

"After three days they found I had three blocked arteries. When this business came up, I said I would not be going racing again until it was resolved. Now I've been cleared I'll probably go racing when I get back to England in the New Year."

It was a rare public comment from Wright, who the following March was the subject of an international arrest warrant as a result of one of one of the largest ever seizures of cocaine in Britain. His son Brian, known as Briany, was one of 10 people charged in connection with the seizure of almost half a ton of cocaine from a garage at Leigh-on-Sea in Essex. The seizure, worth £100 million, was so big it was expected to impact on the availability of the drug in Britain.

Gallagher, meanwhile, was told on New Year's Eve 1998 that his bail had been further extended until March. "It is very unfair to keep someone in limbo like this," said his solicitor Douglas Fordham.

It was a miserable end to a miserable year. But by no means an end to the madness.

TRIO ARRESTED

This one made the front pages. Two more jockeys, Ray Cochrane and Graham Bradley, and a former trainer, Charlie Brooks, all arrested.

The jockeys were big-time – perhaps even more so than Osborne. They out-achieved Gallagher for sure, and were in a different class to Aspell when it came to kudos.

Ray Cochrane, the first connection the investigation had thrown up to Flat racing, was a Derby-winning rider, aged 41 at the time of his arrest. He had joined the elite relatively late in his career, gaining Classic successes on Midway Lady in the 1986 1,000 Guineas and Oaks. His biggest moment came after winning the 1988 Derby on the Aga Khan's Kahyasi, when newspapers seized on the fact that he had sought the advice of Lester Piggott, who was in prison at the time.

In 1997 Cochrane made the headlines again when he was reported missing by his wife Anne. He turned up safe and well, but without explanation, three weeks later.

Graham Bradley was the most charismatic figure in the National Hunt weighing room and the man who had led home Bregawn in the Cheltenham Gold Cup when Michael Dickinson saddled the first five horses. In 1996 he won the Champion Hurdle after a chain of events that fitted neatly with Bradley's harlequin image. He had originally been booked to ride the hot favourite Alderbrook, but overslept and missed an important morning workout on the gelding, handing the golden opportunity to Richard Dunwoody. Bradley instead partnered Collier Bay, who pulled off a shock by beating the odds-on Alderbrook.

Both Bradley and Cochrane were arrested at their homes between 6.00am and 7.00am on 8 January 1999. The police also turned up for Charlie Brooks but he was away on business. He later reported voluntarily at Charing Cross police station and was arrested for his troubles.

Brooks, a personable Old Etonian, achieved some notable successes as a trainer, winning the Hennessy Gold Cup twice and playing a pivotal role in the training of Fred Winter's Champion Hurdle winner Celtic Shot. His 'Champagne Charlie' nickname, and possibly a lifestyle to match, may have hindered his progress, as did self-acknowledged bouts of depression. He retired as a trainer in 1998, shortly after Suny Bay finished runner-up in the Grand National for the second year running.

PARANOIA RETURNS

Once more racing was soaked in paranoia and uncertainty as a result of these arrests. A surreal touch to an already unfathomable situation was added by Cochrane's wife Anne, who rang the police station in an attempt to find out what she should do with the tomatoes in his carefully nurtured greenhouse.

Cochrane, who missed a winner that he had spent two days starving himself for, said after being released on bail that he was "amazed" at his arrest. "They asked me a few questions and then they let me go," he said. "I had no inkling it was going to happen. I've done nothing wrong. My solicitor was with me and she looked after me. The police were quite good about it but I have got to come back on 10 March."

He was initially quizzed about two races he had participated in. Like those Osborne and Gallagher were involved in, there is no evidence of any malpractice. The first of those races was the four-runner Stanley Wootton Stakes at Epsom on 24 September 1996. Cochrane rode the runner-up Double Leaf, who was waited with but could not peg back the winner Magellan when asked to.

Cochrane stressed there was nothing untoward about the race, but two bookmakers, Stephen Little and Colin Webster, told the police of their unease at the betting on it. "I expected Double Leaf to be favourite, but all the money was for Magellan (who started at 8-11 having opened at 11-10) and there was nothing for Double Leaf in the ring," said Webster. Little announced his intention to step down from the betting ring after 25 years. "I have never been so uneasy about racing as I am now," he said.

Cochrane was also asked about the Stardom Stakes at Goodwood on 11 September 1998, in which he partnered Fantastic Light, trained like Double Leaf by Sir Michael Stoute, one of Britain's very best trainers. The race attracted only three runners, and was won by the 100-30 shot Mutaahab, who beat the odds-on Glamis by half-a-length with Fantastic Light two lengths away back in third. According to the *Racing Post* Fantastic Light did not appear to handle the track. The colt went on to prove himself one of the most successful horses recruited by Sheikh Mohammed's Godolphin operation, his career culminating with victory in the Breeders' Cup Turf.

It later emerged that an all-weather race was under investigation, the Dunston Claiming Stakes on the all-weather at Wolverhampton on 21 November 1997, in which The Happy Fox made all to beat the fast-finishing

Sea-Deer, ridden by Cochrane, by a head. Cochrane was never charged over these incidents.

Graham Bradley had a wry approach to his arrest. When he had first heard of the arrests of Osborne, Gallagher and Aspell, he had joked to himself that it was surprising he, too, hadn't been lifted. "It had already crossed my mind on several occasions that with my reputation it was surprising that they hadn't given me a tug as well," he said in his biography, *The Wayward Lad*.

"But if I thought the police had overlooked me I was wrong. During 1998 my name had never been seriously linked with the on-going inquiry except for the odd joke in the weighing room or pub, which I would have expected.

"But the rumour factory was still active and certain journalists were sowing malicious seeds of doubt about the integrity of particular jockeys. By Christmas (the initial arrests had been the previous January) the whole sorry affair had found its way off the news pages and, although I secretly thought it was a miracle that I'd never been interviewed, I was well aware that if enough mud is thrown then some will stick. With my record, surely I was overdue. I needn't have worried. The boys in blue knew my address."

Bradley picked up the phone on the morning of his arrest at 6.10am. He thought it was a local trainer, aware of Bradley's Olympic-standard ability to oversleep, ringing to remind him of a schooling session he had booked the jockey for that morning. It wasn't. "When I picked up the receiver a deep unpleasant voice said: 'Mr Bradley, it's the Serious Crime Squad here. We're outside your house and have been banging on your door for five minutes but couldn't wake you up. Could you come down and let us in, please?'"

That's one way of waking somebody. Just as they had with the other jockeys, the police searched Bradley's office and files, which were neatly and alphabetically organised. Like the other jockeys, he was taken to Charing Cross and put in a cell.

Charlie Brooks, on the advice of his solicitor, also said little of his arrest. His partner Miriam Francome, ex-wife of champion jockey John, had been asked by police when they raided their Lambourn home at 6.00am why she appeared so relaxed – "I said the reason was that under-age drinking was the sum total of Charlie's criminal activity."

Both Brooks and Bradley were asked about the running of Man Mood at Warwick on 5 November 1996. According to Bradley it was the sole focus of the police's questioning.

It was a race that caused real fireworks. With only one rival, Man Mood, trained by Brooks, started the 4-7 favourite, having opened even shorter at 1-2, for the Oliver Cromwell Handicap Chase but was pulled up by Bradley with much of the race still to run.

Brooks may have muddied the waters by making the perfectly legal suggestion to the gelding's owner Julian Robbins that he should back Drumstick as a 'saver', so that Robbins couldn't lose financially, a rare occurrence for an owner in the expensive world of horseracing.

In his biography, Bradley admitted that Brooks' advice backfired. "Charlie is a very straight-forward man with no side and his views to Julian Robbins may not have been the wisest in hindsight," he wrote. "As Robbins stood to win £4,000 in prize-money, Charlie said he should put £500 on Drumstick to balance the books and make it a no-lose situation. It was poor advice given the subsequent turn of events."

Bradley also strongly denied any attempt to fix the race; he pulled Man Mood up because the horse was struggling for breath.

Much of the kerfuffle that followed the Man Mood race overlooked the fact that three runners had actually been declared, only for the Venetia Williams-trained Mine's An Ace, the likely hot favourite ("obvious chance in a bad race," said the *Racing Post*) to be withdrawn on the day, for entirely legitimate reasons.

Bradley had already ridden two winners before the Man Mood race, but had not been confident of a treble. He let Man Mood bowl along in front and it was only entering the back straight that he became concerned. Man Mood began to falter, then choke and lose his action. Determined not to risk his own or the horse's safety, Bradley pulled Man Mood up with six fences left to jump. As soon as he did so, the other runner, Drumstick, galloped past him on his way to inevitable victory.

The Warwick stewards held an inquiry in which Bradley reported that Man Mood "fell in a hole, started to choke and lost his action," something he had done at Leicester the previous season.

A storm was brewing, yet Man Mood's run attracted little adverse comment in the next day's papers. He went on to run 14 times after Warwick without ever winning. Charlie Brooks told the stewards of Man Mood's troubled medical history and reminded them that Man Mood had only been aimed at the race after it was re-opened because of a low original entry.

The gelding had undergone what is known as a soft-palate operation to aid his breathing. "With this particular infirmity only one person can tell when a soft palate operation is needed," Bradley said in his book. "And that is the jockey, because it is not until the horse is put under racing conditions that the palate displaces. This stops oxygen getting to the lungs, brain, and muscles, which in turn makes the animal falter and lose its action, but after the trauma of racing subsides the palate then rights itself.

"The racecourse vet, Peter Thorne, explained this to the panel of stewards, who then heard from the betting intelligence officer monitoring transactions in the ring.

"He appeared a bit agitated and said one major firm had taken a phone bet of £3,000 for Drumstick but could only get £1,000 on. No big deal there, I thought, and it didn't surprise me when the stewards accepted our explanations after they deliberated for a short while. If I thought that was the last I'd heard about Man Mood I was badly mistaken."

Very badly mistaken.

The race had attracted the attention of the Betting Office Licensees Association, the trade union for bookies. It reported its concerns to the Jockey Club, whose spokesman David Pipe reported the next day: "Our security department has been having discussions with the Betting Office Licensees Association and is examining betting patterns."

BOLA weren't the only ones disgruntled. Peter Stevens, a punter from Welwyn Garden City, questioned the decision of the Warwick stewards to accept the explanation that Man Mood had choked. "As there was clearly no evidence of this occurrence – as stated by the racecourse vet – how could that explanation be accepted?" he asked.

In a letter to the *Sporting Life*, Stevens provided a vivid indication of the irritation the race had caused among punters. "Better evidence was perhaps provided in the betting ring before the race where, it seems, some knowledgeable punters were well aware of this 'problem'," he wrote. "This issue should be of concern to the stewards and security services. How can anyone on the ground know whether or not a horse choked or gurgled?"

Stevens' malcontent was picked up by the *Mail On Sunday*, which devoted a feature to his ire. The article described him as a "respectable and respected charter surveyor" and "a seasoned follower of horseflesh, a punter of 20 years' standing who meticulously studies form". He placed £350 on Man Mood and apparently found the course "alive with gossip" after the race.

With the hullabaloo continuing, Charlie Brooks spoke out in support of Bradley's decision to pull Man Mood up. "A good one and a quarter miles from home, with a considerable number of fences in the way, the horse lost its action so the jockey did the right thing and pulled the horse up," Brooks said. "The horse lost his action because of the gurgling. It has a history of wind problems. Our explanation was confirmed by the vet and the stewards accepted our explanation."

A month after the Warwick race, it emerged that the Jockey Club was still investigating the incident, even though the local stewards on the day had accepted the explanations of Man Mood's connections. As part of the investigation, Bradley and Brooks were asked to hand over print outs of calls made from their mobile phones. Bradley refused on legal advice and on a matter of personal rights; Brooks complied at the request of Andrew Cohen, the owner of the famous Uplands stables from where Brooks trained.

In the end the Jockey Club decided not to hold an official inquiry into whether there had been any breaches of its rules. The news failed to appease Charlie Brooks who had been unhappy about the Jockey Club's handling of the case. "As far as I am concerned the whole matter has been a highly unsatisfactory 'fishing trip'," he said. "Having had our explanation accepted on the day, I was disappointed that the Jockey Club informed the press that there was to be an investigation into the matter before they notified me."

The arrests, meanwhile, continued. Five days after the shock of Cochrane, Bradley and Brooks; Nigel Troth, a Chesterfield-based bookmaker and punter was arrested and bailed. He was later cleared without charges ever being brought.

D-days for those arrested arrived and fizzled out with depressing regularity. The next one looming was on Wednesday 10 March 1999 – the week before the Cheltenham Festival, at which Istabraq was to succeed in his quest for a second Champion Hurdle.

Suddenly things were starting to happen.

By now it was 407 days since Dean Gallagher had made his first acquaintance with Charing Cross police station. He was getting a little restless as he left his Newbury home to catch the train to Paddington.

As Gallagher headed for London, Graham Bradley was already making his way through the Charing Cross station doors. He arrived at 10.48am smiling and looking relaxed. He left at 11.43 with his head bowed. Bradley had been re-bailed for another month. Saying nothing as he walked away, the look on his face was expression enough of his feelings.

Bradley was well gone by the time Gallagher arrived later that afternoon, 10 minutes after Ray Cochrane had pulled up in a black Mercedes to answer his own bail charges.

Both jockeys were called into the interview room together and emerged after five minutes having been told they had been ruled out of the doping and race-fixing inquiry. "I am delighted and relieved, it has been a difficult and frustrating 14 months for me," Gallagher said.

Cochrane added: "I'm glad it's all over and I can get on with life. I have known all along that there has been nothing in it, but you can't put your mind at rest until it is all over. Thankfully, it is now."

In somewhat eerie fashion, neither Gallagher nor Cochrane found much peace once they were cleared from the inquiry. Gallagher faced hefty legal bills, for which he could not claim compensation because he was never charged, and was forced to sell his house to pay them. He was drinking too much in an understandable bid to erase his problems. That wasn't enough and soon he turned to drugs – cocaine. "I took it to give me a lift and take me away from reality."

The further away from reality that Gallagher was taken, the greater his troubles became. The jockey lost his riding licence for six months after twice testing positive for the drug when racing in France, where he had a successful retainer with a leading French trainer, Jean-Paul Gallorini.

Even after those tests, Gallagher continued to take the drug. "Cocaine gives you delusions, and I thought that as I had been caught I might as well carry on and escape from the depression," he said in a frank interview with the *Racing Post*.

Relief often comes only through being caught, but before he returned to the saddle, Gallagher had to undergo rehabilitation treatment at the Marchwood Priory Hospital near Southampton. It was emotionally brutal, soul-searching therapy that Gallagher underwent. It worked so well that he was able to help another talented but troubled jockey, Timmy Murphy, when he had to confront alcohol dependency following an incident on an airline that led to a six-month imprisonment in July 2002. Gallagher celebrated a happy follow-on from his trials when he gained the biggest win of his career in the 2002 Champion Hurdle on Hors la Loi III.

Ray Cochrane suffered even greater distress than Gallagher, although his was not self-imposed. It was on an unheralded, early summer's day, that Cochrane's life changed even more dramatically than it had on the day of his arrest. Fifteen months had passed since then and Cochrane was on his way to Goodwood with Frankie Dettori.

They never made it. Their plane, a Piper Seneca, took off at Newmarket beside a local landmark known as the Devil's Dyke, near the town's two racecourses. The light aircraft crash-landed soon after take off. Cochrane and Dettori both saw their lives flash before them before hitting the ground with a split-second thud. The plane's pilot, Patrick Mackey, was killed. Cochrane saved Dettori's life by dragging him from the wreckage seconds before it burst into flames. This had been a miraculous survival. Cochrane has received several awards for his heroics.

He somehow defied his injuries to return to race riding but was forced to retire that October after a couple of falls left his back in a parlous state. He took over as agent to Dettori and a star for the next generation, Jamie Spencer. He also acts as an expert paddock and form analyst for the BBC.

Arrests, flirtations with death and one jockey dependent on cocaine. Who would accept such an implausible script? Who can yet believe that, actually, it's all true.

BRADLEY'S LICENCE SUSPENDED

And still the drama continued . . . It's easy to forget that amid the celebrations of Cochrane and Gallagher's release that five men – Ray Butler, Glen Gill, Adam Hodgson, John Matthews and Jason Moore – were charged in connection with the doping of racehorses.

They were committed for trial under the Betting and Gaming Act of 1845 in that they were accused of conspiring to defraud "by interfering with the fair running of horseraces by administering a performance-enhancing drug." The charges related to the period between 1 March and 1 April 1997, during which Avanti Express and Lively Knight were doped.

It was starting to look as if the police were switching their focus to races that they knew had featured doped horses instead of races that had allegedly been fixed by jockeys stopping horses. You can't lie about an ACP test. Even if a jockey had 'pulled' a horse, proving it seemed almost impossible.

The five men accused of doping were back in court to appear in front of Bow Street Magistrates, also in London, a month later. To widespread surprise, they were joined by another man, Graham Bradley.

Bradley was the only jockey still under investigation and was charged with conspiracy to defraud on 14 April 1999. He was accused of deliberately stopping Man Mood in that contentious race at Warwick. It just wouldn't go away.

The police statement was chillingly simple: "Graham John Bradley, 38, a jockey, has been charged that on or before the 5th of November, 1996, within the jurisdiction of the Central Criminal Court he did conspire with others to win for himself or others from bookmakers sums of money through wagering on the event of a horserace, the 3.25pm at Warwick on November 5, 1996, by fraud or other unlawful devices in that together he agreed that Man Mood, ridden by him, would not win the said race." The charge was made under section 1(i) of the Criminal Law Act of 1977. It all sounded so serious.

The charging of Bradley meant that six of the total 15 people arrested were facing trial. He also become the first jockey to face court on a racing related matter since John Williams appeared on four counts of conspiracy to obtain property by deception (i.e. prize-money) following the case of the 'ringer', In The Money, which was a winner at Newton Abbot in 1978. In The Money was in fact a far superior horse called Cobbler's March.

The judge directed the jury to find Williams innocent, but In The Money's trainer, John Bowles, was fined and handed an 18-month suspended sentence, and later warned off by the Jockey Club for 20 years after being found guilty of two counts of conspiracy.

With Bradley's future under a cloud, there was better news for Man Mood's trainer Charlie Brooks, who was released without charge on the same day. The day after he had appeared in the dock at Bow Street, Bradley was back in familiar, healthier surroundings at Cheltenham to ride a horse called Country Star. If this was to be Bradley's last ride it was an appaling way to go out. His mount started favourite but broke a leg in the race and had to be destroyed.

Bradley felt something similar was about to happen to his riding career as he entered the Jockey Club's headquarters at Portman Square the following day.

He had left Cheltenham amid emotional scenes, not knowing whether he should be saying his goodbyes to the riders and the valets he had been with behind closed doors, day in, day out for 23 years. It's hard to get a handle on how he must have felt.

After a 45-minute hearing and 90 minutes of deliberation by three Jockey Club stewards – Gurney Sheppard, David Oldrey and Michael Wyatt – it was decided that his licence should be taken away. Unlike the other jockeys who briefly suffered the same fate, Bradley had actually been charged, not just arrested.

"The Stewards have not made a judgement on whether or not Graham Bradley is guilty of the charge laid against him," said the club's senior steward Christopher Spence, "but have decided, in view of the nature and gravity of the charge, it is inappropriate for a licensed jockey to continue race-riding." As compensation, the Jockey Club agreed to pay Bradley £29,000 a year, the same amount he would have received had he been injured.

Bradley, who could still go racing but was barred from the weighing room, promised to "fight and fight" to clear his name and ride again, but the legal process of bringing him to trial promised to be a lengthy one.

The sense of outrage that the National Hunt community felt on Bradley's behalf was summed up by his close friend and champion jockey, Tony McCoy. "If this decision finishes his riding career, it will be one of the worst things to happen to racing in a long time," said McCoy, who was staying with Bradley at the time.

Racing found it hard to adjust to a situation where one of its own – without question one of its favourite sons, and probably its most lovable rogue – was caught in such a serious web. Words of support for Bradley ran as free as a river that had burst its banks. The consensus among professionals was that he should have been allowed to carry on riding.

Spence, who had succeeded Lord Hartington as senior steward at the Jockey Club the previous July, countered: "It is our job to maintain confidence in the racing product, otherwise it becomes a farce.

"So much emotion surrounds jockeys that the heart sometimes rules the head. At the end of the day, racing is finished if people get the impression that it is a corrupt sport and that nothing is being done about it.

"If a banker, solicitor or accountant is charged with a serious offence within their line of business, they are suspended on full pay until they have been found either innocent or guilty. The situation is the same in this case."

On the advice of Brian Wright, who was one of his closest friends, Bradley prepared for his trial by recruiting a legal firm that was already representing John Matthews, one of the men accused of conspiring to dope Avanti Express and Lively Knight. Others close to Bradley were unsure about this move, but Bradley implicitly trusted Wright, who offered to help him with what threatened to be considerable legal fees.

Bradley's new legal representative, Paul Rexstrew, of Law Mooney solicitors, did his job well, insisting that there had been no concrete reason to charge him. On Monday 7 June 1999, all charges against Bradley were dropped on the grounds of insufficient evidence, leaving a major question mark in many minds over why all these jockeys had been arrested in the first place.

Bradley certainly had right to feel confused. Having suffered the ordeal of being charged with an offence and appearing in court, he was then to learn that the Crown Prosecution Service had changed its mind about the strength of the evidence against him. CPS representative Clifford Chance said: "If, after further police investigations I alter my assessment of the evidence, the proceedings could be re-instituted. But it would be unjust on Mr Bradley to proceed while evidence does not exist in an admissible form."

Party time. Bradley celebrated with a few bottles of champagne and in his typical, charmingly brazen style went round to the Jockey Club that night to pick up a form to reapply for his riding licence.

Not everyone felt like celebrating this development, though. The Jockey Club suddenly found itself on the back-foot and about to topple onto its wicket. Its insistence that Bradley should not be allowed to ride because of the seriousness of his situation became the subject of further condemnation. Amid the relief for Bradley and condemnation for the Jockey Club, a significant letter to the *Daily Telegraph* went almost unnoticed.

David Calvert-Smith QC, for the CPS, defended the handling of the Bradley case. "The police have a duty to investigate suspected crime," he said. "They are entitled to arrest suspects in good faith if they have reasonable grounds to suspect complicity in an offence.

"If the CPS believes that the evidence is strong enough to make it probable that a court will be sure of guilt, we normally take the prosecution forward. If not, we drop it.

"The police charged Graham Bradley on April 13 with conspiracy to cheat at betting and he appeared the next day at Bow Street Magistrates Court. The prosecutor asked for a remand to June 9 and stipulated in court that the decision to charge Mr Bradley was subject to CPS review.

"The police evidence was subsequently reviewed with extreme care and on June 9 it was judged that the evidence did not meet the standard requested and so the charge had to be withdrawn."

The letter added that "if further evidence emerges" the proceedings against Bradley might have been reinstated. They never were.

"The police and the CPS have independent but complementary functions in all criminal cases," Calvert-Smith wrote. "It is wholly misleading and inappropriate to suggest that we would ever support prosecutions without proper foundation."

That attempt to put a hose to the flames of rancour had only a limited effect. The Jockey Club continued to feel the heat and, in particular, there were calls for the resignation of its head of security Roger Buffham; the man seen as the link between the Jockey Club and police investigations.

Roger Buffham was unusual in racing. He cared not about what the major players thought of him, and he had no desire to be part of any of racing's 'sets'. He was convinced that racing was collectively refusing to face some major corruption issues, and if nobody else was prepared to tackle them, he most certainly was. Buffham was closely involved in a seminal 1991 speech that Christopher Spence made at the annual Gimcrack Dinner. For the first time, a senior figure in the Jockey Club warned of racing's links with criminal elements and its vulnerability to corruption. Buffham also pushed for the introduction of the unpopular 'fit and proper persons' rule that allowed the Jockey Club to issue warnings to trainers and jockeys who it felt were mixing with 'undesirables'.

Buffham was a man who got up noses. He was seriously disliked within the weighing room and treated with contempt practically everywhere else. Unusually, he had minimal links with racing before he joined the Jockey Club in 1992 and he soon became distrustful of Jockey Club member's close links with the rest of the sport. Practically everyone in the Jockey Club had horses in training and thus knew many trainers and jockeys well. Buffham's view was that this relationship barred the Jockey Club from being an effective regulator of the sport.

Buffham's CV at the time of his appointment read well, if a little mysteriously. He was a former bomb-disposal expert and intelligence officer whose time in Northern Ireland earned him an MBE. Later, he worked as a scientific staff officer at the Army's research and development centre before setting up his own security company dealing in CCTV, and served as a local magistrate in Lincolnshire.

But Bradley's release from the doping and race-fixing investigations could not have left Buffham's stock with a lower value in racing. A smug demeanour leaning towards arrogance did not help his cause. Regardless of all his initiatives – bringing in senior policemen to boost the Jockey Club's investigative team, launching the reward line Raceguard, introducing video surveillance cameras at all racecourses – Buffham was branded a failure who had spearheaded an embarrassing corruption investigation that itself ensured that racing had been brought into unnecessary disrepute. After nearly three years of investigations, no one from within the sport had been charged despite a chain of arrests.

Buffham was held responsible but he wasn't going anywhere. The Jockey Club stood by their man. For now. His racing enemies – it wouldn't take you long to name his allies – fed well on stories linking him with a South

African called Dr Wouter Basson, also known as Dr Death.

Basson, a respected cardiologist, was arrested in 1997 on accusations of multiple murder, fraud and drug dealing, as well as laundering stolen money through a British company unbeknown to but set up by Buffham.

Basson headed South Africa's secret chemical and biological research programme during the apartheid years. Buffham, who had met Basson through his former company Contemporary Designs Systems, which he sold in 1991 was asked to give evidence at the trial but declined to travel to South Africa. He provided a statement for the prosecution and had been willing to give evidence from the UK. Basson's case had no links to horseracing, but that didn't stop Buffham's critics using it as a further stone to pelt him with.

Graham Bradley had his riding licence returned on 21 June, 14 days after the charges against him were dropped. He returned to winning ways in a celebrity race at Stratford, which lacked official status. His next winner under rules was his final one, Ontheboil, who won at Haydock on 13 November. That was it. Bradley announced his retirement in order to concentrate on a successful bloodstock business that had seen him recruit high-class horses from Germany to run over Jumps. His clients included the England international footballers Robbie Fowler and Steve McManaman.

A colourful and brilliant career had come to a close. Yet Graham Bradley's appearances in the dock were a long way from over.

DIRTY MONEY

In the meantime, Bradley found himself the subject of further unwanted attention, even in retirement. This time it was over a horse called Night Fighter.

He had bought the horse from Germany for a man named David Chopra, who had paid him for his share in the horse by handing him £10,000 of chips at a London casino. Bradley was filmed on the casino's security camera cashing in the chips. The transaction was significant enough to be reported to the National Criminal Intelligence Service, as is mandatory for deals above a certain sum.

Soon afterwards Chopra dropped out of the deal – he was said to be on the run from the police – without ever having been registered as Night Fighter's owner. The gelding was then sold on to permit-holder Norman Mason, later to win the 2001 Grand National with Red Marauder.

But the *Sunday Times'* Insight team said that Night Fighter was being used as a money laundering vehicle by criminals on the Costa del Sol. The article, dismissed by Bradley as "a load of bollocks", highlighted Night Fighter's run at Market Rasen on 5 May 1999, when he started an unexpectedly warm favourite at 11-8 and finished second. "It is impossible to say how much more money was placed on Night Fighter through bookmakers away from the track. Any each way money placed on him by money launderers in the illegal gambling bars of the Costas would come on top of that," the article alleged. Job done. Although backing Night Fighter each-way at 11-8 would have yielded little reward, the exercise could be judged a success in that dirty money had been laundered.

Whatever the merits of the *Sunday Times'* story, other papers 'ran' with it. A shady world was portrayed in which jockeys were offered a "ready supply of cocaine, cash, and prostitutes" in return for helping to fix races. All the quotes were anonymous, all the allegations were big and blurry.

The only real focus was on poor old Night Fighter who had somehow become a cipher for stories that ran wild on allegations but always pulled up short on proof. Nonetheless, the Jockey Club announced an inquiry into the ownership of Night Fighter.

Richard Guest, who assisted Mason with his training and rode Night Fighter at Market Rasen, denied any wrongdoing. "Mr Mason has the receipt and he owns him 100 per cent," he said.

Guest was unaware who had backed Night Fighter down to 11-8, but added: "He ran too freely on soft ground, which didn't suit him, and so we gelded him. That turned him round at home . . . and it was no secret that he went to Market Rasen on better ground, well-handicapped."

The Jockey Club eventually decided not to hold an inquiry into Night Fighter, although its security team did interview Bradley. Yet racing's vulnerability to money laundering rang loud and clear in the words of Christopher Spence, who said: "We can't ignore it and we don't. I'm on record about it being my biggest worry for racing. If racing's integrity breaks then everything breaks.

"What the newspaper the *Sunday Times* (which may well have been briefed in the first place by a Jockey Club source) said is what we have been saying for months. Nothing in it was news to us. It is all part of the under-regulation of betting. The money involved in drugs is horrific and as it gets harder and harder to launder the money the criminal element are bound to be looking at different methods. We want to keep them out of racing."

It was too late for that, however.

5

A CONFUSING CASE

How Jamie Osborne must wish he had never come across Bob Harrington. And if Norman Williamson hadn't been sleeping with Kim Bailey's wife Tracey, he might never have done. That's the bummer of it all.

Soon after his arrest in January 1998, during the initial burst of activity in the police's doping and race-fixing inquiry, Osborne received a call from Kim Bailey. The trainer said he knew of a man who might be able to offer some advice on his predicament.

That man was Bob Harrington, a former Thames Valley police officer, who had earned a series of commendations for his undercover work prior to taking early retirement from the force after suffering from ME.

Harrington first met Bailey after a charity auction, at which he had successfully bid to spend a day with the trainer at his Old Manor Stables in Lambourn. Harrington went on to own horses with him but there remained something of the racing groupie about him. He looked up to Bailey, describing him as "the Alex Ferguson of Jump racing" thanks to his rare triptych of successes in the Grand National with Mr Frisk in 1990 and the Cheltenham Gold Cup and Champion Hurdle with Master Oats and Alderbrook, both at the 1995 Cheltenham Festival.

Bailey and Harrington had reason to be close. They ended up being jointly accused of breaking the law together . . . as you do. Bailey's marriage to Tracey had ended in the aftermath of her affair with Williamson, who, in a prime example of the social incest that seems to spread itself around Lambourn like horse manure, was Bailey's stable jockey at the time. Whether through expediency or magnanimity, the two men resumed their partnership soon after their initial break-up. Tracey, meanwhile, teamed up with John Francome, the former champion jockey turned TV presenter.

In the midst of all this social upheaval, Bailey was arrested on 12 October

1998, and charged seven weeks later with conspiracy to burgle Williamson's home at nearby East Garston. Harrington faced the same charges, although they were subsequently dropped against both men.

Looking back, it might seem strange that Bailey and Harrington happened to be under police surveillance at the time of this incident. But when Bob Harrington was involved, nothing was ever quite as it seemed.

I first came across Harrington in December 1998 at a bail hearing at Bow Street magistrates court in central London. Harrington was the man given bail, after four months on remand following his arrest by officers of the Criminal Investigation Bureau, the branch of the police force that investigates its own.

Harrington was intriguing; a big, shambling, silver-haired man with a knowing glint in his eye. He appeared keen to present himself as a stash of secrets. And you were left in little doubt that he would quite like to talk about them.

Talk he did, although not quite in a manner he would have chosen. On 3 June 1999 Harrington was committed to trial at the Old Bailey. He faced two charges: firstly, of attempting to obtain dishonestly £500 in cash from Jamie Osborne on 21 July 1998, by claiming he was in a position to influence the police investigation involving the jockey; secondly, of corruptly soliciting for Detective Sergeant Richard Wall the sum of £2,000 as an inducement for him to show favour to Osborne during the same police investigation. Harrington denied both charges.

At the time of the allegations, DS Richard Wall was the Metropolitan police officer in charge of the doping and race-fixing investigations. He was later recruited to work for the Jockey Club's security department. If Harrington was the stash of secrets, Wall was the man who put them there.

He, like Kim Bailey and Jamie Osborne before him, found out to his cost that Harrington was a beguiling figure. While you sang, he listened. And never forgot a thing. So why did he end up in the dock? We have to move forward, to January 2000, to find out. During a stop-start, five-week trial, Harrington's behaviour and motives were scratched and picked at with all the intent of a cat ridding itself of fleas.

Two cameras. That's the key to the whole thing.

"Two cameras": words that Jamie Osborne will never forget. Not because of any so-far concealed interest in photography, but because that was the price of freedom that he was being quoted by Bob Harrington. Two cameras is slang for £2,000. Or it is in Harrington's world. And it was the sum he claimed was needed to allow him to help bribe Osborne out of the investigation.

Not that Osborne had asked for such advice. The two men met initially at Kim Bailey's house with the intention that Harrington would assess the evidence against Osborne. That first meeting left Osborne unimpressed, but after several calls from Harrington they met again. Osborne may have felt

Making his point: Dermot Browne in his riding days.

Tales to tell: Browne at Doncaster railway station.

Man Mood, ridden by Graham Bradley, has an early lead in the Oliver Cromwell Handicap Chase on 5 November 1996. The horse was eventually pulled up, leading to a race-fixing charge against the jockey that was subsequently dropped.

Man Mood is overtaken by Drumstick.

Man Mood is pulled up as Drumstick goes on to win.

Josh Gifford:
trainer of Lively Knight.

Charlie Egerton:
trainer of Avanti Express

Cleared: Dean Gallagher (on the left, with fellow jockey Jamie Osborne).

Cleared: Leighton Aspell.

Cleared: Charlie Brooks (left), with his solicitor Monty Raphael.

Cleared: Ray Cochrane at Charing Cross police station.

The five men who were cleared at Southwark Crown Court of conspiring to dope racehorses. Above left: *Glen Gill;* above: *Adam Hodgson;* above right: *John Matthews;* below left: *Jason Moore; and* below right: *Ray Butler (right), with his solicitor Danny Soloman.*

I'll fight on: Graham Bradley after the Jockey Club took away his riding licence. It was later re-installed after charges of race-fixing against him were dropped.

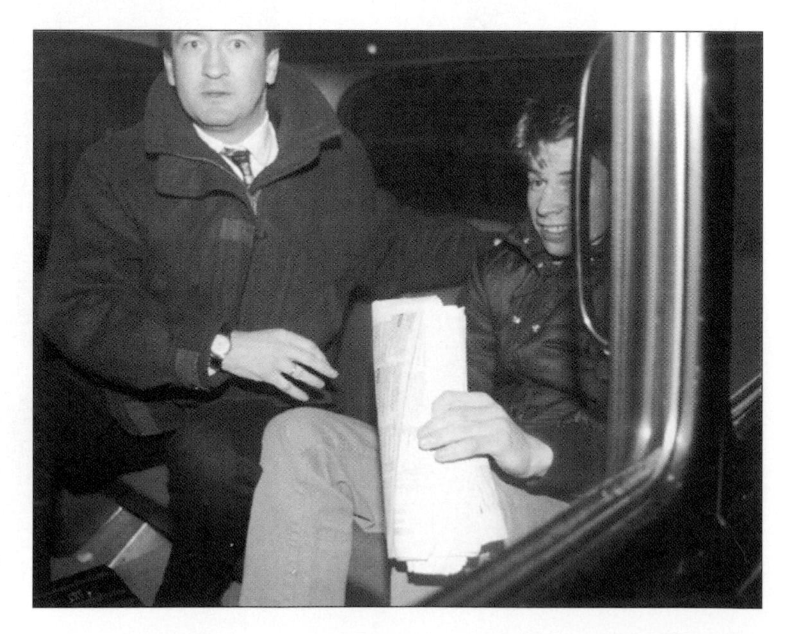

Cleared: Jamie Osborne.

Good cop, bad cop?: Bob Harrington.

A doping gang was under police surveillance when it failed to nobble the Irish-trained chaser Elegant Lord at the 1998 Cheltenham Festival.

Mr Big: Brian Wright.

Off the street: Customs' cocaine seizures were so significant they were expected to affect the supply of the drug in Britain.

Under surveillance: Brian Wright junior.

In the bag: some of the cocaine seized by Customs during its raid on a lock up garage in Leigh-on-Sea.

Not so lucky: one of the boats used to smuggle cocaine.

The Wright gang used extensive contacts to purchase suitable vessels to bring the cocaine ashore.

Out of the saddle: Barrie Wright in his riding silks.

In the saddle: Barrie Wright with celebrity friend Pamella Bordes.

Racing's reputation in his hands: Mr Justice Morland made a significant high court ruling.

Ferdy Murphy: one of the three trainers to feature in Kenyon Confronts.

Standing out from the crowd: bookmaker Victor Chandler.

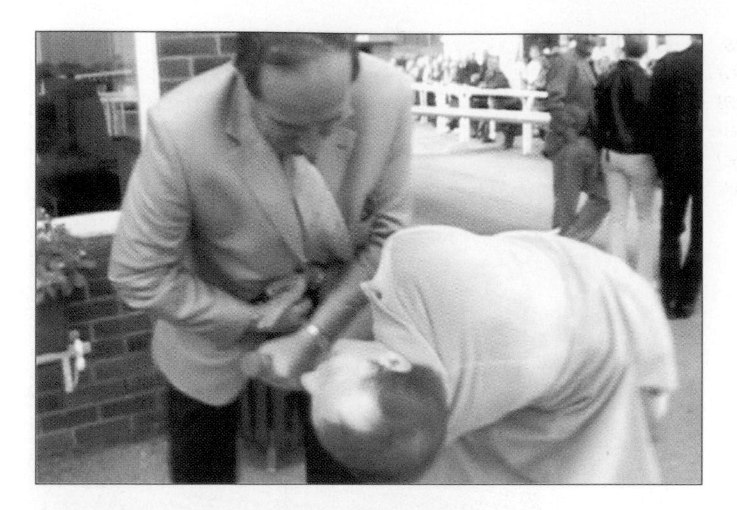

Come racing: David Wintle introduces TV reporter Paul Kenyon to the subtleties of the sport in this sequence of photographs.

In happier times: Jockey Club senior steward Christopher Spence with former security chief Jeremy Phipps.

On the spot: Jockey Club Chief Executive Christopher Foster

Roger Buffham, ex-security chief of the Jockey Club, outside the London High Court

BBC Panorama producer Steven Scott.

confused by these approaches. He was right to be. Harrington was weaving a tangled web. Plenty of people got stuck in it. Including, ultimately, Harrington himself.

Unbeknown to Osborne, Harrington had by this point signed up as an informant to help the police with the same doping and race-fixing investigations that Osborne was part of, but later released from without charge.

Well after his court case, Harrington told me that he had been working as an intelligence officer since 1992 for "various departments within New Scotland Yard, predominantly the Flying Squad".

One of his tasks involved monitoring money laundering through racecourse betting rings. Harrington said the suspects included Brian Wright and "other very, very notorious and major criminals".

According to Harrington, he was asked by a senior police officer if he would be an operative on the race-fixing inquiry, which was said to be making little progress in its investigations. He agreed.

Harrington's codename was Sid. DS Wall was his handler. He had assigned Harrington to keep his ear to the ground in Lambourn, to "get information in advance" about fixed races or dopings. According to Wall, "he never did. He gave us mainly anecdotal stuff."

Harrington had another brief; to persuade Osborne to act as a police witness. He had an unusual way of going about that role. There he was, stretched across Jamie Osborne's sofa sipping a glass of lemonade. Illicitly recording everything that was said. That was his 'm.o.'. To tape every meeting, every conversation he was involved in. Osborne had no idea Harrington was a police informant. The police had no idea of the lengths Harrington was about to go to in his efforts to test Osborne's statements of innocence.

Rather than tell Osborne of his dual role, he instead memorably described himself as someone who specialised in "keeping people out of trouble, getting people into trouble, providing alibis – anything to do with defence work."

Osborne would have thought his defences probably needed some work on them (whether they did or not) when he heard what Harrington had to say next. He told the jockey he was done for. Not only was Osborne in the frame – he was about to be framed. "They (the police) are going to try to put something together here, no doubt about that," Harrington said to him, matter-of-factly.

Can Bob fix it? Yes he can. Harrington offered Osborne a way out of his troubles, which the former jockey just couldn't believe.

"You want him (Wall) to go away," Harrington said. "Perhaps he would."

"What! He wants a few quid. You are not serious," Osborne replied, in a manner more incredulous than John McEnroe ever achieved.

"He wants a few quid and he will go away," Harrington insists, leaving Osborne's head spinning with shock. "That happens? I can't believe that. Nothing surprises me any more," he said.

DS Wall was unaware that Harrington was making these approaches, and it did not take long for CIB to realise that Harrington was acting on his own in offering Osborne a financial way out. To reiterate, Wall's brief to Harrington was to find out about future bent races and to try to persuade Osborne to come forward and give a statement. Not imply that Wall was bent.

Harrington put other options to Osborne, such as becoming a prosecution witness. He rejected them emphatically. "I am not going to pretend an involvement in something I am not involved in," Osborne said. "This is madness, isn't it. Stupid. Ridiculous. I couldn't bring myself to pay for my freedom again when I am not guilty, no way."

Harrington calmly told him: "You will get five years and that will be the end of you."

Osborne rejected Harrington's claims. Instead, with a "combination of shock, anger, and dismay" he contacted his solicitor, who promptly referred the approach to the CIB.

Game on.

THE CORDUROY CAVALIER

For now, though, put yourself in Jamie Osborne's shoes. His emotions could hardly have been through a more vigorous tumble dryer. Less than 24 hours after winning a big race at Cheltenham, the Murphy's Gold Cup on Senor El Betrutti, he had suffered that awful fall from Space Trucker. Two months later he was taken away by police in a dawn raid on his Lambourn home, arrested and kept on bail for nine months. During that time he had to come to terms with the loss of one of his closest friends, John Durkan, to leukaemia, while another, Rose Nugent, was killed in a road accident. His wrist, meanwhile, continued to have the strength of spaghetti.

The word was going around that Osborne would never ride again. Tales circulated about how he couldn't even operate a knife and fork let alone half a ton of heaving horseflesh. So low was he that Osborne considered quitting racing. Neither the pain nor the police allegations against him would go away. "I found myself in this void where the hand was at its worst. At the same time I felt there was someone out there who was trying to wreck my life and I was powerless to do anything about it," he said.

In an interview with the *Racing Post*, once the police charges against him had been dropped, he neatly put his situation into context. "I'm sure there are some out there who believe there was some truth in the allegations. I suppose, if I'm honest, if it had happened to someone else I wouldn't have believed that a person could have been kept on police bail for nine months without there being a grain of truth in it. But I knew there was no truth in it."

A self-confessed "tart for the big occasion", Osborne was being starved of oxygen by being left on the sidelines. The 1998 Cheltenham Festival came and went without him, but while most of the racing world made merry and bet and drank with abandon, Osborne had to contend with Bob Harrington saying "coo-ee". It was his special, little secret that he could tell no one about. It didn't matter what Harrington's motives really were: they left a blizzard of doubts and turmoil in Osborne's mind.

Osborne was nicknamed the 'corduroy cavalier' – surprising, really, as it encourages an un-Osborne-like image of carefree, gormless charm; like the Harry Enfield character Tim Nice-But-Dim. And it simply wasn't like that in 1998. Life was anything but carefree.

Somehow he came through it. Perhaps because he became hardened to such drama, for Osborne's life has had a knack of being played out in vivid colour. Not many jockeys have been slapped by Jenny Pitman, not many jockeys, with their arm in a sling, are said to have literally hit back when provoked by a goading Premiership footballer. Even when he finally returned to the saddle, on 31 October 1998, his comeback ride was swathed in emotion, coming as it did on Coome Hill, one of the jockey's two Hennessy Gold Cup winners, in a race at Ascot run as a memorial to John Durkan.

Finally, after another injury, this time to his right wrist in a fall at the 1999 Cheltenham Festival, Osborne decided to call it a day. In typically dramatic, emotional circumstances, he announced his retirement at the annual 'Lesters' awards, a black-tie, gala dinner at London's Hilton hotel.

The tributes flowed, the many analyses of his career reflected on a clever guy, a natural at getting horses to jump, stronger than he was generally received credit for, and brave with it. A career that yielded 800 winners over 15 seasons had come to an end.

As Osborne reflected on all the moving tributes that greeted his retirement, nothing could have prepared him for the scrutiny that was to follow. That's the thing about nightmares. They never really go away.

CARRY ON DETECTIVE

From June 1998 onwards, in a plot that could easily have been nicknamed Carry On Detective, Harrington had become the taper taped. He was now the one left in the dark. All of his subsequent meetings and telephone calls with Osborne were recorded by the CIB, with the jockey's full co-operation.

Having established that Harrington was working alone, and that Dick Wall was unaware of the "financial option" which Harrington had presented to

Osborne, the CIB set out to snare their man. On a sunny June day, Harrington turned up at Osborne's Dances Barn cottage near Lambourn. Inside was a secret camera. Outside, in a shed, was a CIB officer with a disco full of recording equipment. Two others were lurking in a nearby bean field.

Osborne was wired. Harrington was worried. Despite having his own secret recording equipment in his briefcase, Harrington started looking under cushions and asked whether a security light was in fact a camera.

Things had moved on. Osborne's tone, inevitably given the circumstances, had changed. He told Harrington: "I want to get back and ride at the earliest opportunity. I couldn't care about the others (under arrest). I'm selfish to the end.

"How do we make it go away?"

Harrington was ready for the question: "Well, what do you want me to do, go and see Wall and ask him if he can go away? Is that what you want me to do?"

Osborne: "Yeah, I'd be willing to do that I think."

Harrington: "I can do anything. I can, that's my game."

Harrington asked Osborne for a £500 "sweetener" for Wall, to take the detective out to dinner, to find out the latest news on the doping and race-fixing inquiry.

A day later, Osborne, still wired, handed over the £500 to Harrington in the car park of a Reading hotel.

Problem: the money had been given to him by the police. They had a record of the serial numbers.

"As I see it, the purpose of parting with this money is for you to get Wall," Osborne said to Harrington.

Back came the reply: "I shall be treating matey and I shall leave the balance with him – if he will take it. You're a bit naïve at this game. You've got to rely on me whatever happens. There's no comeback whatsoever. You've got your life, your health, your future – you've got every chance of getting it back."

Before you start wondering whether Harrington and Wall concluded their meal, courtesy of the tax payers, with a bottle of 1971 or 1975 Chateau d'Yquem, forget it. It was a meeting that never took place. In fact, Harrington told police the payment had been made in lieu of expenses incurred while helping Osborne. All he had been doing with Osborne, was "trying in a genuine and honest way to get as much information as I could . . . by telling him what he wanted to hear." The "financial option" had been used to test whether Osborne was guilty, Harrington said.

OLD BAILEY APPEARANCE

Before he was arrested outside Osborne's home in August 1998, Harrington had no idea of what was in store. The same could still be said of Jamie Osborne.

When the case finally reached the Old Bailey in January 2000, Osborne knew he would have to appear as a witness. Like everybody else, he could not have anticipated the ogling focus he would find himself under, so much so that the Judge, David Paget, had to remind the jury: "Jamie Osborne is not on trial."

By this point, Osborne had embarked on a new career as a trainer, but the evidence in the case was to focus like a laser on various aspects of his time in the saddle. At times you would sit in court not quite believing what you were hearing. And you certainly wouldn't have believed the unexpected helping hand that Harrington was about to receive. It may have been Bob Harrington who was on trial, but in a manner that took the breath away, horseracing's reputation was shoved into the dock beside him.

Being in a courtroom can be a tedious experience. No matter how 'juicy' the trial, there are often long, soporific sessions of infuriating detail. You can only sit, suffer, and suppress the yawns – or entertain yourself watching the jury try to do the same – as the trivial and the unfathomable are elevated to the status of rocket science.

The trick is to be around for the good bits. The courtroom pros who spend their journalistic lives sniffing out headlines of the unexpected can do it with unerring skill. With a little help, mind you. It is not unusual to see a barrister, remembering the favourable publicity he received during his junior days, discreetly slip a piece of paper into one of these stalwart's hands. The message is simple: "It's about to kick off in Court 13. Be there."

For the rest of us it's pot luck and a long haul through the drudgery. After several days of dreary legal talk, the jury was sworn in and Harrington's trial began. It was a nondescript February afternoon. Not a day to remember. Until, that is, the smiling, willowy figure of Sir John Nutting, QC, rose to his feet, and the revelations began.

Boom! Well-known horseracing names bounced around the courtroom. Such is the privilege of reporting what was said in court, that these names would soon explode into the public domain.

There couldn't be any other way. Not when Sir John, perhaps unaware of the thrilling tales that lurked within his words, calmly and charmingly told the jury in his opening speech as to why they were gathered here today.

He told them it was a "case about corruption". He wasn't kidding, either. But as the allegations tumbled out, not just about Bob Harrington, but about horseracing's integrity as well, you were soon left wondering: who or what is corrupt? Sir John made references to Brian Wright, a "well-known" criminal; Dean Gallagher, who "accepted money for pulling horses", and the bookmaker Victor Chandler.

Say what! What the hell was going on here? Sensation on a plate, that's what. Sir John's opening speech was made in open court and as such could be reported, but it's also worth making a few things clear. Victor Chandler was questioned but never charged in the doping and race-fixing investigation. It was not part of the prosecution's case that anybody named in the evidence – be it Chandler, Dean Gallagher or Brian Wright – had committed any offence

Still, Brian Wright, eh? His was a name that was being whispered in salacious circles as a man with a keen and close involvement in racing, which may have seen him cross the line.

Journalists were able to report that Harrington told Dick Wall that eight of Britain's top 10 Jump jockeys at the time had been entertained by Wright, who also, it was alleged, set out to corrupt younger riders. "He befriends them when they are starting out and bungs them a few quid. Then four or five years later he calls in favours," Harrington claimed. Speaking in May 1998, he told Wall that Wright was "the most important person in all these moves" to fix races.

Could it be true? How could Harrington be so sure that Wright was this 'Mr Big' who had silently but effectively made racing his own personal fiefdom of nods and winks and 'naughty' races?

Say what you want about Bob Harrington's motives – and you could never be sure what they were; the more you listened to the evidence, the more your head span with the possibilities – he was a master craftsman when it came to cajoling people into spilling the beans. "I was very impressed at the thought of having such a contact," DS Wall said, "and treated him like a colleague on the team. I took the very, very unusual step of telling him much more than a normal informant – what we were thinking and in what direction we were going."

"It was an unusual situation that the proposed informant was a police officer," Sir John Nutting told the court.

Unusual situation, unusual methods. Wall was later to find out – much to his horror – that Harrington had secretly taped their conversations using a machine within his briefcase, the same trick that he employed when recording his conversations with Osborne. Wall is a big man with a walrus moustache and a heavy, hanging face to match. It is not difficult to imagine those features drooping even further when it emerged what Harrington had done. The rest of us just sat and listened open mouthed.

Bob Harrington, the man with the tall tales and sneaky briefcase, had allowed reporters to write of allegations that would not otherwise have been made public. Suddenly, his battle of wits with Osborne, and his attempts to imply that a senior police officer could be bribed, became a secondary tale within a much bigger one. Just like the players at the court of Elsinore.

An ironic corollary of Harrington's clandestine taping was that we got to hear in court exactly what information he prised out of Wall. This information mattered. Wall was head of the doping and race-fixing allegations at the time. We got a crucial portrait of the nature of the investigation. Not just in its detail, but its validity.

Straight away we could see Wall's influence on the investigation and just how closely the Jockey Club was involved with it. For example, Wall told Harrington that he was behind the decision to take away the licences of Osborne, Gallagher and Leighton Aspell. "All three of them had a little bit of a shock by having a suspension. Maybe next time I won't give them back," Wall is heard saying on tape.

Wall wanted to be seen as "the man in control" yet when later questioned in court said he had in fact very little input in to the decision to withdraw the trio's licences temporarily. Never could you be truly sure just what was going on.

All that seemed consistent was Bob Harrington's ability to get people talking. His taped conversation with Wall reminded you of an indiscreet comment Osborne made during one of his 'chats' with the double-dealing detective, the one at Kim Bailey's place. "The Jockey Club has known what they (the police) are doing the whole way through," Osborne said, while later referring to a "big rift" that was building up between the two sides. Osborne also made a curious reference to the Jockey Club, insisting: "I don't give a fuck about the Jockey Club. If I have to blow the thing open I fucking well will."

He was asked in court about that remark and said. "There are things I know about members of the Jockey Club that probably wouldn't look very good for racing." That wasn't all that Jamie Osborne said. He also told Harrington of the only time he had been offered money to get horses beaten.

"I was offered £20,000 when I was 19 to stop the last two favourites at the Cheltenham Festival. The probable name behind it was Brian Wright. I know where he lives but never met him.

"I didn't take it and I've never been asked since, on my life. I had a £5,000 overdraft and didn't sleep all night, but I decided in the morning that I was not going to ruin my name to go hooky."

Osborne had in fact written, in less precise terms, about this same approach in the *Racing Post* weeks before his arrest. "The timing was too awful," he recalled.

During his time in the witness box, Osborne was asked by defence counsel Richard Ferguson about the £20,000 offer. "Who offered you the money?" asked Ferguson, his face stern, his jaw strong and pointing right at Osborne.

"A fella called Dermot Browne," Osborne replied.

Lovely. The phrase shooting fish in a barrel sprang to mind. Sometimes you see a front-page story and marvel at the work that must have gone into it. Sometimes you write one yourself and are almost ashamed at the ease with which it is spawned. Open the notebook, click the pen into action and let it rest between your finger and your thumb, snug as a gun, until it's time to fire.

"A fella called Dermot Browne." That'll do. Now it's just a case of relaying this news back to the office and let them decide on the point-size of the headline. But you know already: it'll be big.

True enough, there it was the next day: "DERMOT BROWNE OFFERED ME £20,000 TO GET BEATEN," and below it, in lower case, the equally dramatic subhead: "Osborne claims former jockey asked him to stop two Cheltenham favourites."

When he was aspiring to be a jockey, and used to hang around the weighing room at his local course, Wetherby, an ambitious kid who had the nickname "gums and teeth", Jamie Osborne used to look up to Dermot Browne; he had been a "childhood idol".

Back in court, his view of him was rapidly changing, as Richard Ferguson, with his face of polished granite, continued his questioning. Ferguson, like Sir John Nutting, was a joy to watch in action. You honestly felt privileged to be in the same court as them. They were big time. Sir John had successfully prosecuted the paedophile Sidney Cooke and Britain's first war criminal, Anthony Sawoniuk. Ferguson specialised as a defence counsel and clearly liked a challenge. His former clients had included Rosemary West. Since Harrington, he has represented jailed property tycoon Nicholas van Hoogstraten, and REM guitarist Peter Buck, who was cleared of an air rage attack.

Ferguson was preparing to use all his skills on Osborne. "This is the only occasion you have had any direct contact yourself with corruption in horseracing, am I right?" he asked.

"Yes," said Osborne, agreeing with the barrister that it had a "pretty profound impact" on him.

Ferguson recalled one such conversation between the two men, in May 1998. "What you were telling Mr Harrington was that you always thought Brian Wright was behind it (the £20,000 offer)."

On hearing this at the time, Harrington thought he had "cracked it", so did the journalists sitting in court.

"That was a guess," Osborne told Ferguson.

"Why did you guess that?" Ferguson asked.

"Because he was a friend of the person (Browne) who offered me the money," Osborne told him.

"Are we to understand the only reason you had thought it was Brian Wright was because he was a friend (of Browne)?" Ferguson persisted.

Osborne's reply hammered home the feeling that this case was the starting point of something big. "There were a lot of stories going around about things that were going on with racing. That man (Wright) was linked to a lot of them."

The pen could hardly keep up. Ferguson said it was "a serious matter" to raise Wright's name "in this connection unless you have some reasonable basis."

Osborne agreed.

Brian Wright, he said, was "somebody who might have been connected with things that might have been going on at the time in the 80s that were corrupt."

People had talked, people had wondered, people had whispered. People could now sit up and listen. Here was one of Britain's most talented and most successful jockeys saying, yes, while he was not involved, racing had its 'moody' side.

It was just the kind of thing that those who like to peer through racing's privets had been itching to discover.

OSBORNE TAKES THE STAND

So what was a jockey supposed to do to earn £20,000 in the 1980s?

According to Osborne, the offer that he spurned would have required him to stop two horses at the Cheltenham Festival, both on the final day. Raise An Argument, trained by Monica Dickinson, started the 15-8 favourite for the Cathcart Chase but was pulled up by Osborne. Half an hour later Regal Castle fared little better when unplaced in the County Hurdle, despite starting co-favourite.

Aged 19, Osborne had not known what to do about the approach. He told only the two trainers of the horses what had happened, and "possibly a friend".

"No one in authority?" Ferguson asked him.

"No."

"There was no inquiry into the matter?"

"Nobody knew the matter existed."

"You didn't think it was appropriate to notify the authorities?"

"No, I was 19," Osborne said. "If it happened now, yeah, I would have done. Aged 19, you don't understand the implications of something like that. Plus there were things going on in the 1980s that no longer go on in racing. There were some corrupt activities going on. Nowadays it isn't like that and if somebody came to you with that sort of approach you would go straight to the Jockey Club."

There we go again. "Corrupt activities". It mattered little that Osborne thought they were no longer going on. You wanted to know what *had* gone on.

Osborne left the witness box with Judge Paget reminding the jury that he was there, simply, to give evidence against Harrington as a witness for the prosecution. It must have been a nice feeling to get out of there. No more scrutiny, no more harassment, no more Dick Ferguson tapping away with his questions, steely eyed in search of weakness.

Finally Jamie Osborne could go home and relax.

Like hell he could. You know those films where a secret figure makes his entry into the plot. He might be spying on the hero and heroine as hand-in-hand they try to escape from danger, yet unwittingly are heading towards it. All you get is a back view of this shadowy character, maybe you see his hands. But then you hear his wicked, dark, delighted laugh. And you know he is about to exert an influence on the plot that is as unwelcome as it is unexpected.

Someone, somewhere was reading the following day's *Racing Post* and decided he, too, would make a dramatic intervention. He picked up the phone and dialled the number of the paper's newsdesk. "This is Dermot Browne," the voice said. "I'm ringing about your story."

Dermot Browne had plenty to say about the story, the story that outlined Jamie Osborne's recollection in court of the £20,000 offer. In fact, he left his number, so that it could be passed on to Dick Ferguson so that he could call Browne back. That task fell to me.

Ferguson, although regarded as extremely affable outside the courtroom, scared me. He knew his way around the Old Bailey. I didn't. I was terrified of messing up one of his quotes. So commanding was he at his job that you would secretly hope for his approval. His displeasure just didn't bear thinking about.

Ferguson had his stern face on as I walked towards him with Browne's number. "He wants to get in touch," I said. I almost saw a smile. "Thank you," Ferguson said, and then he walked away. You knew that he was already planning his next line of attack.

And so it was that Jamie Osborne returned to the witness stand, eight days after he thought he had seen the last of Court 4 of the Old Bailey, of Bob Harrington, of Richard Ferguson, and of the line of journalists sitting in front of him like French widows with their knitting at the guillotine.

As he returned to the stand, you noticed that Osborne had a fierce red spot on his nose, an apposite peephole for the fury that no doubt lay within.

Ferguson welcomed him back to the crease with a wicked bouncer. "When you last gave evidence you told us about a man who had offered you £20,000 on two races at the Cheltenham Festival.

"The point that you were making is that you refused the offer," Ferguson said.

"That's right, yes," Osborne replied.

Ferguson continued: "I suggest to you, in fact, that it is not true, and, in effect, you took the £20,000."

"That is not true."

"And not only did you take the £20,000, but you asked for an extra £10,000."

Osborne laughed quietly at the suggestion of the extra £10,000, but then could not contain his anger. "Mr Ferguson," he said. "I don't know where you are making this up from but it is categorically not true."

Ferguson said: "I suggest it was in Cheltenham and the year was 1988. Was that the year?"

Osborne responded: "I don't know. I can't remember. Probably."

Ferguson continued: "I suggest what happened was this: that you received the phone call offering you the £20,000 and your initial reaction was that you would think about it and, thereafter, you indicated that you would do it, but you wanted an extra £10,000."

Osborne's frustration at the allegations continued to manifest itself. "Mr Ferguson, this is a fairytale and, to be perfectly, honest I am fed up with it. I came here as a witness and I am not on trial."

He then named Dermot Browne as the likely source of these new allegations. "He had phoned all the press telling them that I took the money, which is categorically not true," Osborne said. "I presume you have been in contact with him. It is absolute nonsense. If you want to take his word for it, that is absolutely fine. I am not on trial here. This did not happen. You are trying to mislead everybody."

"I am just trying to get your evidence," Ferguson told him. "Not only did you take the money, i.e. £30,000, but I can suggest to you the circumstances and the manner in which the money was paid out to you."

Ferguson alleged that a meeting was arranged on a lay-by on the road between Lambourn and Great Shefford. "What happened is that you were in a car and the man who was paying you the money was in a car.

"Both cars drove towards each other with the drivers' windows side by side, and then the money was passed over to you."

"Absolute rubbish," Osborne said. "A figment of someone's imagination . . . Mr Ferguson is attempting to mislead the jury and he is going to mislead the public . . . "

Suddenly everybody jumped a little as Mr Justice Paget intervened. "Stop," he told Osborne. "It isn't Mr Ferguson's fault. He has to act on instructions."

Osborne had already made an appeal to Judge Paget over Ferguson's questioning. "Is he allowed to make accusations like this with no substance?" Osborne asked.

Mr Justice Paget replied: "Mr Osborne, I can understand your frustrations. The short answer is 'yes'."

Osborne, reminding the court of his new profession, said: "There are wider implications for me because it reaches a wider audience. This will be reported in the papers." Too right.

"There is absolutely no truth in it and I am absolutely defenceless. It is absolutely appaling." Osborne then told the court how the prospect of riding a winner at the Cheltenham Festival – remember Raise An Argument was the 15-8 favourite – was "comic book stuff. The thought of throwing the chance to do that for money would just never have entered my head."

You had to feel for Osborne as he once more finished his evidence and marched out of court, while the French widows scuttled off to the bunker that is the Old Bailey press room to file their copy.

It was a raw deal. Osborne wasn't on trial yet he was stuck in the witness box while accusations were pelted at him like rotten tomatoes. And they had to be reported; this whole story could not be ignored on the grounds of Osborne's sensitivities. Harsh, but true. All the same, "just doing my job" seems a bit feeble in comparison to the treatment he was singled out for.

HARRINGTON JAILED

Five days after they were asked to consider their verdict, the jury found Bob Harrington guilty of both the charges he faced. His sentencing was delayed pending psychological reports, although he was told by Judge David Paget: "I am afraid I have no alternative as I see it, but to remand you in custody."

As Harrington was sent down, the black cat brooch that he wore on his jacket lapel having brought little luck, you could only reflect on a court case that, for all its giddy revelations and salacious detail, finished on a sad, unsatisfactory note.

Jamie Osborne certainly suffered. He had found himself the subject of some explosive claims. His fear, as he embarked on his new career as a trainer, was that the allegations, however unfounded, would prove indelible. It was a heavy price he paid for coming clean, although at least he could start that new career with a nearly full stable of 60 horses.

Osborne quickly made it clear he had no regrets about reporting Harrington. "Any rational man who was innocent and in my position would have done the right thing," he said when I spoke to him afterwards. "I'm glad this is over once and for all and I hope it hasn't done too much damage to my credibility. It wasn't the sort of publicity that I really needed."

Osborne found trenchant support from DC Shaun McLeary, who was one of the CIB officers who investigated Harrington. "One thing this does is completely vindicate Jamie Osborne," said McLeary. "The easy option for Jamie would have been just to ignore Harrington. It is to his credit that he came to us and not once has he wavered, despite a tremendous amount of hostility towards him."

While the rest of us felt uneasy confusion as to Harrington's motives, DC McLeary was unambiguous. Harrington, he insisted, was a pain in the backside, "a most difficult man" who had used the system cleverly to try to dismantle the case against him and distract his adversaries.

"He knows the system as well as I do. You have seen how he behaved during the trial. He has tried to grind me down," McLeary said, adding that Harrington had made numerous complaints about him. It was he added, the longest and most frustrating case of his career, involving the documenting of more than 4,500 pages and the cataloguing of nearly 1,100 exhibits.

Returning to the Old Bailey for sentencing was a grim affair. Suddenly, Harrington was no longer the nitty-gritty, rough-and-tumble, wheelin-an-a-dealin, duckin-an-diving, furtive man of undercover means that he would have liked us all to believe.

Sir John Nutting, in a manner that rolled off his tongue to golden effect, had called him "a braggadocio", a braggart, a man of empty boasts. You thought back to the tapes of Harrington being interviewed after his arrest, and how he had told an officer that he and Osborne had been "conning each other and kidding each other along."

He was told: "It sounds a very murky world."

And Harrington replied: "It was a Walter Mitty world. I was trying to get as much information as I could by telling him (Osborne) what he wanted to hear."

Never was anything quite what it seemed, a view endorsed in the summing up of Judge Paget, a man who presided over the confusion with incredible patience and skill. "An unusual case," he called it. "A case of double bluff. That is how it is being presented by all sides."

Harrington was portrayed as a shell of a man, a wreck, suffering from acute depression. Psychiatric reports described him as a man of lower-than-average intelligence with the memory of an 80-year-old. He was 58 at the time. Concern about Harrington's mental health meant he had been placed on the 'at risk' register while in Belmarsh prison in south-east London – home of some of the criminal fraternity's biggest hitters and as depressing a location as you could imagine.

Before his early retirement, Harrington had been a widely respected policeman for 27 years, receiving several commendations in his role as an undercover officer. Brian Ward, a former Thames Valley colleague, spoke of Harrington's "unique ability to cultivate informants in every possible way".

Harrington's ex-boss, former Chief Superintendent Anthony Webb, described him as an exemplary detective. "I worked very closely with him and would have trusted him with my life," Webb said. Harrington had "special abilities within the criminal network", meaning he kept things "very, very close to his chest".

It also meant he was a marked man. As a former cop, Harrington was at risk, not just from himself but his fellow inmates. He needed to be checked on every 15 minutes while at Belmarsh. "There are people actually being tried in this building at the moment who have made it their business to make it clear to Mr Harrington that they know about him, that they know about his background, and left him in no doubt whatsoever what they would do to him," Ferguson said.

Concern for Harrington was clear. Judge Paget, who had received a "very moving" letter from Harrington's wife Linda, said an 18-month sentence for both charges, which were to run concurrently, were "as low as they possibly can be, considering my public duty."

He told Harrington: "What you did was a very serious perversion of all you have apparently stood for all your life."

During his time as a policeman, Harrington was credited with the successful conclusion to 60 murders. He earned 23 commendations but retired from full-time service aged 48 as a result of his virus. His former boss, Superintendent John Clements, described him as a "tough but fair" sergeant, "the finest in the Thames Valley".

"A man like him makes other detectives look less effective," he said.

So why had he risked so much for so little? If, in fact, he had.

Harrington, who failed to overturn his conviction in the Appeal Court, blew a kiss to his wife Linda in the public gallery once the sentence became known. He was led down, a guilty man.

Left behind him was a trail of incredible allegations and a sense of disbelief.

STEP FORWARD DERMOT BROWNE

The effects of Harrington's trial should not be underestimated. It gave an insight into the thinking of those in charge of the doping and race-fixing investigations, however unimpressive that insight was.

Perhaps more importantly, it caused Jamie Osborne to rub the lamp that released Dermot Browne onto an unsuspecting world. Even at this point, February 2000, very few people – perhaps only two others – knew the full extent of Browne's mischief. Certainly no one knew the horrific detail of his claims that are contained in this book.

For six years the Jockey Club had been trying to get Browne to tell of his secrets. The Harrington trial persuaded him that the time was right. Browne had even been lined up as a prosecution witness at the trial of the five men accused of conspiring to dope racehorses. Unsurprisingly, given Browne's very chequered track record, that idea was reported to have been dropped on the grounds that he would not have been viewed as a reliable witness. The defence counsels would have made mincemeat of him.

It was during the preparations for that Southwark trial that Browne gave the interview to police that has been included here.

Besides Dermot Browne, the Harrington trial also revealed that the dopers who occasionally blighted British racing were prepared to go to the very top. Even at the Cheltenham Festival.

One of Wall's indiscretions to Harrington concerned a failed attempt to dope a horse at the meeting in 1998. The horse was Elegant Lord, who started the 5-4 favourite for the Christies Foxhunter Chase.

The dopers' plans became known to the police and the Jockey Club meaning that the security was too tight for them to proceed with their plan.

Wall, who was unaware that he was being taped, told Harrington that for the first time every trainer was given their own padlock and key for each stable.

"The guy said 'I just can't get in there' and it all fell apart. Everything was set. They had the package, they had the man, they had the horse," Wall said. "I spent 72 hours with the team watching the horse. The doper was on his way down. He was actually there. They just couldn't get into it.

"Cheltenham was just too well covered, tighter than any racecourse, even tighter than Liverpool."

Elegant Lord, ridden by his trainer Enda Bolger, could only finish fifth and the race went to the 3-1 shot Earthmover.

Bolger described the thwarted doping attempt as "a complete surprise".

He added: "I rode him myself that year and he ran badly," he said. "He made a couple of bad mistakes and was a well-beaten fifth. As far as stable security at Cheltenham is concerned, it's absolutely top-class. It would be easier to get into the White House than to get in there if you weren't entitled to."

6

FARCE ON THE THAMES

We could have done with some of Bob Harrington's firecrackers at Southwark Crown Court later that year when the trial began of the five men accused of conspiring to dope racehorses.

The court is situated on the banks of the Thames near London Bridge and next door to the new offices built for the Mayor of London. Those very same glass-fronted offices have been rather witheringly compared to a giant testicle, in which case there could hardly have been a more appropriate backdrop for this particular trial. For the more you sat in court, the more you struggled to escape the view that someone had made a complete balls-up of the case, and as a corollary the entire doping and race-fixing inquiry.

After more than three years of police and Jockey Club investigations, and after 16 arrests, it had come to this. The trial of five men: Ray Butler, 52, from Cricklewood, North London; Glen Gill, 33, from Fareham, Hampshire; Jason Moore, 30, from Woodford Green, Essex; Adam Hodgson, 38, from Slough, Berkshire; and John Matthews, 36, also from Slough.

They stood in the dock accused of conspiracy to defraud by "interference with the fair running of horses in horseraces by the administering of a performance-inhibiting drug." They all denied the charge, which related to dates between 1 March and 1 April 1997, the period in which Avanti Express, at Exeter, and Lively Knight, at Plumpton, were both doped with ACP.

Someone had clearly tipped off the awaiting jurors as to how unsatisfactory this trial would prove, as it took four days to swear in a panel. An original pool of 25 potential jurors had been whittled down to 17, seven of whom found excuses – "some of them extremely feeble excuses", according to Judge Elwen – leaving only 10 candidates and a problem. You need 12 for a trial to begin.

This one finally did begin after five days in front of a jury of seven men and five women.

THE ROAD TO PERDITION

The opening speech made by prosecution counsel Richard Whittam was noticeably light on hard evidence.

He told the jury that ACP was found at Butler's home at the time of his arrest in January 1998. Police found a small white paper bag in a kitchen cupboard. It contained two unused plastic syringes and three hypodermic needles, along with another two syringes that "appeared to have been used and fitted with needles which had been adapted to stop the syringes leaking which were found to contain traces of ACP."

Asked about the syringes, Butler said a friend used them to keep greyhounds quiet in transit from Ireland. "When it was pointed out the bag was from Bliss the chemist in Kilburn and not a shop in Ireland, he [Butler] didn't reply," Whittam said.

"Later he explained the gentleman in Ireland was called Ryan and was from Waterford but he couldn't provide a telephone number or address."

Whittam stated there was no evidence that this equipment was used on Avanti Express or Lively Knight. The syringes were found 10 months outside the timescale of the charges. The Jockey Club's senior vet, Peter Webbon, said the needles found in Butler's flat were of the right size to be injected intramuscularly into horses, although, in line with Whittham's opening speech, a forensic scientist said there was "no evidence" that these particular needles had ever been used on an animal.

The betting habits of Glen Gill, John Matthews and Jason Moore were examined in court. All seemed serious players – Moore was one of spread betting firm Sporting Index's top 10 clients, with a special gold line straight to the trading room – but none of this linked them to the doping of Avanti Express and Lively Knight.

The most startling evidence came in the second week. It was pretty damning – of the police that is, certainly not of any of the accused.

One of the officers leading the investigation, DC Peter Kelly of the Organised Crime Group, said he had been "a bit green" about betting when he started on the case. This, it has to be said, seemed extraordinary for a case that was about the doping of racehorses. During questioning of Glen Gill shortly after his arrest in February 1998 Kelly had referred to " . . . my lack of knowledge of racing and betting".

Inevitably, this statement was seized upon in court by Gill's QC, Jeremy Gompertz. He asked Kelly about the concept of 'value betting', which Gill had referred to during his interviews when he was questioned about why he had placed a series of bets on a three-horse race in which he had left out the 1-7 favourite Lively Knight.

Kelly said in court: "I couldn't understand why he was leaving out the

1-7 shot. I couldn't understand it."

Gompertz asked him: "Do you still take the view that opposing odds-on favourites is folly?"

"I am not a gambling man, but yes I would," Kelly replied.

"Your position, Mr Kelly, is this: that only a lunatic or a fraudster would oppose odds-on chances?" Gompertz continued.

"It is not an easy question to answer."

Not for Kelly perhaps, but for millions of punters it is a no-brainer.

Gompertz asked him: "Do you accept, as a rational punter, it was a reasonable thing to do?"

"No," Kelly replied.

"Do you realise that if you are constantly backing horses at 1-7, to compensate for one loser you have to have seven winners? That's your idea of sensible betting?"

"He was ignoring a 1-7 shot and backing two others who, on form, were not good enough. If the bookmakers have made a horse 1-7, they must have thought it was going to win."

Kelly admitted he didn't study horseracing form. Gompertz did. He had kept a record of all odds-on favourites over a month and found that a £10 stake on all of them would have yielded a net loss of £96.32.

"Automatically backing odds-on chances is the road to perdition, isn't it?" Gompertz asked Kelly.

"Possibly," he replied. "But it's not something I would know and that's why I couldn't understand Mr Gill."

Hearing this exchange, you could sympathise with those who had criticised the apparent lack of understanding among police of the subject they were investigating. Whatever his merits as a copper, DC Kelly was never going to give John McCririck any sleepless nights.

CASE COLLAPSES

It was becoming pretty clear that the case was drifting away from the prosecution. Something was missing: evidence.

The trial was proceeding at a faster rate than expected. It had been due to last four to five weeks. It collapsed after two. Once the prosecution had completed its case, the defence teams – each of the five men had their own briefs, ensuring the courtroom was a sea of white wigs – joined forces to argue there was no case to answer.

Judge Elwen agreed. The jury was called in and instructed to return not guilty verdicts. The five men in the dock were free to go, having not been required to give evidence. The whole thing was over. Let the rancour begin. "No defendant has a case to answer," Judge Elwen said damningly.

His ruling was based on the prosecution's failure to prove that the defendants had conspired to dope Avanti Express or Lively Knight, or to provide evidence showing who doped the horses and how.

"Central to the charge of conspiracy is the idea that they [the defendants] were in some way involved in the doping or arranged for horses to be doped," he told the jury. "My conclusion is that there is no evidence from which you can confer that part of the plot took place."

Out of 16 arrests there were no successful prosecutions and DC Kelly admitted: "I am not surprised by the judge's decision. It was always going to be a difficult case because there is no physical evidence. We know horses were doped but not by who and how."

Look back on the case, you can only wonder how it even got to court. The evidence presented to the jury had the solidity of soup. The discovery of syringes with traces of ACP at Butler's home counted for little. There was nothing to link them to the doping of Avanti Express and Lively Knight or to the other four defendants.

The court had heard how the five defendants had phoned each other frequently on the day Avanti Express was doped. This is hardly a crime, and it was surprising that their mobile records had not been checked on other days to see if this pattern of phone traffic was anything unusual.

The evidence that John Matthews had placed £400 on Stormhill Pilgrim, the winner of the race in which Lively Knight was doped, was hardly persuasive either, especially when his barrister, John Kelsey-Fry, sought to "put that bet into proper context" by explaining that his client's regular stake was closer to £4,000.

Ray Butler's QC, Francis Gilbert, accused the Crown's case of "starting on the basis that anyone who bet on the race [which Butler had] was involved in the doping." He described the evidence in court of just two of the 32 bookmakers at Exeter on the day of the doping as a "totally incomplete picture" and "very dangerous for the jury to look at". John Kelsey-Fry, in the legal argument that preceded the trial being halted, also referred to "an insufficiently exhaustive investigation" into the Exeter betting.

After talking to some of the police officers involved in the case, it quickly became clear that the doping and race-fixing inquiries had been treated almost as a side-show to other investigations that they regarded as more important. Other journalists, having met privately with some police officers in charge of the case, spoke of their alarm at an ignorance of racing and betting matters and a conviction that racing was essentially bent. If it was the police's job to prove it, they failed miserably. The collapse of the case had cost at least £500,000 of taxpayers' money.

One undoubted problem was the way in which responsibility for the case was passed along like a hot potato. DC Kelly was only the last in a line of four officers put in charge of the investigation.

JOCKEY CLUB BAN TRIO

As damning an outcome as it was for the police, racing had only one picture stuck to its dartboard. Roger Buffham was the man it was aiming its bile at. As head of security, Buffham had been responsible for preparing the evidence of possible corruption in racing to be handed over to the police. One of his sternest critics, Michael Caulfield, the chief executive of the Jockeys' Association, was first out of the traps in calling for Buffham to go. "Buffham has staked everything on this inquiry and he believes that everyone in racing is bent. I think he should make his exit from racing. I say it with passion," Caulfield said . . . with passion.

"I will not accept that it is all down to the police; initially it [the enquiry] was Jockey Club-led. They are simply not able enough."

In fact, Buffham did offer his resignation – unbeknown to his critics – and it was not accepted by the Jockey Club.

Both the police and the Jockey Club said it had no plans to re-open their investigation into the dopings. But the hassle was not yet over for three of the five cleared men.

Ray Butler, Adam Hodgson, and John Matthews were all banned indefinitely from setting foot on Britain's racecourses, despite the 'not guilty' verdicts at Southwark.

The decision was taken at a Jockey Club Disciplinary Committee hearing in February 2001 when the three men were told there would be no review of the ban until 2006. The decision continued the bans placed on the three men since their arrests. The bans on Jason Moore and Glen Gill were lifted.

Matthews, speaking on behalf of the trio, said: "I went to the hearing believing the decision had already been made. I was proved right. I felt like a naughty schoolboy in front of a kangaroo court. I am unhappy with the evidence that was used against me."

They were angry that evidence was used against them that came from Dermot Browne. They were further upset by the use of evidence from an anonymous informant known as 'Nureyev'.

I met the trio for a coffee after their hearing and they were seething at being warned off by the Jockey Club despite being cleared in court. "I don't think it was right that it should use an anonymous informant (Nureyev). Even one of the Disciplinary Committee said he wasn't happy with that evidence,"

Matthews said. "The Jockey Club seems to think it can do what it wants, even disregarding the opinion of a Crown Court judge."

In its defence, the Jockey Club argued: "The doping trial was a criminal case heard before judge and jury, where the issue was whether or not there was sufficient evidence to prove a conspiracy to defraud.

"The Disciplinary Committee were making judgement with regards to the Rules of Racing, which give the senior steward the power to exclude someone from licensed premises purely on the basis that they consider the presence of such a person undesirable in the interests of racing."

By now, though, there was a growing feeling that the interests of racing weren't being particularly well looked after. Still, at least a scapegoat, a head on a pole, was about to be produced.

7

AN ANGRY MAN

Roger Buffham lost his job as head of security at the Jockey Club following an internal inquiry into "serious allegations" against him, made by members of Buffham's own security team of 30 full-time and 34 part-time employees.

The specific reason for his departure, which came 10 months after the collapse of the Southwark trial, was inevitably the subject of considerable speculation and dispute.

This is how the Jockey Club tell it: the allegations covered a number of incidents that occurred between 1993 and 2001. At the same time a complaint was made against Buffham's style of management. Prior to an appeal by Buffham against his dismissal, a confidential settlement was reached.

Buffham argues differently. The "serious allegations" against him included one of sexual harassment by a female colleague that occurred in 1993 that he strongly denies. No complaint was made at the time and that person continued to work with Buffham until his departure.

According to Buffham, the complainant declined to give evidence against him at his disciplinary hearing. That said, the Jockey Club deny his claim that any witness statements against him were withdrawn, relating either to the first complainant or another woman who alleged that Buffham made what he himself described as "a minor inappropriate comment" in 2001.

Buffham, meanwhile, says that the second allegation was not upheld at his hearing, when the complaint about his management style was also thrown out. He insists he left the Jockey Club by "mutual agreement", having received a "full and flattering" reference together with compensation (£50,000) "for loss of office".

Whatever the circumstances of Buffham's departure, he wasn't happy about it – as you might expect. Elsewhere, you would have struggled to fill a thimble with the tears that followed his exit. "I can now get on with the rest of my life without him hounding me. I'm very pleased indeed, like a number of people in the racing industry. I'm very glad to see the back of him," said Graham Bradley.

Bradley was convinced that Buffham had been out to 'get' him and devoted much of his time – too much time, perhaps – in attempting to do so. Bradley's delight was personal.

Yet the neutral voices, such as that of John Reid, the respected joint president of the Jockeys' Association, were just as disdainful. "There are no tears being shed in the weighing room – he certainly didn't have the confidence of the jockeys," Reid said. "We didn't know what he was doing most of the time, he seemed to be barking up a lot of trees without cats in them."

The visceral distrust of Buffham overshadowed the fact that his time at the Jockey Club was by no means without achievement: improved information systems, better qualified staff, greater use of new technology, better links with the police, a restructuring of his department and the recruitment of investigative officers with a strong police background can all be credited to him.

He was also closely involved with many of the Jockey Club's rule changes that were made in response to the Wright Organisation's involvement with racing, yet proved so unpopular with jockeys and trainers. They will feature in a later chapter.

Racing thought it had seen the last of them man it lampooned as Roger Buffoon and Inspector Clouseau.

But it hadn't. By now, Buffham was an angry man, adamant that he had been badly treated by the Jockey Club. And if his critics thought he had caused enough upset while working within racing, they hadn't reckoned on what he might do now that he was standing on the outside pissing in.

There was a loud smack of hands hitting foreheads inside the Jockey Club's headquarters at Portman Square, central London, when news filtered through that Buffham was working as an advisor to two BBC programmes into alleged corruption within the sport, *Kenyon Confronts* and *Panorama*. Like so many characters and twists in this extraordinary tale, by no means have we heard the last of them.

Buffham had supposedly signed a confidentiality agreement. The Jockey Club argued that by advising these two programmes he was acting in breach of that agreement, which consequently "could have the potential to undermine our ability to regulate racing effectively".

It swooped on London's High Court to take out an injunction preventing Buffham from divulging the confidential and privileged information he had gathered while at the Jockey Club. It was a move that Buffham initially challenged before agreeing to accept the terms of the injunction.

So he is unable to tell us what he knows, but you can imagine how he felt.

Which was pretty pissed off.

Buffham's problems began in the spring of 2001. In the aftermath of Southwark, the Jockey Club had introduced a series of measures aimed at not only protecting racing but also ensuring that Buffham and his team were made more accountable by reporting to a new internal group, the Security and Investigations Committee.

The committee had, amongst other things, the power to demand sensitive information such as betting and telephone accounts from owners, trainers and jockeys. Anyone who refused to provide the information risked being warned off.

Buffham was closely involved with the formation of this committee. Once it was in place, he took a holiday. On his return, he was told of the complaints that had been made against him.

On 8 August 2001 Buffham attended a disciplinary hearing and was told on 15 August that he had been dismissed from his job.

Buffham appealed, and a hearing was held on 8 September. Three weeks later came the offer of a settlement from the Jockey Club and a £50,000 pay off for Buffham.

PHIPPS' INDISCRETION

Around this time, Buffham said he was approached by Steven Scott, a *Panorama* producer who he had known for "many years". Scott was aware of the court cases involving the Wright Organisation and wanted Buffham's advice on its racing links with a view to making a programme on the issue.

He decided to help. "My motives for doing so were to attempt to restore my own reputation and bring into the public domain serious shortfalls and inadequacies in the Jockey Club's ability to regulate racing properly," Buffham told me.

"In January 2002 I was also approached by the producers of *Kenyon Confronts* and assisted them as a consultant. The extent of my consultation with Kenyon was to ensure that they understood the dynamics of horseracing and how it worked.

"When Kenyon and *Panorama* began to interview people within the industry, it became clear to the Jockey Club that they had inside help and even they managed to deduce that it might be me.

"In June 2002, I received a telephone call from Jeremy Phipps, my successor as head of security at the Jockey Club, who said he would like to talk to me on the context of seeking advice from me. So he arranged to meet me at a Wine Bar known to him near Victoria Station.

"In the context of what was happening, I informed the BBC of the meeting and they suggested it should be recorded.

"We met at Tapster's wine bar where Phipps, full of bonhomie, very foolishly attempted to ply me with lots of wine and even more foolishly was extremely indiscreet about his new found colleagues in the Jockey Club and his own views on corruption in horseracing.

"He rightly acknowledged that a whole generation of jockeys may have been compromised by members of the Wright gang. He also spoke of his concerns about the Jockey Club's lack of 'backbone' in dealing with corruption within the sport. I was quietly surprised that after four months in the job that he had come to the same conclusions as I had about corruption, in particular the considerable difficulties of achieving any support from the Jockey Club.

"Many people have asked why I have been prepared to be so forthright in revealing to the makers of *Panorama* and Kenyon information that many people thought should be confidential and secret information.

"I have searched my soul and thought long and hard about my participation. During my 10 years at the Jockey Club, I tried very hard to get people in the industry to realise the extent to which racing was susceptible to corruption.

"I am restricted by the contents of the constraints order issued by the court on 31 May, 2002, from providing all the evidence at my disposal. But what I can say, because it is now in the public domain, is that there is a powerful body of evidence that arose from the Woolwich and Southampton trials which clearly showed that racing had been infiltrated by a gang with serious criminal links.

"Also, one of the particular problems is that members of the Jockey Club and its officials are actually allowed to participate in that which they regulate, which may have an effect on their objectivity when faced with serious matters of regulation; i.e. the problem is that some of them, particularly those who have horses in training, may not be without sin themselves, given the nature of horseracing.

"Essentially, my view is that there has been cogent evidence of serious corruption in horseracing and that by its actions, or its lack of actions, the Jockey Club could be accused of institutionalising that corruption."

So that's what Roger Buffham's has to say. Many in racing felt saw reds under every bed. He, though, remained convinced that there were serious corruption issues that the sport, and in particular the Jockey Club, was failing, perhaps even refusing, to address. Significantly, many people outside of racing were starting to believe strongly that he had a point.

Ultimately, you could not blame the Jockey Club if it regretted its decision to let him go, simply because of the damage it caused.

Buffham's involvement with *Panorama*, in particular, sparked unwanted publicity for racing; and not just the actual broadcast. The build up to the programme was intense, with speculation about what revelations it would make – and about whom. Practically each day would bring different rumours about the latest racing figure said to be shifting uneasily from foot to foot.

The anxieties and curiosities were enhanced by a delay of several months in the transmission of the programme. This was because of a series of expensive, time-consuming legal challenges from the Jockey Club as to whether *Panorama* could use the material supplied to it by Buffham.

You would have thought that racing had spent enough time in the dock, wouldn't you? Not a bit of it.

When you consider that it is the Jockey Club's brief to protect racing's integrity and reputation, its decision to fight *Panorama* so furiously in the High Court would prove to be a questionable one.

Suffice to say for now that the Jockey Club's attempts to gag *Panorama*, just as it had already gagged Roger Buffham, was to backfire. Badly.

And it was all because of an angry man.

But before we find out the tempest that awaits the Jockey Club, it's time to put on the lifejackets and face a different kind of tumult.

8

A STORM BREWING

We have the weather to thank for the exposure of Brian Wright's racing secrets. He would have remained a man of intrigue and rumour had it not been for a boat that went astray amid stormy seas in September 1996.

Having embarked on an arduous journey from Venezuela, stopping off in Trinidad, the *Sea Mist* steered off her intended course for the south of England and ended up instead in Cork, southern Ireland. A routine search by customs found 599kgs of cocaine worth £80 million on board. The stash of narcotics, which had been welded inside a disused goods lift, proved the spark point for Operation Extend, a Customs and Excise investigation that lasted six years and was later described as "without parallel in UK drugs law enforcement".

OPERATION EXTEND

Operation Extend disrupted a massive, global drug-trafficking gang that became known as the Wright Organisation. Brian Wright was named by Customs as the 'Mr Big' behind it.

The complex investigation led to the conviction of at least 16 people worldwide, who between them were sentenced to 215 years. In Britain, the case featured five separate trials, one of which, at Woolwich Crown Court in south London, lasted 14 months, making it the second-longest criminal trial in English legal history.

It was during the Woolwich trial, and another at Southampton Crown Court, that the full, incredible, extent of Wright's racing network became clear, even though it was mainly as a sideshow to the more serious and more pertinent matter of drugs smuggling.

Horseracing and drugs makes for a pretty sickening combination. Brian

Wright is said to be the link between the two. Drugs first.

The five trials took place against high levels of security and amid strict reporting restrictions. Those restrictions were only lifted in June 2002 – the Woolwich trial had actually started in May 2000 – when a South African member of the Wright Organisation, John van Staden, pleaded guilty to charges of drugs importation at Bristol Crown Court. He was jailed for nine years.

When the *Sea Mist* was searched, and the unexpected drugs booty uncovered, no one had any idea that it would be the start of the dismantling of one of the most successful drugs smuggling gang ever to target Britain. As the extent of the operation started to unravel, the Customs investigations took in stops in Ireland, the Caribbean, the US, Mexico, Venezuela, Australia, France and South Africa.

On board the *Sea Mist* a parachute was found, leading Customs to believe the cocaine had been dropped on to the boat, or nearby seas, by a light aircraft in the Caribbean.

They were proved right. The *Sea Mist* had, in fact, set off from Venezuela in August 1996 and headed for Trinidad, where, 100 miles offshore, it picked up cocaine contained in 17 bundles from an airdrop.

The *Sea Mist* had been due to meet a small boat off the south English coast in order to 'cooper' the drugs onshore. This is the process by which the drugs are transferred to a local ship, which would inevitably attract much less attention than an international vessel.

The Wright gang targeted 'the Howards' Way set' to hire or buy boats from or even help bring the drugs into Britain. Coastal areas it used included Salcombe in Devon, Poole in Dorset and Lymington in Hampshire.

The captain of the *Sea Mist*, John Ewart, who had been using a false passport with the name Gordon Richards, was handed a 17-year jail sentence in Ireland for drug running. The rest of the crew were acquitted. Ewart went on to give evidence for the Crown at Woolwich.

As well as the drugs and a parachute, important mobile phone records were found on the *Sea Mist* that linked the abortive smuggling enterprise to Brian Wright. One of the acquitted crew members of the *Sea Mist* was monitored by Customs meeting two influential members of the Wright Organisation, Kevin Hanley and Godfried Hoppenbrouwers.

Hanley soon emerged as a close associate of Brian Wright's, a 'hands-on' trusted lieutenant. Hoppenbrouwers was a Dutch national who lived in Brazil. He organised the global transport for the drugs, securing the yachts and crews.

Hanley and Hoppenbrouwers purchased one of the boats used to cooper the drugs, the *Selina*. She had picked up 600kgs of cocaine offshore at Poole from a boat called the *Casita* in July 1996. The *Casita* was then due to cooper the drugs from the *Sea Mist*, meeting it in the English Channel 200 miles off Brest on the French coast. Of course, that never happened.

Hoppenbrouwers was subsequently arrested in Miami in February 2000, as a result of a Customs international warrant, and sentenced to 30 years in prison for money-laundering and drug offences that related to the importation of two tons of cocaine into Fort Lauderdale, Florida, in May 1998. Two other men – James Goodrich, an American, and Alain Deland, a Canadian – were involved.

In December 1999, the US Customs Service told their British counterparts that Goodrich and Deland were already serving prison sentences in America, having been arrested in May 1998. Goodrich subsequently became a witness for UK Customs and told them that it was he and Deland who had sailed the *Casita* from St Maarten in the Caribbean to Lymington. He said Kevin Hanley had crewed the *Selina* when it met them to cooper the drugs. They also waited to meet the *Sea Mist*, but after learning of her fate, abandoned the *Casita* and returned to the States.

The Customs surveillance proved to be incessant in its detail. Suspects were followed almost everywhere they went. Brian Wright's son, also called Brian, was tracked to the Caribbean, with customs believing he was helping to prepare a shipment of drugs on the *Sea Mist*.

Customs also registered trips to the Caribbean made by former Jump jockey Barrie Wright – no relation – who was to become the subject of one of the five trials involving the Wright Organisation. He was arrested in Belgium in May 2000, when the subject of an international warrant, and was acquitted of all charges at a trial at Southampton Crown Court in September 2001 in which he was accused of conspiring to import cocaine.

Other members of the gang were soon identified. Brian Wright's ex son-in-law Paul Shannon was marked down as a "gofer", as was Ian Kiernan, who travelled to the Caribbean in connection with the *Sea Mist* importation. John Gurney was said to be an associate of Wright senior who provided finance for the purchase of the *Sea Mist* and supplied the gang with mobile phones.

During their surveillance, Customs kept a close log on Brian Wright senior's movements. On 7 July 1997, when Barrie Wright was logged returning to Heathrow from the West Indies, Wright senior was seen meeting Kevin Hanley at 1.30pm at the Conrad Hotel in Chelsea. The hotel was near to his hired apartment and was thought by Customs to have been used regularly for his business meetings. The two men were logged being joined by Barrie Wright.

Members of the Wright Organisation were extremely careful about making telephone calls. Often they would make a call using their mobiles from a phone box, read out the number of the public phone and hang up before being called back. That would allow meetings to be arranged without fear of their personal phones being bugged. Details of contact names and numbers were carefully coded so as not to be easily detectable.

Shortly before another importation of drugs on a boat known as the

Moonstreak – which carried £30 million worth of cocaine – Wright senior was observed in Hampton, in August 1997, meeting Hanley and Brian Wright junior. He returned to Spain the day after drugs were believed to have been offloaded from the *Moonstreak*.

During the Woolwich trial, the jury heard that the Wright Organisation was trusted with credit when buying the drugs because Wright senior had a reputation as a prompt payer. Once the drugs had been brought in and sold, the profits would be split 50/50 between the Colombian-based supplier and the Wright Organisation. This information came from a witness for the Crown who had previously had links to the Wright Organisation.

In August 1998 Wright senior and Kevin Hanley were seen at a telephone box in Turnham Green, west London, from which they made calls to Spain and Portugal. They then walked to another telephone box to call Spain, and then another.

Despite being under such intense surveillance, the Wright Organisation was thought by Customs to have made at least seven successful cocaine smuggling ventures, using vessels other than the *Sea Mist*, worth £300 million between 1996 and 1998.

"I WANT A SOLICITOR..."

A breakthrough came in October 1998 when two key overseas members of the gang – Gary Boshoff, a South African, and Ronald Soares, a Brazilian – were secretly recorded talking about future deals. Soares was said to be the linkman between the Wright Organisation and cocaine barons in Colombia. A month later, Kevin Hanley was arrested while driving a car that contained 29kgs of cocaine, worth £1.5 million, following an anonymous tip-off.

Hanley, driving a blue second-hand Rover, was stopped by police near Paddington Station having been followed there from Bryanston Square just off Oxford Street. Hanley was asked by the arresting officers: "Do you know why we have stopped you?" To which he replied "yes". He was asked "where's the gear?" and answered: "I'd rather not say. I want a solicitor."

Told that the car was about to be searched on suspicion of it containing drugs, Hanley was asked: "Is there anything in the car before I start searching?" Hanley replied: "If you look you will find it."

The boot was opened and inside was a black holdall containing 29 packages wrapped in tape. Hanley's arrest was a major blow to the Organisation. He was thought by Customs to have played an important role not only in arranging the transportation of the drugs but also their onward sale within the UK.

Brian Wright flew in to London from his Spanish home to assess the implications. Having checked into the Conrad Hotel under a false name, Wright was unaware that he was being bugged by Customs, who secretly photographed him on the balcony of his suite. It was this picture that appeared in the dailies when the reporting restrictions were lifted – Mr Big, deep in thought. The photo was taken from a distance but you could still sense Wright's charisma within its fuzzy frame. A stylishly dressed, good-looking man, you could imagine him attracting friends in racing like a magnet.

The Customs bugging devices, meanwhile, were picking up the Wright Organisation's plans to move the drugs that remained unsold in the aftermath of Hanley's arrest. Soares had also returned to Britain and agreed to take over the distribution of the drugs.

On 11 February 1999, Soares, the linkman to the Colombian suppliers, was under observation with another man buying 13 holdall bags from an Oxford Street shop at 11.00am. These bags were all placed into a larger holdall at the shop.

Later on, at 1.17pm to be precise, Soares was followed to Leigh-On-Sea railway station, carrying the large holdall. He met another man, Roger Newton, to whom he handed over the bags within a bag. He was then seen catching a train back to London at 1.50pm.

Newton was followed driving to a lock-up in Leigh-On-Sea, Essex. The next day he was arrested at 7.28am and a raid on the garage revealed a major stash of cocaine, some of which had been filled into the bags bought at Oxford Street.

With careful planning, Brian Wright junior was arrested at his home in Weybridge on the same morning, just 20 minutes after Newton. He told detectives he had a "couple of grand" stored in the house – it turned out to be £46,170.

That was followed by the arrest, at 8.20am, of Barry Fennell, who was thought to have liased with Soares and helped move the drugs around. Customs officers searched a farm in Laleham, Middlesex. A white van that had been hired by Fennell was found with 29 packets of drugs inside. The packaging was identical to the drugs found at Leigh-On-Sea.

Between them, the Leigh-On-Sea and Laleham raids had unearthed 427kgs of cocaine with a street value of £61 million.

That's gotta hurt.

Eleven arrests were made in total, involving British, Colombian, and Brazilian nationals.

Brian Wright junior was one of seven men in the dock at Woolwich. Customs alleged he had often travelled to the Caribbean to "arrange for drugs movements and was also involved with meeting others essential to the running of the scheme."

Wright junior pleaded not guilty to conspiracy to import and supply cocaine between 1996 and 1999. He was jailed for 16 years. At the same trial, Ronald Soares was found guilty of importing drugs and was sentenced to 26 years; Ian Kiernan was sent down for 20 years for the same offence; and Paul Shannon was found guilty of conspiracy to supply and sentenced to five years.

Separately, Kevin Hanley was given a 15-year sentence after being found guilty of conspiracy to import and supply; Barry Fennell received 10 years for importing cocaine; and Roger Newton nine years for possession with intent to supply.

Four more trials were to follow, after which Government minister John Healy said: "Customs have dismantled one of the most significant global drugs trafficking networks ever known to UK law enforcement.

"This network was a menace to the UK, targeting enormous quantities of drugs to our streets. Customs have put them in jail where they belong and will continue to hunt down the profits they've made from this evil trade."

But the man that those in charge of Operation Extend really wanted remained on the run, apparently in Northern Cyprus.

Let's hear a bit more about Brian Brendan Wright.

9

MR BIG

There is no middle ground with Brian Wright.

There are those who swear by him. There are those who swear at the very mention of his name. There are those who see him as a flamboyant, generous entertainer, a shrewd and fearless punter adored by those he has befriended. And there are those who see him as Britain's most wanted man, the fugitive head of an international cocaine smuggling gang.

In the main, Wright keeps out of the debate, wisely believing: "Your mouth is your most dangerous weapon."

Once more we have to thank Graham Bradley's autobiography, *The Wayward Lad*, for a rare and valuable insight into the man – and for once it comes from his own mouth . . . Wright in his own words. They are words worth noting.

This is Brian Wright's story as told by him.

He was 12 when his family move to London from Ireland in 1958. They settled in Cricklewood, north London. Wright described himself as "a little bit of a tearaway early on until I had my wings clipped with a sharp dose of borstal, which didn't do me any harm".

He used to act as a bookies' runner for the builders who worked in nearby Kilburn, which had a strong Irish community. Working out that he rarely returned as much money as he took, Wright started to stand some of the bets himself.

His first serious win came on Indiana in the 1964 St Leger when he staked five bets of £1,000 to £70, landing him £5,000. Watching horses work at Epsom, Wright began to specialise in handicaps, following certain trainers, noting their patterns, and backing horses when he thought they had "got one ready".

"Racing is all about opinions," Wright said. "And I'd back mine against anybody's." He thrived during the high-rolling 1980s. One night at Windsor he won £40,000 and decided to play up the lot in the final race. He backed Harry's Bar, trained by Michael Stoute and ridden by Walter Swinburn, at 7-4. It started at 11-10 and won by half a length.

The more successful Wright was with his betting, the harder he found it to get bets on, leading him to "cut down considerably". He also spoke out against his alleged involvement in the doping and race-fixing investigations. "Mine's the first name that's put in the frame," he said. "I couldn't believe what I was meant to have done and even though I was annoyed, I couldn't help laughing at some of the things that were put in the Press.

"Just like Victor Chandler, I was never charged with anything when the corruption investigations were going on. But whenever Victor's name came up in court it was always reported that he had been completely exonerated of any wrongdoing. Quite right, too. But with me it's different. Whenever my name crops up it's always with an additional comment of 'well-known criminal' . . . and never that I am a serious gambler who has made a lot of money backing my opinion."

But was there another side to Brian Wright? Apparently so.

Reports were linking him to people that you really wouldn't want to mess with. One of them was Roy Adkins, a man with whom Wright raced horses under the syndicate name Running Horse. One day at Kempton they were seen with another man – Charlie Wilson, the Great Train Robber. Two of those men ended up murdered, one of them held responsible for the killing of the other.

In April 1990 a man wearing a baseball cap knocked on the front door of Wilson's Spanish villa in Marbella. A minute later, Wilson was dead. The word, underground, was that Wilson had advised a drug dealer called James Rose to name Adkins as the head of a narcotics ring and that Adkins had responded by having Wilson 'bumped off'. That may or may not be linked to the events of September the same year when Adkins, sitting in a bar in Amsterdam, where he had arranged to meet two Colombians, was shot dead.

Two weeks after those allegations were reported in the *Racing Post* in February 1999, Brian Wright became the subject of an international arrest warrant as a result of the same £100-million drugs swoop that saw his son Briany and 10 other men arrested.

The lifting of the court reporting restrictions in June 2002 saw a further hammering of Wright's reputation. Suddenly the talk was of how he laundered the proceeds of his drug dealing through horseracing – "with huge bets placed on dead cert winners in 'fixed' races." *(The Sun)*

Or how he was, "the mastermind behind a global drug smuggling enterprise worth hundreds of millions of pounds, has been linked to several gangland murders and is responsible for nobbling hundreds of horse races in the past decade." (*The Observer*).

The papers told of how he built up his drugs network when moving to Spain 10 years earlier, with a Customs source saying: "Brian Wright was a menace and remains a menace. No one should have any doubt we want to get him."

CELEBRITY FRIENDS

Wright was said to have been "treated like a Mafia Don" by those around him, and it was *The Observer* that best summed up the dilemma of the man known to police as The Milkman – because he always delivered – and to his friends in the racing fraternity as Uncle: "It is almost impossible to find anyone to say a bad word about him. Customs officers say Wright managed to dupe many celebrities and sports people so thoroughly that they are unwilling to admit they could have been so wrong about him."

One of those celebrity friends was the comedian Jim Davidson, to whose son Wright is godfather. He also played an active role in the placing and management of Davidson's string of racehorses. Davidson had appeared at the Woolwich trial as a character witness for Brian Wright junior and spoke up for Wright senior while he was there, describing as "laughable" claims that he was a drug dealer. "I still count myself as a good friend of Brian's. I have known him very well for 19 or 20 years," Davidson said.

Wright was estimated to have laundered around one-tenth of his drugs proceeds through racing – so god knows how many millions of pounds that amounted to. At this time, Customs were noticeably shy about linking Wright to washing his money through the betting rings; the Jockey Club was less so. "The revelations of the activities of the Wright gang underlined racing's vulnerability to corruption by criminals and the potential of betting as a vehicle for money laundering," said its senior steward Christopher Spence.

And according to a briefing statement from the Jockey Club at the same time: "In view of Brian Wright's own interests in gambling and racing, it is no surprise that his organisation chose betting as a conduit for laundering drugs money. It is also no surprise that Wright's gang actively attempted to cultivate jockeys, trainers, and stable employees with a view to obtaining information from them about horses. Such information helped Wright's gang not only to clean dirty money but to increase their returns from gambling as well."

The evidence at Woolwich Crown Court, if to be believed, of Wright's son, also called Brian but widely known as Briany, indicated the extent of Wright senior's friendships in the racing world.

Entertaining, for instance, was important to Wright. And when he entertained, he entertained well. Brian Wright junior's evidence told how some of Britain's very best jockeys would be treated to nights out. "They would go out with my father, they might go somewhere like Annabel's, somewhere like that and my father might get the bill," he said.

None of the jockeys mentioned by Wright junior were aware of the Wright Organisation's cocaine smuggling links, and not all would have been involved in its corrupt activities in racing. But it is an early reminder that Brian Wright senior mixed with racing's elite.

Nights at Annabel's didn't come cheap. Wright junior said he had never been there, but paid his father's membership because "my father has not got a bank account". Membership initially was £500 a year, although it became free because Wright senior was "a good customer there".

Wright junior had, however, been on nights out to Tramp. They were "quite expensive" evenings, the bill cruising past four figures.

Two address books/diaries gave further clues to the extent of Wright's racing friendships. One of them belonged to Brian Wright senior, the other to his son. Both were taken in police raids and were used as evidence in the Woolwich trial. The racing names were largely mentioned in passing without further comment on why they were in both diaries. Their presence, of course, in no way suggests any complicity in racing corruption or illegal activity but it shows how credible a person Brian Wright could appear.

Brian Wright junior's own address book included the names of: Graham Bradley, Barrie Wright and Victor Chandler, as you would expect of a bookmaker prepared to lay bets of the size that Brian Wright junior alleged his father was making.

Brian Wright's address book, a *Channel 4 Racing* diary for 1996, also contained those names, as well as many other leading Flat and Jumps jockeys, bookmakers and TV presenters.

While the names listed in both diaries were read out in court, no evidence was produced to confirm that some of them had actually known or even spoken to Brian Wright senior, Brian Wright junior or their associates in any context.

Wright senior's *Channel 4 Racing* diary had been given to him by a man widely known in racing as 'Yarmy', who had written inside it: "To Brian, Happy Christmas and good luck in 1996. Yarmy."

Yarmy is regarded as something of a racing legend. His real name is Steve Dyble, his nickname coming from his hometown of Yarmouth. A 10-times stable lads' boxing champion who worked for Henry Cecil for 20 years, he has since made a career out of persuading reluctant horses to enter starting stalls, a skill that has earned him widespread respect. His technique is based on that of the 'horse whisperer' Monty Roberts. Whenever you see a horse entering the stalls with a great big blanket over its withers, chances are it will have been schooled by Dyble.

The court heard that Yarmy was paid by Wright's racing organisation, as

Junior told the Woolwich jury: "How my father pays Yarmy, I am not aware of that. I know Yarmy is basically looked after by my father. Yarmy works for himself anyway, he has got his own business."

Parroy asked Wright junior: "So basically, what are we to get a picture of, your father passing a bundle of notes to Yarmy on appropriate occasions, for services rendered?"

"Yes," Junior told him.

It was not just Wright's racing contacts that Woolwich provided an insight to. The betting habits of the Wright Organisation were also laid bare. For example, Wright junior said it had "no real need" to keep business accounts; neither were all its bets recorded.

"That is sometimes the case, sometimes not. It depends who you bet with. There are lots of private bookmakers on the track," he said. "It is something that was apparent during the Jockey Club inquiry into horse doping and that. There are a number of private bookmakers such as ourselves, we are in a position to lay bets to people."

Private bookmakers? Change that to illegal bookmakers. To lay bets legitimately, you need a bookmaker's licence. The Wright Organisation didn't have that.

It was a point that Michael Parroy was quick to seize on during his questioning of Wright junior. "Private bookmakers. Do you mean unlicensed bookmakers?" he asked.

Wright junior confirmed that he did.

"And off course bookmakers have to be licensed."

They do.

"So when you said that what you were doing was all entirely legal, that is not right, is it?"

Wright junior replied: " . . . We are doing nothing illegal as such, it is something that goes on in racing, it is something that we have done and people have done before us."

The court at Woolwich also heard that Brian Wright senior would set up two or three big bets a year. According to his son, there were "multi-thousand pound bets . . . anything in excess of £25,000."

Bets of £5,000 or £6,000 would regularly be struck. These were "not peanuts as such, by no means. But it would not be what we would classify as a big bet," Wright junior said.

Were these bets placed legally? "It all depends on the price available and the position we are in at the time," Wright junior said. "If we are owed money by a particular bookmaker we may use that particular bookmaker, to save us carrying the cash to the track."

Parroy asked if the bets were "just as likely to be placed with an unlicensed as a licensed bookmaker?"

Wright junior told him: "It is the price that basically dictates to us who we bet with, the price available."

"If you are betting with a legitimate bookmaker, like Victor Chandler, there will be records?" Parroy asked Wright junior.

"In most cases, yes", he said, but added that sometimes Chandler or his representative would record the bet as being placed by "myself".

Wright junior explained: "They like a nickname. It could be an initial. It is how everyone works in racing. If I had a bet with Victor, Victor might look down and say 'to myself' and the bet would be registered as 'myself'."

This method was the subject of some surprise in court.

Parroy asked: "To 'myself'? . . . He writes in the book as though he is betting against himself?"

Wright junior said: "Yes, it would be 'myself'. It is just a term that we use in racing, Mr Parroy . . . maybe it is a question that you should ask a bookmaker."

To which the QC said: "Well, you might ask the question: 'Why are you not putting down my name? How do I know if you want to welsh on the bet? How do I prove it is me not you?'"

Junior responded: "Someone like Victor Chandler, I have the greatest respect for, Mr Parroy, and I would like to think it is returned with me, and I would never expect him to welsh on a bet. He would never expect me to welsh on a bet."

He was then asked "what is the point" of placing a bet that wasn't in his own name.

Wright junior insisted: "It is something that happens, it is a nickname. As you are running down the line (of bookmakers) they will just do it. They will register in their books like that. It happens all the time, my Lord. It is not just with us. It is with any number of gamblers on the track."

The possibility of bets placed but registered in another name prompted questioning from the judge in charge of the trial, Mr Justice Mitchell.

"Have I got it right," he asked, "that really, although he is a licensed bookmaker and of course keeps records, that the records will not really be much use because it may well be . . . that you are not being recorded under your own name?"

"That is basically the case, My Lord," Wright junior replied. "There would be lots of occasions when he would put it down to me or to Ian (Kiernan), or down to Paul (Shannon), but there would be some occasions when he will not have."

Wright junior had no doubts that such a form of betting was legitimate. "It is something that I have been used to for the last 15 years of my life, 16 years of my life. It is something that I have become used to," he said.

In 1997, the Wright Organisation was in bookmaker-bruising form. Brian

Wright senior did not mess about with his betting – as a £20,000 bet at 6-4 on Istabraq to win that year's Champion Hurdle can testify. That bet had been struck with an unlicensed bookmaker, someone who was working as a tic-tac man, according to Wright junior.

Wright senior also heavily backed Sleepytime at 5-1 to win the 1,000 Guineas, while 2,000 Guineas winner, Entrepreneur, was another major punting success, as was the sprinter Danetime.

Wright backed Danetime to win the NGK Sparks Rated Handicap at Newmarket's July meeting. Sparks certainly flew when the colt won by two lengths from Elnadim carrying £30,000 of Wright's money. Danetime was the only horse backed in the race, attracting a torrent of recorded bets ranging from £400 to £2,000 stakes – and that's just with the licensed bookmakers.

Yet the same horse had cost the Wright Organisation dear on his previous start, when beaten a head in the Wokingham Handicap, when he was regarded as an unlucky loser. Danetime had been drawn wide in stall 19, before being dropped in at the rear of the field and was tracked across to the stands' side. He and jockey Gary Stevens made up huge amounts of ground in the final furlong and just failed to catch the winner, Selhurstpark Flyer. Wright had staked a bet of £15,000 at 6-1. Ouch.

If Wright placed his bet in one hit, it was done so illegally as the largest single recorded bet on Danetime at Ascot was £16,000 to £2,000 each-way.

Impressively, Danetime was said to be the Wright Organisation's only losing bet where more than £10,000 had been staked. There had been "quite a few", between 10 and 15, losing bets of £5,000-£10,000.

Brian Wright's betting tapered off in 1998 because, according to his son, "he basically just walked away from it and wiped his hands and walked away and that is what he was wanting to get me and Ian (Kiernan) to do." This was at the time of the police and Jockey Club investigations into race-fixing and doping allegations when Brian Wright senior himself was arrested, although released without charge.

"What it really comes down to is this," Parroy said to Wright junior. "That effectively from what you are telling us, in 1998 the organisation had no income."

Wright replied: "Basically, my father never had no big bets, he would still back a horse . . . he was basically playing."

To help with his betting, Brian Wright employed a full-time form expert, Arthur Shaw, a former Arsenal footballer who was in his seventies at the time of the Woolwich trial.

"My father will always make sure Arthur has got the money . . . Arthur would be looked after," Wright junior said.

Further racing evidence was heard at Woolwich through Peter Teffler, a friend of Brian Wright junior who became involved with the Wrights' betting empire and would often be on nights out with jockeys.

"We used to go to the big meetings," Teffler told the court. "Ascot and York, racecourses like that. We would normally walk in with at least £10,000 each (in cash) to bet with."

Often Teffler and other members of the racing organisation such as Brian Wright junior, Ian Kiernan and Paul Shannon would finish the day with three or four times that amount. The key was to synchronise their bets. In a manner that almost mirrors the famous Arsenal offside trap, the Wright punters would line up, step forward to the rails, and place their bets down the row at exactly the same time. The aim was simple: to hit the bookies hard and fast before they had time to react and shorten the price.

Teffler described nights out when anything from "one to 10" jockeys would be entertained. "Almost all of the sort of big-name jockeys I met at one time or another," he said.

"I have been in clubs when he has been entertaining jockeys and also they were regular visitors to the house and to the flat in Chelsea Harbour. Tramp was where we would go most often."

Jockeys would be entertained "almost weekly" and "a great night out" would be had by all. "They were also some of Brian (junior)'s closest friends, jockeys. So . . . you would naturally be out with your friends regularly and his friends were jockeys," Teffler said.

Of course, at Woolwich such evidence was not produced in order to brag about the Wright Organisation's betting exploits, or its friendships with jockeys. Betting was a way of explaining the vast amounts of cash that were generated by the gang.

"They have chosen to explain their wealth (as) derived from betting on horseracing," Michael Parroy said during the trial.

You could say, in the parlance of the steward's room, that their explanations were not accepted.

"A VERY NICE GUY..."

Brian Wright junior's evidence also revealed how his father was involved with a number of horses that weren't registered in his name, one of them being Jibereen, who became famous for providing jockey Declan Murphy with a comeback at Chepstow in October 1995 following a horrific fall at Haydock the previous year.

Jibereen was by no means Wright's only secret. His biggest secret, of course, was the allegation that he was the main supplier of cocaine to the UK. Whatever topics were discussed on his nights out with jockeys, that was not one of them. Say what you like about Brian Wright – and by now he has probably had plastic surgery on his burnt out ears, such is the discussion he attracts – there are, and were, people in racing who regarded him as nothing other than a very good friend.

It is well known just how highly Graham Bradley rates him: "I make absolutely no apology for my friendship with him. Brian Wright has been a very good friend of mine for 15 years and during that time he has never compromised me," he once said.

The jockeys' weighing room has been described to me as "the most exclusive club in the world". There's a lot of truth in that. It really was a case of 'one for all, all for one'. Jockeys stick together; the risks that they take ensure a unique, unbreakable bond.

So when one of their own offers a night out, as the guest of a friend, questions are not necessarily asked. If that friend is good enough for one jockey, especially someone as well liked as Bradley, then he is good enough for plenty more.

It's something to bear in mind when trying to work out how Brian Wright could befriend so many jockeys, and how, indeed, they could be hoodwinked into thinking this man of cash – who according to one rider "looked like a gangster" – had somehow achieved his manifest wealth through legitimate means.

Don't think for one moment that Bradley is on his own in regarding Wright as a good friend. Check out the words of another top jockey, genuinely one of racing's high achievers. His thoughts are expressed anonymously, not because he is ashamed of his friendship with Brian Wright – he isn't – but to save him the hassle of having his outstanding reputation wrongly impugned.

"It was the early 90s probably when I first met him," the jockey said. "I met him through Brad (Bradley).

"Brad would have said to me 'why don't you come along' and we'd go for a night out and it went from there.

"Once a year or twice a year, I might come up to London and go out to dinner with him, maybe have a few drinks and we might go down to Tramp or something like that afterwards.

"He (Wright) was a very likeable guy, a very personable guy. I wasn't aware of any problem. Brad said he used to bet heavily but by the time I started to get involved with him he didn't any more.

"That's why I was never sure about people making Brian out to be such a big punter. After the nights out we'd had and the hospitality he'd have more reason to ring me more than almost anyone but he never did.

"We hardly ever talked about racing. I think he only ever once, through

Brad, asked me about a horse. Brad on one occasion asked, 'How is such and such? Brian wants to know – he might have a bet on it.' But that is the kind of information you get asked all the time. What I would have said to Brad would have been no more than I would have said to anyone else. And I can only remember that one time."

Jockeys, especially one as successful as the one who is talking here, attract their fair share of 'starfuckers', people who want to be seen with them not because of who they are but because of what they are, and what they have achieved.

"It wasn't that unusual if you were a jockey to be taken out to dinner, a lot of the owners would do it," he said. "I suppose there are people who want to take you out to be seen with a leading jockey but Brian Wright was not one of those. He would be a long way from being one of those."

So why do it? Why spend thousands – in cash – keeping jockeys well fed and topped up with champagne at one of London's swankiest nightclubs?

"I think he enjoyed it," the jockey said. "Brad's company, our company – Brad obviously knew him a lot more than I did. I enjoyed it because I liked him. I thought he was a nice guy.

"He was a very generous guy. He was charismatic but also he was, well, an ordinary guy."

The jockey was not a sponger. He regarded Wright as a friend not a sugar daddy. He knew Wright well enough to visit him in hospital when he was recovering from a triple heart bypass.

The jockey would also be entertained by Wright at racecourse boxes, mainly at Ascot. He found the company interesting. "There were a few people in there that were quite high up, I'm not saying in racing in this country, but were senior in other racing institutions around the world. Officials. I won't say where from but they were officials," he said.

The jockey also confirmed that Wright's weighing room friendships were widespread. "A good percentage of the top jockeys knew Brian, and I wouldn't say you'd have any one of them saying a bad word about him. Whatever the truth about Brian's morals, he's a very nice guy."

Wright clearly inspires loyalty. He is an alleged drug dealer, but to this particular friend he remains above all else, "a very nice guy".

Interestingly, the more we talked, the more it became clear that the jockey had much less time for Roger Buffham, a man whose job it was supposedly to protect racing's image, than for Wright, even though the latter had been unmasked as a suspected drugs dealer.

"When I first heard that Brian was involved (in alleged drugs smuggling) I was quite surprised as obviously you would be," the jockey said. "I thought whatever he had his business in, it wouldn't have involved that.

"If he walked in here now and sat down at this table, you'd enjoy his company. Simple as that. And he'd be actually, almost quite shy, you know.

"I'm just disappointed that his business was actually what it was. It does seem as if the case is fairly well proven against him.

"But it would be good to hear his side of the story."

10

THE ONE AND ONLY

Graham Bradley stepped into the witness box and was asked: "You are Graham Bradley, the jockey, are you not?"

"The one and only, yes," he said.

It was a response that would surprise none of his many friends in racing; in fact, it would probably delight them. "Typical Brad," they'd tell you.

Graham Bradley, The One And Only. It would make the perfect epitaph. For it is not in Bradley's nature to be overawed by any occasion. It is not his style to be coy. It is not his role in life to 'toe the line'. Whether or not it has been his intention, he has spent much of his life causing a stir. And he saved his biggest stir 'til last when giving evidence at the Southampton trial of his friend and former colleague, Barrie Wright.

Barrie Wright, who is no relation to Brian Wright, was acquitted of all charges of conspiring to import cocaine during his trial in September 2001.

Bradley appeared as a character witness. It was a loyal thing to do. You could say it was a stupid thing to do. Because by the time he had left the witness box, Graham Bradley had stuck up for Barrie Wright, but in doing so had badly besmirched his own reputation.

Talented, stylish, irrepressible, loveable Brad had admitted to secretly passing on sensitive punting information to Brian Wright in return for his own financial reward. That was not the sort of thing you are supposed to do as a jockey.

Bradley spent a frustrating amount of his time as a jockey being accused of things he wasn't supposed to do. It was part of his charm that he appeared to sail so close to the wind – and what's more appeared to enjoy doing so. The controversial moments, though, could not cloud the fact that above all he was an outstanding jockey.

Like Dermot Browne, he made his mark through his association with the famous Dickinson yard, from which Tony and then his son Michael dominated Jump racing.

Bradley's first big break came when then stable jockey Tommy Carmody returned to Ireland and Michael Dickinson decided not to replace him, instead putting his faith in the nascent talents of the lads already in the yard, mainly Bradley and Robert Earnshaw.

As a 22-year-old, having already ridden Bregawn to finish second in a Cheltenham Gold Cup, he got into an early scrape when, at Cartmel in August 1982, he placed a £50 bet on a horse. Jockeys bet – be in no doubt. But if you get caught, you are fucked.

Less than a week after winning the Hennessy Cognac Gold Cup on Bregawn, Bradley was banned for two months at a Jockey Club hearing, just when his career was starting to go places. The ban meant Bradley missed the winning ride on another of the stable's star chasers, Wayward Lad, in the King George VI Chase at Kempton, and also his part in history when Dickinson trained 12 winners in one day.

But he returned in time to renew his partnership with Bregawn for one of the most amazing achievements there has ever been in Jump racing, when Dickinson trained the first five home in the 1983 Cheltenham Gold Cup and Bregawn led the way.

Two seasons later, Michael Dickinson had switched to Manton, his mother Monica had taken over the licence, and Bradley continued his links with Poplar House but combined them with new commitments to southern trainers, particularly Toby Balding. He also had a brief retainer with Sir Philip and Lady Harris, owners of the enigmatic, Balding-trained chaser Kildimo.

Bradley's time with Balding coincided with one of the low points of his career. In November 1986, Bradley was publicly accused of 'stopping' the novice hurdler Robin Goodfellow at Ascot. The accusation was made by the colourful gambler and trainer Barney Curley, who had backed Robin Goodfellow and was concerned that, for all his money, the price drifted.

Curley first made his accusation in a phone call to Monica Dickinson. Curley knew the Dickinsons well and used to sell them horses from Ireland. However, she was unimpressed by Curley's claims and forewarned Bradley that Curley was planning to ring him. So when Curley did, Bradley was ready and he taped their conversation. Despite Bradley telling him that the allegations were completely untrue, Curley threatened to report the matter to the Jockey Club.

He fulfilled that threat, although the Jockey Club decided there was no evidence to support an inquiry into Bradley's riding of Robin Goodfellow. In fact, Curley's protests backfired when he was banned from training for what the Jockey Club considered to be 'threats of a serious nature' made in telephone calls to Bradley and Monica Dickinson. Curley later successfully appealed against the ban, although the Jockey Club maintained that his actions were "reprehensible".

It was rotten period for Bradley, who had also picked up a three-month non-triers' ban for his riding of Deadly Going, beaten 10 lengths into second at a Bank Holiday meeting at Market Rasen in April 1987. Two years later he faced the same allegation, but was cleared, when riding Starjestic, the 5-4 favourite in a three-runner race at Southwell. Starjestic had actually made a serious blunder and unseated his rider, but the fact that Bradley had to attend a Portman Square hearing, months after the race itself, before being cleared illustrates his unfortunate position as a 'marked man'.

In the meantime, Starjestic had reappeared at Southwell and won. Bradley was so incensed by the boos that greeted the success that he actually lost his renowned cool, responding to the heckling racegoers with a one-fingered salute.

By the 1991/92 season, Bradley had teamed up with Charlie Brooks in Lambourn. He was riding as well as ever, as demonstrated by his performance on former champion hurdler Morley Street, trained by Toby Balding, in the Martell Aintree Hurdle on Grand National day in April 1993.

It was absolutely brilliant, the perfect portrayal of Bradley's talent. Perhaps only he would be so cool as to toy with his rivals before, 50 yards from the line, slipping Morley Street into the lead and thus allowing a tricky horse to win as he pleased.

Bradley was in his pomp. Other big wins followed, notably with Collier Bay in the 1996 Champion Hurdle. The 1997/98 season brought him wins in the Hennessy Cognac Gold Cup on Suny Bay, the Tripleprint Gold Cup on Senor El Betrutti, and Supreme Novices' Hurdle at the Cheltenham Festival on French Ballerina. Bradley and Suny Bay also put in a heroic effort in the 1998 Grand National, finishing second to Earth Summit when conceding 23lb.

An Indian summer for a by-now veteran jockey turned stormy with his arrest in January 1999 and the loss of his licence when charges were brought against him over the Man Mood race. When the charges against Bradley were dropped and his licence returned, there was little sign that he intended to resume his riding career at full pace; you sensed that he had made up his mind to quit. He took only 15 rides during the 1999/2000 season, waiting until he could bow out on a winner. He did just that when Ontheboil won at Haydock in November 1999.

The weighing room had lost one of its dominant, best-loved characters. Bradley was adored not just for his own talent, but for his willingness to offer guidance to those around him. He was mentor to some of the very best, among them Tony McCoy, who made it clear that this was a retirement that no rider wanted to see. "The weighing room has lost a little of its sparkle," he said.

Graham Bradley was never going to fade away. Thanks mainly to his purchases for Steve McManaman and Robbie Fowler, Bradley's second business as a bloodstock agent continued to keep him in the headlines. So, ultimately, did his appearance at Southampton Crown Court.

But these were the wrong headlines.

PRIVILEGED INFORMATION

Producing a hand-written note from his pocket, Graham Bradley told the court how he had first met Barrie Wright, or "Baz" as he called him, at Folkestone in the early 1980s.

He was certainly making his mark. Relying on notes from the witness box is an irregular practice. Bradley was quickly told this. "Just wanted to be precise," he said. Bradley, in fact, is incredibly organised. The police discovered this when they turned up to arrest him and found all his records immaculately filed; he also kept detailed and exhaustive notes on his career to help compile his biography.

Perhaps it's because he's a Virgo.

Having been born and raised in nearby Wetherby, Bradley told the court – without notes – that he was a devoted fan of Leeds United. It was through his links to the club that he met Barrie Wright's brother Tommy, a professional goalkeeper who was based at Elland Road at the time. He introduced himself to Barrie Wright as a friend of his brother's and also an admirer of his riding skills. "I have known him for 20 years. He has been a very special friend," Bradley said.

Brad and Baz became not just mates but housemates and the balance of their relationship was soon established. "He asked if he could move in for the weekend while he got himself sorted out . . . and he ended up stopping about three-and-a-half years," the court heard.

During that time, Bradley's phone bill trebled. "Barrie was addicted to the telephone . . . it started annoying me in the end."

Wright's achievements in the saddle never came close to matching the newspaper exposure he received when named as one of the less likely conquests of celebrity shag Pamella Bordes. Yet although he became well known for his amorous instincts – "a real ladies' man," Bradley said – Wright's time on the phone was more professional than social.

His landlord recalled: "Because Barrie never got to the top as a jockey he had to supplement his income. Basically punting is the only word for it . . . He is collecting information from different people in the racing industry, which is privileged information that the public can't generally get hold off.

"The public can read the form book in the *Racing Post* or the *Sporting Life* and look at how a horse has run and its form generally, and form experts do that. But to collate sensitive privileged information – like the well-being of a racehorse and if it has been coughing, how fit it is, how it looks, has it missed any work, is it going well, etc – is very sensitive, and very privileged."

Barrie Wright used his privileged position as a jockey, and his invaluable access to the weighing room, to sell information to heavy hitting punters, who would pay him in return. It was information unknown to anyone sitting hopefully in a betting shop; it was information denied to anyone walking through a racecourse turnstile with their rolled up newspaper gripped in their hand like a weapon. It was information that belonged to racing's other world, the world of nods, winks, backhanders and brown envelopes. Information for the elite.

This is how it worked. "He (Barrie Wright) would ring different people – head lads, stable staff, fellow jockeys, some owners he knew, some trainers he knew," Bradley said. "He was in the racing game and everyone liked him and he was respected. He could get this information. He would just pass it on to different people, professional punters etc, who would use that and their own information. It is important to know that the horse hasn't trod on a stone or something, or bruised a foot and missed four days' work.

"It is just like putting a jigsaw together and if all the bits in the jigsaw fit, everything is well. (If) the horse hasn't been coughing, he hasn't missed any work, (if) it is flying, it looks well in its coat, the form is there, the ground is right . . . then you have a few quid on."

And that's what Barrie Wright's punters would do. They would have quite a few quid on. Armed as they were with "very privileged and very sensitive" information, how can you blame them?

One of Barrie Wright's biggest punters – almost certainly *the* biggest – was Brian Wright. In fact, it was Barrie Wright who introduced Bradley to the man who would soon become his close friend and play such an influential part in his life.

They were introduced at a two-day meeting at Sandown racecourse in 1984. Bradley remembered it well. "Barrie said, 'You'll have to come and meet a very good friend of mine, he's a very good judge.'"

Bradley and Brian Wright hit it off straight away, had dinner that evening and met again at Sandown the following day. "I have liked him ever since," said Bradley.

He told the jury that they "got on very, very well" and were "still close friends . . . I like his personality, his charisma. He was very knowledgeable, very intelligent, very affable. He was a very good-looking guy. Just generally helpful, kind, nice, generous. I couldn't say a bad word about him and anybody I've ever met have all said the same . . . For a man with no formal education whatsoever, he is a very intelligent guy."

Bradley would use Wright's knowledge of the form book to help him decide on a choice of big race mounts. "He is that good a judge. I would ring him and ask him which one to ride. That is how highly I regard his knowledge of the form book, on tracks, on ground etc."

He would also ring him for advice on "lots of things, worldly things" and Brian Wright would also introduce Bradley to leading owners, a crucial opening for a rider of his undoubted charm. "Meeting someone on a personal basis would give the edge in getting the ride over somebody like (Richard) Dunwoody or (Tony) McCoy or Scu (Peter Scudamore) or (John) Francome," Bradley said.

The more the two men knew each other, the more they would meet at the racecourse and the more nights out they would have. Bradley once said Wright would always be seen with a huge roll of notes, big enough to "choke a donkey".

"I have seen lots of money in all the times I have seen him. He was never a credit card man, a cheque book man. It was always large amounts of readies," he told the court.

At the big race meetings such as Ascot, Kempton, Newmarket and Sandown, Brian Wright would have with him plastic bags full of £50 notes – "hundreds and thousands of pounds – a big, big gambler he was," Bradley said.

That's how Bradley viewed Brian Wright. As a big, big gambler, someone who had won £100,000 in a bet in 1973 – "that is some amount of money in 1973 to win".

For a jockey, Bradley had a surprisingly intimate knowledge of Brian Wright's betting habits. During his evidence, he described Wright's gambling successes as a case of "swings and roundabouts". Once he had owed £1 million to an unnamed bookmaker, soon after the same bookie owed him £2 million. He estimated that Wright's average bet would be between £10,000 and £20,000; his biggest stake was £100,000.

That's a lot. "To coin a phrase it is telephone numbers, isn't it," asked Jerome Lynch, the QC for the defence.

"It is. Out of my league," said Bradley.

"My personal experience of seeing him was massive, massive amounts of cash which he frequently, every day, would have on horse races. That's why it was so important to get everything absolutely spot on.

"He didn't want to be having (bets of) £10,000, £20,000, £30,000, £40,000, £50,000 if the horse had been coughing for three days, if it had missed a piece of work, if it had trod on a stone. Everything had to be professional," Bradley said.

"It is very difficult to get it on these days, but in the mid-eighties, early nineties you could get that sort of money on. It is a commonly known fact that Victor Chandler, a big bookmaker fielded £1 million for one day on a Monday night meeting at Windsor. People could get bets of £40,000, £50,000, £60,000 on. He (Brian Wright) was betting in those amounts regularly."

Bradley was asked by Lynch: "In putting those sort of bets on, you could not just go along to the bookies with £100,000 in a Sainsburys' carrier bag and say 'here you go', could you? How did you do it? Did you have to give the money to other people to put it on? How did it work?"

The court was told of "a precise operation", whereby if the money wasn't down quickly the price would go, because of the sheer size of the bets involved. Bradley's evidence brought to mind that of Peter Teffler's at Woolwich.

"Basically," Bradley said, "he has to get friends to go down (to the betting ring) with sort of £10,000 apiece, and all walk up at the same time to all these bookmakers that are stood in a line all offering 2-1 and you have to go £10,000, £10,000 in synch.

"It has to be a very precise operation to get the best price, the best value – to maximise winnings."

Bradley was also asked about Brian Wright's influence on young jockeys, to which he gave a telling reply: "It is always fairly impressive to see large amounts of money and he has lots of friends, lots of acquaintances. Lots of people in the know.

"He knew other trainers, he knew the big owners, he knew other jockeys. You would be a little bit in awe of him, definitely. In fact, I was, maybe, for a while."

Whether he intended to or not, Bradley ended up telling us as much about Brian Wright, his friend the gambler, as he did about Barrie Wright, his friend the jockey. Prosecution counsel Michael Parroy, QC, who had taken the same role at Woolwich, was keen to explore Bradley's friendship with Brian Wright.

Parroy asked Bradley if he was "a man who literally was rolling in cash".

Bradley agreed, saying: "Yes, he was when I knew him."

Parroy: "A man with no apparent means of making a living beyond gambling . . . who can afford to risk huge sums of money?"

"That is what gamblers do," Bradley said.

Parroy then asked Bradley if there was "money to be made, if the horse is definitely not going to win."

"Probably," he replied. "You are talking about doing a criminal act . . . so you have to weigh up the consequences, whether you want to spend 10 years in prison. Or do you want to run everything by the book. That is the decision you have to make when you are asked to do something like that."

The court heard that Bradley's phone number was found in a number of diaries – Brian Wright's, Brian Wright junior's, Barrie Wright's, and that of Ian Kiernan, a member of the Wright Organisation who was found guilty at Woolwich. Bradley said he regularly exchanged racing information with them.

His number was also in the address book of another imprisoned member of the gang, Kevin Hanley. Bradley said he had no idea why Hanley had his number.

Crunch time. Remember Brian Wright's wise words, of how your mouth is your most dangerous weapon? Bradley should have considered them more carefully during his time in the witness box.

"Let us be clear," Parroy said to him. "It is not only Barrie John Wright who is providing information to Brian Brendan (Wright senior) and his team. You were as well, were you not?"

Bradley said that he was.

"The sort of information which, let us also be clear, the average punter would probably give his eye teeth for?"

"Yes, very privileged information."

"Information which the trainers and the owners you were riding for expect you to be giving to Brian Brendan Wright?" Parroy asked Bradley.

"Not generally, no."

"What you are actually doing, Mr Bradley, is providing information which is in essence in confidence. Are you giving it to other people for their financial advantage?"

Yes, Bradley said. He was.

"In the end, also for your financial advantage?"

Yes again.

"Because when you give a good tip to somebody like Brian Brendan Wright, you get a 'present', do you not?"

He did.

"Thousands of pounds sometimes?"

Bradley disagreed. "Not that sort of money," he said.

"What is the biggest amount he has paid you?"

"Different nights out and hotels etc etc. I can't recall the exact biggest present he has ever given to me."

Parroy continued: "Let us see how the system works. It is known that you and others like you have access to this privileged information, which you should not be disclosing."

Bradley then claimed that "every jockey in the country" – up to "300, 400" people – "probably does the same".

"Who they give it to, of course, depends on who they know and how they are treated by the people they know," Parroy said, describing a "you scratch my back and I'll scratch your back situation".

He said to Bradley: "And how you got your back scratched was, apparently, nights out at expensive nightclubs . . . all the drinks paid for, all the meals paid for, all the rest of it paid for by Brian Brendan (Wright)."

Bradley agreed.

But that wasn't all. Parroy asked if he had ever received "an envelope with cash if you had given him a good tip?"

"Occasionally," Bradley said.

"Holidays paid for?"

"Flights occasionally. Not generally holidays, no," Bradley told the court.

"Flights to Spain? Did you ever go to his villa down there?"

"Yes, a few times."

Asked how much information he had passed on to Brian Wright in the 1990s, Bradley's answer was to the point. "Lots," he said.

Oh dear. Bradley is not stupid. He had to have known that this evidence would make its way to the Jockey Club. Sure, reporting restrictions were in place but they were not going to be so for ever. Besides, his evidence was still heard in open court. There was absolutely nothing to stop a Jockey Club security official sitting in and listening. Chances are, one did. Having spent much of his career believing, rightly or wrongly, that the Jockey Club had it in for him, Bradley virtually offered them his head on a plate.

Surely he knew this? And if he didn't, he soon would.

The damage was done, but Bradley's evidence was not complete. The questioning returned to the salad days of a jockey's career.

"Of course, all jockeys start off at one stage in their careers as struggling apprentices," Parroy said. "Nobody starts at the top, do they?"

"No everybody starts at the bottom as stable staff," said Bradley.

"When you are at the bottom money comes tight, does it not?"

"Extremely"

"Stable lads are poorly paid and work very hard?"

"Yes."

Bradley may have been wondering what all this was about. No doubt, you are wondering what the poor plight of stable lads has to do with a trial about alleged cocaine smuggling.

Parroy knew what it was all about. It was about establishing how far Brian Wright's tentacles spread in racing and how carefully he aimed his reach.

He asked Bradley: "If someone comes along and starts flashing lumps of money at them, being generous to them when they are apprentice jockeys, there is going to come a time when the favour is going to have to go back the other way, is there not?"

"It depends on the individual," Bradley said.

"With Brian Brendan Wright," Parroy said. "He was proven to be very generous but he was also expecting to receive something back, was he not?"

"He was expecting the privileged information, yes," Bradley replied.

By the time Bradley retired from racing in November 1999, the court heard that Brian Wright had "done a runner".

Bradley said he "hadn't got a clue" that Wright was wanted in connection with cocaine smuggling and added that the two men continued to talk: "To be honest, I don't really know what his situation was but I still spoke to him regularly and still talked about horses and horse racing and punting and numerous other things."

Bradley had once asked Wright what he did for a living and was told: "This and that." He never asked the question again.

"Did that mean, Mr Bradley, that you assumed that there were other things he did and it was wise not to ask about them?" he was asked.

"Not wise, I just didn't bother any more. I had asked him the question once and that got an answer, so that is the way that I am. There is no point in pursuing it, but it didn't worry me."

Bradley was also asked in court about *The Observer* newspaper article of June 1998 that claimed: "The shadowy Mr Big at the heart of Britain's biggest horseracing investigation is Brian Wright, a businessman long identified by customs as an associate of the country's most powerful organised crime family . . . the much-feared Adams family."

He said: "I don't know any of them."

"Did you know what Brian Wright did?" Parroy asked him.

"No, not at all."

"Mr Bradley, this man was known, was he not, not merely to be involved with horseracing, but to be involved with other unlawful enterprises?"

"I certainly don't know anything about it, whatsoever," Bradley said.

He was asked again if he knew of Brian Wright's alleged criminal links. "Definitely not," Bradley said. "I think he is totally, totally innocent, I really do . . . I don't know anything about it because he has never mentioned anything to me."

One thing Bradley did know about Brian Wright was his habit of owning horses that ran in other people's names. "I don't think he ever owned one in his own name," Bradley said. "He managed a few horses, he probably had private or secret shares in a few. He has owned a few over the years, I think."

Graham Bradley bought one of those unofficial horses for Brian Wright. A horse called Border Tinker. Both men have reason to remember him.

Wright, together with one of his associates, the deceased Roy Adkins, had asked Bradley to buy them a horse. Like Wright, Adkins was never registered as owner, although his wife Brenda was.

No one knew at the time that horseracing was doing such heavy flirting with the criminal element. Had Graham Bradley known of the allegations surrounding Wright and Adkins, he might have stalled on his purchase of Border Tinker. As it was, he had identified the gelding as a likely 'job horse' for the pair; one to watch when the money was down.

Bradley's original attempt to buy Border Tinker failed when he was sold at the 1987 Doncaster sales for 1,000 guineas more than Bradley's 24,000-guinea limit. But the successful buyer broke his back in a fall soon after, and

Bradley was offered the chance to buy it for the price it raised in the sales ring. He took it, paying for the horse with a Co-op bag full of cash. "The deal suited me grand. I still hadn't found the right article for the touch, but Border Tinker was it."

Border Tinker, who ran in the name of Sally Hainsworth, the fiancé of a friend of Bradley's, was lined up for a race at Sedgfield nearly a year after his purchase, during which time there had been a couple of figurative false starts.

Bradley, whose father Norman trained the gelding, had jocked off Barrie Wright to ride Border Tinker himself. At least then, if something amiss happened, he could only blame himself for the gamble going astray.

Which it didn't. Wright and Adkins each put £30,000 on Border Tinker at odds between 5-1 and 7-2. It was a job well done. Bradley received £10,000 for his part in the coup – "and another £4,000 to square up the people we hadn't told."

Bradley was asked during his Southampton evidence why Wright's horses ran in others' names, or "false colours".

He said: "He probably didn't want to be known as the owner because of all his contacts. If his name was down and people knew he owned it, the price would be ridiculous. He wouldn't be able to get a big bet on it.

" . . . it is not really deception. It's just a way of hopefully maximising your profits and it is the way things are done, that is the way he did it."

Wright also played a close role with the six to eight horses owned by the comedian Jim Davidson, who as we know gave evidence on behalf of Wright and his son during the Woolwich trial.

"Brian organised them (Davidson's horses), where they should run," according to Bradley. "He was an adviser. Whether Brian owned shares in them I don't really know."

Again, Bradley knew of a "definite association" with Newmarket trainer Willie Musson, although again, "whether he had shares in horses there I really don't know."

Soon afterwards, Bradley left the witness box and could have been excused a quick look round to where he had been standing – just so he could work out how much of his iconic status he had left behind him.

WEIGHING ROOM CONTACTS

Other jockeys appeared at Southampton to speak up for Barrie Wright. One of them was a Grand National hero, Richard Guest.

He was regarded as a superb horseman but a maverick jockey. He was certainly in the Bradley league for natural talent; the way he had nursed Red

Marauder to victory at Aintree earlier that year in appalling conditions was one of the most skilful, most considerate rides ever seen over the famous fences, particularly as his mount was not a natural jumper.

Yet Guest, who also partnered Beech Road to win the 1989 Champion Hurdle, so nearly missed out on Red Marauder's triumph, and he would have had only himself to blame, having quit riding on the spot when he was found guilty of riding a non-trier by the Perth stewards in 1998. His self-imposed retirement last six months.

As well as knowing Barrie Wright and Brian Wright, Guest was also a good friend of Bradley's. He was Toby Balding's conditional when Bradley was based there. Guest subsequently proved himself an invaluable assistant to Red Marauder's trainer, Norman Mason in County Durham. So highly did Bradley rate Guest, that he put him forward as a successor to Charlie Brooks at Lambourn's famous Uplands stables.

During his evidence at Southampton, Guest gave an account of Brian Wright that was not nearly as warm as Bradley's. Guest was asked if he had come across the phrase, "he who dines with the devil must use a long spoon?"

"I haven't no," he told Michael Parroy.

"Dealing with Brian Brendan Wright, you would understand what I mean, would you not?"

"Yes," said Guest. "I wouldn't advise it."

"And he had the look of the gangster about him?"

"Certainly," Guest told the court.

"He had people around him who rather matched the mafia-don scene?"

"I would agree with that, yeah. He was charming, always very clean. He looked like a gangster – sharp."

Guest told the court he had met Brian Wright between 20 and 30 times, mainly through racehorse owner Leslie Garrett, one of Wright's best friends and the man for whom Guest rode Romany King to finish second in the 1992 Grand National. "He (Wright) was supposed to be a very good judge of horses and got information from here, there and everywhere," Guest said.

He portrayed Brian Wright as a networker, someone who would use Barrie Wright's popularity among jockeys to make his own connections. He would regularly put in calls to jockeys, to "see how they were, what they were doing, ask them how their football team got on, and whether they got their leg over on Saturday night and then slip in: has this (horse) got a chance today?"

Brian Wright kept in touch with his jockeys. He had even spoken to David Dutton, a former northern-based rider and trainer, days before Dutton made an appearance of his own at Southampton Crown Court.

Dutton was not nearly as successful as Bradley or Guest, riding 140 winners during his time in the saddle, the biggest success coming on Cockle Strand in the 1982 Scottish Grand National. He turned to training in 1989 although later quit to run a pub.

He knew Brian Wright well. "He was a very quiet person; very generous," Dutton said. "He was a wealthy man and a very likeable man. I was based in the north of England. I used to have a lot of telephone conversations with him regarding racing . . . we would discuss, you know, the day's racing . . . would basically try to mark his card for him by telling him that, you know, one would like certain conditions, one wouldn't like other conditions. He was a big gambler. So I would basically try to mark his card for him.

"I wasn't gambling. I wasn't asking him to put any money on for me. It was just advice I was giving him. As far as I knew it was within the rules of racing at that time. There were quite a few jockeys that used to supply him with information."

Quite a few, but not all were chosen. Wright's weighing-room contacts were pretty much hand-picked, according to Dutton, who said that other riders offered their services but were not wanted by Wright's racing organisation. "He used to keep everybody at arm's length. Not all information is good advice which you could rely on . . . I think I was probably closer than most," said Dutton, who as a jockey landed a gamble for Wright's Running Horse syndicate riding Olympic Times to win at Kempton on Boxing Day 1988.

He told the court that he was never paid for his information. Sure, Wright would sometimes put a bet on for him but . . . "the relationship I had with Mr Wright was more friends. Therefore I bet with my money and not with his money."

Dutton had less contact with Brian Wright after he had stopped training. "When I heard that Barrie (Wright) was in a little bit of a problem, that was basically when I heard Brian was mentioned as well," he said.

The news came as a shock. "When you have known someone for 20 years and it is the first time something like that crops up, it takes a little bit of getting used to – quite amazing really."

When the two men had spoken a few days before Dutton's court appearance – while Wright was on the run – Dutton said they hadn't spoken about the Southampton trial: "I didn't know I was coming to this case on Monday."

Dutton further reinforced the image of Brian Wright as a man with so much cash on him that you wondered if it ran through his veins, recalling: "I once got some money off him and we went to go to his car to get it and he opened the boot and there would be a large carrier bag full of money. I wouldn't like to say how much was in there. It was basically a carrier-bag full in the boot of his car."

Wright commanded loyalty. So much so that when Dutton was asked in court whether he would have been prepared to "take some money somewhere" if Wright had asked him, he would have done so and "would not have questioned it".

"I would have done whatever he asked. I trusted him," he added. "I always knew him to be a businessman. I never really probed. I thought he had a snooker club somewhere. I didn't pry into his business."

No one did. Not in racing. Around the weighing rooms, betting rings, and private boxes of Britain's top racecourses, Brian Wright was regarded as a great man, a kind man, a quiet man, a charismatic man, a handsome man, an intelligent-if-uneducated man, a gambling man. Yes, above all, he was a gambling man – a big, big gambling man.

At least, that's what he told people.

WHEN BARRIE MET BRIAN

And Barrie Wright, what about him?

All he wanted to be was a jockey. Just like Dermot Browne, Graham Bradley and anyone else who ran towards that dream but didn't quite know where to pull up.

Wright came from a football orientated family and his size was always going to be a problem for him – "big knees, big bones," according to Bradley. "Why he wanted to be a jockey, I don't know. But he was mad passionate keen and that is what he wanted to do. I had a lot of respect for him because he was a very good rider."

Like his brother Tommy, Wright's dad was a professional footballer, for Sunderland and Scotland. "He was a great footballer but he was finished at 28," Barrie said. "He liked his beer and he liked his dogs and he went back to where he came from."

Perhaps his son spent his own life trying not to follow him home. He made an early mark as a conditional jockey riding in the west of England, linking up with smaller yards, particularly those of Chris Wildman, Rod Simpson and Trevor Hallett. His conditional status, which meant he could claim a weight allowance in races against senior riders, ensured he was in demand from top yards such as Martin Pipe's.

All three of his main yards had gambling owners. Wright had a retainer with the owner John Stone, whose horses were kept at Wildman's yard. Wright was the "general manager" of his string. "My job was to tell these people how good their horse was and then try and run it in a race that was below their class," he said in his evidence at Southampton.

Early in his career, Wright had been due to ride a horse for Jim Davidson called Irish Williams but "smashed my head up a bit" in a fall. Nonetheless, Wright was promised that he would be given the riding fee despite being injured.

He was due to meet Irish Williams' owner at a ball in Cornwall, a traditional curtain raiser to the new Jumps season. Turns out that the horse's owner wasn't Jim Davidson after all.

"It (Irish Williams) ran in Jim's name but it wasn't actually Jim's," Barrie Wright said. "The man that gave me the riding fee was Brian Wright, Brian Wright senior.

"The first time I ever met him was that night at the start of the season ball."

It was to prove a meeting of some consequence.

Because he was a conditional, Barrie Wright was expecting to be given half the riding fee – and he was grateful for that.

Except . . . "Brian gave me an envelope with three notes in it and they were old £50 notes (the equivalent of five or six rides for a conditional). I thought it was Chinese money. I had never seen a £50 note in my life before. He straight away made a great big impression on me."

Funny that. Brian Wright hadn't finished either. He took Baz to one side and said: "The horses are down here not because Trevor trains them, (but) because I've watched you ride now for the last couple of years and we're big gamblers and we want you to ride the horses and that's why they are here."

"That made me feel a million dollars," Barrie Wright said. "For somebody to say that. I knew by the rides I was getting from other trainers that I was starting to make a little bit of a name for myself, but I wasn't near being a champion jockey or anything so for somebody who had horses in the yard to tell me the horses were there for me to ride was a great compliment."

Snared.

Barrie Wright would be told when the money was down, "but nine times out of 10 I was pilot of an aeroplane basically. It was left to me."

He worked hard for his money. "With those horses of Brian's especially, I'd have done all the work on them at home. I decided which way to ride them, which race they would run in, which ground they would like. If I got it wrong, they would lose a lot of money.

"I made up for my lack of ability by my determination to know about the other horses in the race and how they would run. Basically, I had to try and get every angle to make up for my lack of ability with better jockeys."

Brian Wright proved to be a shrewd man manager, inspiring confidence in his namesake. "Whenever I rode his horses I rode better for him than I did for anybody," Barrie said. "He used to tell people like Brad, who to my mind is the best Jumps jockey there has ever been . . . he would say to people like Brad and Richard Dunwoody, who was champion jockey, 'he's (Barrie Wright) as good as you are'. He would say that in front of me and he would mean it.

"I wasn't in the same county as Brad, but he (Brian Wright) made me believe it. When I rode a horse for him, I don't know, I should have been able to ride that way for anybody. But I rode with a lot more confidence in my own ability when I was riding for him. I thought I was a lot better than I was."

Quite touching really, and it probably illustrates well Brian Wright's subtle skills. Even suspected international drug dealers don't get where they are today without having their wits about them. On the other hand, Barrie Wright's self-analysis hints at weakness. You sense that he is going to be one of the fall-guys in this tale.

There is even something undignified about the busy way he hawked around his racing information. "I would pass on (information) to owners, but I would pass every bit of information on to Brian Wright because he became a person who would pay me good presents when I gave him good winning information," he told the court.

Good presents? "A cash gift. When he won money, he would give me a gift."

Brian Wright would hand out cash with the same high speed ease that a croupier flicks out cards. "I have never, never seen him with anything but big wads of cash," Barrie said. "I don't want to give you the wrong idea – he would pull out his money and it wasn't to be flash. It was just his way. If he had to give you some money for information you had given him he would pay you in cash and it was so fluid, the way he'd do it. It was as though he was a natural. He could count notes so quickly and just hand them over and it would always be right. He was just so . . ."

"Used to it?" Barrie Wright was asked.

"Yes, always cash, high denomination notes."

Barrie Wright was asked if the sale of information was a legitimate act for a jockey. "Well, it wasn't entirely permissible," he said. "The Jockey Club rules say to give information about horses you are going to ride, you could get into trouble for it. Jockeys are not allowed to bet, in the same sense they are not supposed to pass on information. But that is not like saying you are not allowed to tell your mum you are going to ride a winner that day. Basically, it is a rule, but a rule that isn't strictly adhered to, I think."

Somewhere amid that muddled thinking lies an indication that not all jockeys keep their thoughts in a safety vault. Amid the exclusive crack and banter of the weighing room, talk isn't necessarily cheap. It can be bloody lucrative.

Barrie Wright, though, was running into a problem – with his reputation. "It wasn't easy because, although you did have certain advantages (such as £500 'gifts' whenever you rode a winner), once you got known as a gambling jockey it tends to put other trainers and owners off. I at one stage went from being quite popular as a conditional to having a reputation of riding for gambling owners. Therefore, the other owners couldn't trust me."

Wright was asked if the other owners were right. "Unfortunately, yes," he said.

Perhaps by now, Barrie Wright had also slipped down the pecking order within Brian Wright's network of racing contacts, something that Graham Bradley recognised during his evidence.

Even though Barrie had introduced Brad to Brian, it was the latter two who became closer. "I was more top profile. I was in the weighing room more often," Bradley said. "I am not saying this in a nasty way but he (Brian Wright) seemed to use Barrie a fair bit. Not in a nasty way, he was just using him to get information from the jockeys, just told him to go to the races when he didn't have a ride and things like that."

Whether Barrie Wright knew he was being used was unclear. "Barrie was a lovely guy, but he is not the most intelligent guy in the world and he is very gullible. I don't think he thought he was being used, but in my opinion he certainly was, yes," Bradley added.

Barrie, meanwhile, continued to do as he was told. "Brian had a lot of Flat horses trained in Newmarket with a fella called Willie Musson," he recalled, "and he told me he wanted me to go up there. I was looking forward to going on holiday but there was no question, I just went and I spent the whole summer working, when a (jump) jockey is usually recuperating."

Basically, Barrie Wright looked up to Brian Wright. He was asked if he was a father figure to him – just like Bradley had been asked – but Barrie Wright denied that he was. He wasn't even sure if he was old enough to be one. "That's the funny thing about Brian Wright's age because you don't know his age actually. He is pretty vain, you know. He is a good-looking guy," he said.

"It was a relationship where I was very much in awe of him. Brian had been like a massive figure in my life for so long. He knew a great deal about racing. He was always saying 'you'll be a good trainer one day', like he'd set me up in training."

Like Vladimir and Estragon, Barrie Wright kept waiting. "It was the thing I wanted to do when I finished race-riding, to be in a position where I could train racehorses. For a long, long time, it was like he (Brian Wright) was the person I was relying on for my future, basically."

Instead, Barrie Wright's future took an unwanted turn. In 1990, when undergoing a compulsory medical because he had reached 35, Wright was refused his jockeys' licence on medical grounds. It was argued he was "punch drunk", having taken too many falls on his head.

Ultimately, the Jockey Club backed down and he resumed riding in 1992, but by then his future was behind him; yesterday's man. Rides were scarce, with only three trainers – Hallett, Simpson and Alan Jarvis – using him on a handful of occasions. He was given leave to sue the Jockey Club for loss of earnings in 1997, but Mr Justice Tudor-Evans ruled that the court should not interfere in the workings of domestic tribunals.

So where did that leave Barrie Wright?

"Devastated", according to Bradley. Financially and mentally devastated. "It just took the legs from underneath him. He just couldn't do anything."

Bradley said he was "always skint", a peripatetic figure. When Bradley became engaged to his now wife Amanda, they asked Wright to move out. At one point he lodged with Brian Wright's son, Briany, with whom he would play a lot of jockeys' charity football matches in the 1990s. Sometimes he would stay with his own brother Tommy.

"He (Barrie) just goes and stops with different friends," Bradley told the Southampton jury. "He has never had a property in 20 years. He's barely had a car. He would come and go. He would stop in Manchester with friends, he would stop in Leeds with friends. He was still riding at the time but he was always running about, here there and everywhere . . . He just relied on his many friends."

According to this evidence, Barrie Wright was anything but the globe-trotting henchman of a cocaine smuggling ring that he was accused of, and indeed cleared of being. He relied on selling on tips and the latest information from the weighing room, where he would always be warmly welcomed. But that proved to be only an "existence".

"He never had any money," Bradley said.

"Now and again these punters would give him 100 quid, give him 500 quid, give him 1,000 quid. But he is the most generous man in the world, from a big family. I think he bought his elderly mother's council house in Scotland for a few quid. He had two daughters, he would give them money. He would give his friends money."

"He would try and build up a pot," Bradley said. "He would be given 100, 200, 500 quid, and he would build up a pot. He was always addicted to the gambling carry on. He would bet on dogs and he would bet on other things, but obviously not in large amounts . . . you couldn't describe Barrie as a mug punter, I don't think. I don't know. You probably could."

His friends pulled together, and had no qualms about giving him information. "He wasn't riding and his income had gone, so he was obviously trying to have a bet to earn a living," Richard Guest told the court. "Every jockey who goes on the Racing Channel and is interviewed about his chances on horses that day would probably say more than I said to Barrie."

Bradley also helped out. "I was still riding Champion Hurdle winners and still had a decent job and lots of friends and he would, not use me as an intermediary, but he would ring up all the time just asking me about different information. He had to continue punting, even more so, and collect information to earn a living," he said.

Barrie Wright was also asked in court about the racing names in Brian Wright senior's diary. One page in particular attracted attention. "Almost every name on the page is to do with racing," the prosecuting QC, Michael Parroy, said.

At the time of his arrest, Barrie Wright was living in Belgium and returned there when he was cleared. The Jockey Club wanted him to travel to Britain to face a disciplinary inquiry into whether he should be warned off for breaching the rules of racing. He declined to do so.

At least he realised his dream of becoming a jockey, even if it led him down an ignominious path.

SUITS YOU

The Southampton trial established that there were punters other than Brian Wright who would cultivate jockeys for information – and reward them.

Step forward Christopher Coleman, a London-based self-employed tailor. Any jockey reading this might know him better as Bosh. That's right, Bosh. Not Bish, not Bash. Bosh, of whom Barrie Wright said: "A big gambler, but the most generous man you would ever meet when you gave him a winner."

Bosh had a lot to say. "I remember the first day I met Barrie," he told the court. "Brad bought him into the shop. He purchased two suits and we just got chatting about racing and he (Barrie) said to me 'There's a horse running on Saturday', I can't recall the name of the horse, just that he said: 'With 10st on his back, he'll think it's his birthday.' He said to me 'you should have a good wager on it.'"

He did: £15,000 each-way at 10-1 . . . "it was a nice Saturday."

Bosh, who first met Barrie Wright in 1987, described himself as a semi-professional gambler who received "quite a lot of information" from Barrie Wright over the years. "He would phone me up and he would say a horse is suited to certain ground. With horseracing, the biggest factor is the going."

Sometimes he acted on Barrie Wright's information; other times he didn't. He bet in "substantial amounts", often to a £20,000 stake. The information he received was privileged, something he recognised when asked in court: "If you were the owner or the trainer of the horse about which he was giving the information, would you want that information given?"

No, Bosh said.

One of his major coups came on a horse he owned called Earth Wood at the then named Devon & Exeter in August 1990, when ridden by Graham Bradley and trained by Trevor Hallett.

How much he paid Barrie Wright depended on the price of the horse. "I wouldn't always give him cash. He would come into the shop and I would give him a couple of suits or whatever I have, an overcoat, a raincoat, and if I had a good touch it would vary from £500 to £3,000."

However, Barrie Wright was so frequently on the move, that Bosh would often find him difficult to contact. "If I couldn't get hold of him somebody would know where he was, and it could be several phone calls before I reached him."

Barrie Wright would sometimes travel with Bosh to Stuttgart, where Hugo Boss – a prized fashion name in the weighing room – had a factory that sold suits at trade prices.

The suits were often cheap because they were out of season. "But everybody loves Boss," Barrie Wright said. "You could actually buy them for £120 and Chris (Bosh) would sell them in his shop for £299, £300, £350. So if you went straight there (to Stuttgart) and bought £100 suits, it was like a supermarket, you would get three or four (suits), take them to the counter and then pay, take them to the car and away.

"It wasn't steady because you could only sell so many Boss suits every week, but it was an income."

Barrie Wright and Bradley weren't his only sources of information. Bosh said that quite a few jockeys purchased their suits from him. Sometimes 'purchase' wasn't quite the right word. Sometimes the suits were in return for information. When he gave his evidence in October 2001, Bosh said that 10 jockeys had given him information within the previous 12 months. And that's a little worrying.

Bosh was also asked to appear at a Jockey Club inquiry. He also declined.

11

BLURRING THE LINES

The gist of Graham Bradley's evidence, although in nothing like the detail that appears here, was revealed to an unsuspecting world on Saturday 15 June 2002. Your mind might have been elsewhere. It was the day England beat Denmark in the second phase of the World Cup

It was also the day that reporting restrictions were lifted on all five trials linked to the Wright Organisation. The last of those cases had been concluded the previous day when South African John van Staden was sentenced to nine years at Bristol Crown Court, after pleading guilty to conspiracy to import cocaine. An accomplished sailor, he had helped with a number of cocaine importations during 1998.

Outside the Jockey Club and those journalists who followed the case, very few people in the racing world knew of Bradley's courtroom confessions.

That soon changed. Bradley's evidence formed part of a seven-page investigation I wrote for the *Racing Post* on the Wright gang and its alleged cocaine and racing links. The report also told how Bradley was facing a Jockey Club inquiry into whether he should be banned from the sport.

The hatch was opened, too, on Dermot Browne's hidden treasures. For the first time, the 23 horses he claims to have doped could be revealed; as could the fact that he was supposedly acting on behalf of Brian Wright, who in turn had been forced out of the shadows by the end of the reporting restrictions.

It was heavy stuff, a wake up call for those who had indignantly insisted racing was a world free of wrongdoing. Here was all the warning you needed that it wasn't. Ironically, these revelations came at the end of a week in which the sport's purity had already been put through the mixer, thanks to the BBC investigative programme *Kenyon Confronts*.

THEY STOP HORSES DON'T THEY?

Compared to what followed, the Kenyon 'charges' were venial; like comparing cocaine smuggling to nicking sweets. But they didn't half touch a nerve. 'They Stop Horses Don't They' was the title of the programme, which rather sensationally set out to expose "the dark underbelly of the sport".

"For some in the sport, it's more about losing than winning," presenter Paul Kenyon said. "In fact, they will go to extraordinary lengths to make sure that a horse goes slower.

"For their brand of fixing, the further down the field the horse comes the better. While they are making money out of it, the losers are you and I, the betting public."

Hmmm. The shock methods the programme was alluding to were attempts by trainers to ensure an effective handicap rating. This was done in a number of ways which the programme found questionable, such as: by running the horse when it is not fully fit, or over unsuitable distances, or on ground, or even courses, that didn't suit.

The iniquity of such tactics is debatable. To many groups – trainers, owners, jockeys *and* the betting public – this is the 'naughty but nice' side of racing, in which those who campaign their horses cutely will be rewarded with a lower handicap mark. Punters prepared to do the detective work – and thus be able to spot when a horse is suddenly running with conditions in its favour when previously they had palpably not been – will be rewarded by backing a winner.

Then there's the other side of the argument. Are horses that are run over a distance too short, or on ground to soft, or on a tight track when it prefers a galloping one, being allowed to run on their merits? Are Jockey Club rules broken because they are being 'schooled in public'? Should punters be expected to spend hours and hours poring over a form book, and goggle over the glut of racing that is shown on TV just to spot all this? How many actually have the time to do it? And if they haven't, are they in any way being cheated by such strokes and wheezes?

Kenyon Confronts took the view that they were. The programme's makers received little co-operation from those within racing, which is not that surprising considering the sport is renowned for curling up in protection whenever outside forces come questioning. Such recalcitrance is often justified as there is no doubt that the sport can be misrepresented by those with a mission to expose but not understand.

Still, it was a surprise that the Jockey Club chose to 'tip off' trainers that Kenyon's investigators were afoot and posing as wealthy antiques dealers in order to establish whether 'cheating' was rife in racing.

Its 'watch out lads' message nonetheless came too late for three trainers, Ferdy Murphy, Jamie Osborne and David Wintle, who all featured prominently on the programme. All were secretly filmed, and all claimed that their conversations were selectively edited and often used out of context.

Wintle, who trains a small string near Cheltenham, sold a horse to the Kenyon team, Seattle Alley, for £4,000. Seattle Alley was described by him as a "fiddling horse" and was featured – unconvincingly it has to be said – being prepared for a gamble after finishing unplaced on two previous starts.

During the making of the programme, Kenyon claimed he was beaten up by an associate of Wintle, who himself was caught on camera grabbing Kenyon by the hand at Stratford races and forcing him to the ground.

Murphy and Osborne came out of it a little better, although neither enhanced their reputations. Murphy claimed to have laid one of his own horses on a betting exchange, knowing it was unlikely to win; Osborne said that he was prepared to "cheat" with his horses and had an "in-house" jockey to help with that plan.

Both men claimed they were duped into presenting themselves in an unfavourable light. Osborne said he was simply being a salesman in front of men he thought were potential owners. "I feel a fool. I talk a lot of bullshit and when I am trying to sell a horse I talk an awful lot of bullshit – that's what I am guilty of.

"I had a salesman's hat on. These guys devised a scenario and were adamant that they would only buy a horse if I would do what they wanted. I need clients. I was purely and simply trying to sell a horse.

"Every time I steered them away from this, they steered me back. And as soon as they got what they wanted they left. It was a con. It was a sting."

Murphy was adamant he had not breached the rules of racing during his time with the *Kenyon Confronts* team. "They were misguided people coming into racing under the impression that it was all about stopping horses and then making a pile of money. I tried to let them down softly.

"Everything I told them was above board. I foolishly said £1,600 was won [on a betting exchange], but I just told an owner that the ground had gone against him at Fakenham and he laid him. But the horse was doing his best."

Within racing, Kenyon was instinctively discredited. Among punters the response was mixed, with some confirming that it was indeed part of their battle with the bookmakers to unearth such ruses; others said they would be more cautious about betting on horseracing.

Some aspects of the programme, such as quoting a jockey and a bookmaker with their identity hidden and their voices distorted, backfired and provided its critics with the ammo to condemn it as clichéd or lightweight.

But that should not overshadow the fact that it prodded some very raw, sensitive areas. You could tell it had by the howls that instantly followed. It took a meeting with Kenyon producer Paul Woolwich to appreciate just how shocked he and his colleagues were by the apparent acceptance that trainers should be allowed deliberately to run their horses in unsuitable conditions.

It wasn't just TV talk; their off-camera disbelief was genuine.

Woolwich, a journalist with a serious, award-winning track record, was also appalled at the defensive, resistant approach of the Jockey Club and its apparent empathy for the practice. To him they were condoning cheating on a widespread scale. "I don't think there is room for any ambiguity, there is not one scintilla of doubt: if you deliberately run a horse over the wrong distance or on unsuitable ground, you are breaking the Jockey Club's own rules – that a horse must be run to obtain the best possible placing. I don't see how you can argue anything else," he said.

"I was quite amazed that people in the industry think this is okay and that they can't believe that anyone could think otherwise. Even if it is acceptable among the racing professionals, it isn't elsewhere. Anyone from the outside thinks it is scandalous.

"The whole of the racing industry; the Jockey Club, the trainers, the jockeys, the bookies all make up into an extraordinarily close-knit community that closes its ranks, in quite an amazing way, the moment anyone from the outside starts to question its practices.

"The National Trainers' Federation constantly attacked us – before the programme even went out – threatening us with legal action and accusing us of breaking our own guidelines.

"Well, I can assure you we didn't break our own guidelines. Everything we did had to be approved by the BBC hierarchy.

"Besides, guidelines are guidelines. They are like blancmange. They can't actually be broken. But you can break a rule and the Jockey Club rules are broken day in, day out.

"Surely it is the job of the racing press to expose this sort of thing? I was amazed at how extremely supine they were.

"Not to put too fine a point on it they are perpetuating a fraud on anybody who goes in and places even £1 on a race. You would never put your money on a horse if you thought it wasn't running on its merits because a trainer is running it in unsuitable conditions.

"When you place a bet you have to believe that there is a chance you are going to win; that is what betting is all about."

As you can see, Woolwich takes a dim view of racing and its participants. The Jockey Club is at the forefront of his condemnation, for refusing, in his opinion, to address cheating on a daily basis because of "incompetence, arrogance, and complacency", and because it is too close to those people it is supposed to regulate.

"The most extraordinary thing was the letter that the Jockey Club sent to all trainers warning them that they thought that some undercover reporters would show the industry in a bad light," said Woolwich.

"Which begs the question: if there wasn't some kind of skulduggery going on, why did they send the letter out? This was supposed to be the regulatory body for horseracing.

"What shocked us was the ferocious criticism we received from the Jockey Club before it had even seen the programme. Why didn't they wait until after the programme had gone out before they started to vilify it?"

Although only three trainers were secretly filmed, four others were approached by the programme, only one of whom, Woolwich said, showed no interest in stopping horses. Despite its unfavourable response to *Kenyon Confronts*, the Jockey Club did ask to see all the unused evidence – including transcripts – with a view to taking disciplinary action against the three trainers who featured.

"Three, four hours worth of material" were shown to one of the Jockey Club's security officers, John Elsey.

Some months after, the efforts of the Kenyon team appeared to have been vindicated when the Jockey Club decided to hold disciplinary inquiries into the three trainers – based on what Elsey had seen.

"His [Elsey's] main concern was that we hadn't taken anything out of context," Woolwich said. "He could see for himself that we hadn't. The evidence was there for all to see."

Murphy and Osborne were accused of bringing racing into disrepute, as was Wintle, whose 'charge sheet' also included acting in a violent and improper manner on a racecourse and whether he had allowed 'fiddling horse' Seattle Alley to run on its merits in two races that had featured on the programme.

Woolwich said that there was enough unseen evidence of wrongdoing in racing to justify a further Kenyon programme on the issue. That is hardly reassuring.

Neither is the news that another TV investigation into racing was secretly being nurtured. Channel 4's respected *Despatches* programme had also looked into racing's malpractices. According to a Channel 4 source, the programme was dropped to avoid any repetition with *Kenyon Confronts* or *Panorama*, rather than because of a lack of material or interest in the subject matter.

PRU'S PROFILE

Whatever you make of Woolwich's views, he is right to have referred to the "closed world of horseracing". It is indeed a sport that does not encourage external audits.

For example, in the minds of many of racing's participants it is the supposed responsibility of those who write about it to 'talk up' and portray it in the best possible light – and certainly not to reveal any imperfections.

I received a reminder of that when writing a comment piece for *Owner* magazine, in which I said: "Regardless of the merits of *Kenyon Confronts*, it presented racing in a pretty poor light. If the Jockey Club could warn off the people it licenses for stupidity, the three trainers who appeared on it would be unlikely to set foot on a racecourse again."

A bit harsh, perhaps, and it swiftly led to a call from one of the Kenyon Three telling me this wasn't on. He called me "a disgrace to the sport" and said that I was "bringing racing into disrepute". You could only admire his gall.

But that trainer's words suggested that *Kenyon Confronts* did hit the target with one of its arrows: it showed that racing operates within a world of its own, and at times its methods are at loggerheads with those of the 'real' world.

An entirely separate example is the High Court case of Pru's Profile, when an experienced judge's ruling was ridiculed by two trainers on the grounds that he may not have understood the intricacies of racing and the sales ring. Pru's Profile was bought as an unnamed, and thus unraced, gelding at the Doncaster sales in May 1995 on behalf of an owner called Gary Heywood, after whose company, Exterior Profiles, he was named.

Heywood had employed the respected bloodstock agent Paul Webber, also a successful trainer, to bid for Pru's Profile. Webber, acting for another client, had paid Ir8,000 guineas for the same horse the previous year.

Webber insisted he had informed Heywood of this; Heywood said he hadn't, and was reported to be "gobsmacked" when he first learned of the connection, in December 1997. Heywood complained to the Jockey Club, not just about this but about the conduct of a leading National Hunt trainer, Oliver Sherwood, prior to the purchase of Pru's Profile at Doncaster.

Heywood said that while viewing Pru's Profile prior to purchasing him, Sherwood had told him that the gelding was the most exciting entry in the sale. Webber, a friend of Sherwood's, gave Heywood the same verdict and advised him to bid up to 25,000 guineas for Pru's Profile.

When he was put through the ring, Webber finally secured the gelding for 28,000 guineas. Sherwood was the underbidder and congratulated Heywood on his purchase.

Pru's Profile failed to live up to his billing on the racecourse. Heywood was so concerned about the circumstances of the sale that he took Webber's then employers, the Curragh Bloodstock Agency, to court.

The case was heard before Judge William Crawford in November 1999. He summed up Heywood's claims thus: "That there was in effect a conspiracy between Webber and Sherwood, his close friend, to run the bidding up falsely on lot 66 [Pru's Profile] to a point just short of Mr Heywood's limit of 30,000 guineas that by so doing Webber was obliging and assisting the vendor, a long-standing client of his.

Also, "by failing to disclose to Heywood that he had bought the gelding himself, the price at which he had bought it and for whom he had bought it, and the nature of his relationship with [the gelding's previous owners], Webber was in breach of his fiduciary [someone who is required to act for another person's benefit] duty to Heywood."

Judge Crawford found in favour of Heywood and awarded damages of £51,480, plus costs and interest, against the CBA. "No competent bloodstock agent would have advised Heywood to pay more than 14,000 guineas for lot 66," he said. In making his ruling, Judge Crawford concluded: "I found Gary Heywood to be a witness of truth". Sherwood, he said, "was prepared not to tell the truth to this court", while in a particular piece of evidence, "Mr Webber, in my view, was not being truthful about it."

Webber said in response: "We'd done nothing wrong and it was a crazy judgement." Sherwood described the ruling as "absolutely scandalous".

In this context, it is not so much the detail of the case that matters as the reactions to it, especially those of Webber and Sherwood when they were fined £4,000 each by the Jockey Club for acting "in a manner prejudicial to the good reputation of horseracing".

After the Jockey Club hearing, Sherwood continued to protest his belief that Justice Crawford had made an incorrect ruling. "I don't think the judge had any understanding of the racing world," he said.

And the solicitor for the two trainers, Justin Wadham, added: "In racing cases it seems the outsider is given an unfair advantage because the judge seems not to understand the issues at stake."

That might well be a view that is shared by Victor Chandler, who discovered for himself that racing folks' idea of acceptable habits is not always viewed that way elsewhere.

Especially in court.

FREE BETTING ACCOUNTS

In June 2002 Chandler went to the High Court to stop *Panorama* using documents that had been taken by police when they raided his office and home addresses during the 1998 race-fixing and doping investigations.

These searches were ruled illegal because incorrect warrants had been used, and a court hearing ruled that all the material seized by police should be returned to Chandler. This included copies of letters that Chandler had written, not all of which were sent, to trainers offering them free bets in return for information on their horses.

Before he was interviewed by police, Chandler, who was cleared of any wrongdoing, was given notice of preliminary areas of questioning, one of which was: "Can Mr Chandler explain why he offered trainers free betting with accounts of up to £2,500? At the search of his private office letters were found which offered these facilities to several trainers – two were named, one of which was Gay Kelleway."

Kelleway, whose father Paul trained Waki Gold, one of the horses doped by Dermot Browne, is a successful trainer in her own right. She took out a licence in 1992, having previously ridden as a professional jockey and been the first woman rider to win a race at Royal Ascot.

The other letter was sent to Jimmy Fitzgerald, a hugely experienced trainer based in Malton, North Yorkshire, who has had major success on the Flat – winning the Cesarewitch and Ebor Handicaps – and over Jumps, training Forgive N' Forget to win the 1985 Cheltenham Gold Cup. He is also famed for his skilful handling of the hot-headed Kieren Fallon, during the champion jockey's early riding career.

Much to Chandler's distress, these letters found their way into Roger Buffham's possession. He in turn passed them onto the BBC programme *Panorama* for its investigation into the integrity – or otherwise – of horseracing. Both Fitzgerald and Kelleway were subsequently door-stepped by *Panorama* reporters.

Chandler went to court in search of an injunction to prevent the letters being included in any broadcast. Lawyers acting for his Gibraltar-based company argued that *Panorama*'s possession of the letters represented a breach of confidence.

Things did not go to plan in court. The Chandler action was heard before Mr Justice Morland. He already had a more than nodding acquaintance with racing's unique ways through his involvement in the Top Cees libel case of February 1998.

During a three-hour, 35-minute summing up of the Top Cees case, he told the jury: "The wellbeing of the racing industry depends upon all involved in it acting honestly and honourably – jockeys, trainers, bookmakers, journalists specialising in racing, owners, stewards and punters." Now, dealing with the Chandler case, he highlighted issues of "serious public interest and concern" that were facing him.

In his ruling, Justice Morland quoted from the letters to Fitzgerald and Kelleway.

The first letter, dated 14 October 1993, said: "Dear Mr Fitzgerald, There will be no tax charged on this account and settlement will be made at the end of the season. However, if the account shows a loss at the end of the season I will clear this. Also you may draw down any time the account shows a substantial credit balance. All these arrangements between us are completely private and confidential."

The Kelleway letter was dated 1 May 1996, and said: "Dear Gay, I wonder whether you would like the same arrangement we had last year. I am prepared to give you £2,500 free credit with the company, and should you lose this amount you do not have to settle."

Justice Morland said: "It is not clear whether these two letters were actually posted. It may be that the financial arrangements between the claimants and the two trainers were concluded orally. In my judgement, it matters not what was the position."

Chandler, in his own statement, said: "Prior to the change in the Jockey Club rules on 6 December 2000, I believe it was common for bookmakers to have various agreements with a number of trainers [all other leading firms denied this]. For my part I agreed with four or five trainers up to £2,000 a year. I often encouraged the trainers to share the free bets with the stable lads.

"The reason why I did this is obvious: if a trainer or stable lad made a bet on a horse in that stable then it is was likely to be because they believed the horse was in form, and such information might be useful in terms of the odds that were set for that horse or as to whether or not bets on the horse should be laid off. Since 6 December 2000 I have had no relationship with any trainer whatsoever."

That date in December is significant because it heralded the introduction of a Jockey Club code of conduct that said trainers should "ensure that their relationships with betting organisations or any person representing a betting organisation do not confer special privileges or concessions which may invite adverse inferences to be drawn."

Justice Morland assumed that the Chandler letters had "probably" been given to Buffham by the police. In his witness statement, Buffham said they had come from an "anonymous source". After he left the Jockey Club in September 2001, he kept copies of the letters, "with a view to bringing to the attention of the public, through the media, evidence of serious regulatory problems within horseracing and deficiencies in the way in which the Jockey Club performed its regulatory role."

Buffham showed the letters to Steven Scott, the producer of *Panorama*, as well as two members of the *Kenyon Confronts* team. Scott said the Chandler letters would play a "very important part" in the *Panorama* investigation into allegations of "a culture of institutional corruption in the racing industry".

He argued: "Whilst I have been given to believe that such accounts have been widely used in the racing industry, the existence of such accounts has never been publicly acknowledged. For example, Charlie Brooks, the well-known former trainer, has in the past said, 'The idea of such accounts is outdated and complete nonsense and one senses these imaginary accounts have the hallmark of Roger Buffham of the Jockey Club security department stamped on them.'

"Mike Dillon of Ladbrokes also denied the existence of such accounts in the *Evening Standard* being quoted as saying, 'I suppose the implied idea is that the bookmaker gets information from his client in exchange for those ludicrous terms. I have been in bookmaking for 30 years. It beggars belief that something like this should exist or ever have existed.' Mr Chandler's account show conclusively that such accounts have existed."

Scott said it was "a matter of concern" that the Jockey Club did not take action relating to the Chandler letters in advance of the code of conduct. "*Panorama* would like to investigate with the Jockey Club why this was. The Jockey Club rules have always provided for disciplinary action to be taken against those who bring racing into disrepute, yet, for example, no action seems to have been taken or contemplated against Mr Chandler or the recipients of the two 'no lose' letters I have seen."

He added that the letters "point to an improper relationship between a bookmaker and a participant in a sport who was privy to inside information of considerable value to those betting or taking bets on the outcome of horseraces. It was clear that an ordinary punter laying bets would have been placed at a considerable disadvantage if his bookmakers had, in effect, purchased inside information about the form or condition of a horse from a trainer.

"I have no doubt that the matters we have taken up with Mr Chandler raise matters of public interest about the way the horseracing industry has been run and regulated in recent years. Roger Buffham, whilst head of security at the Jockey Club, spoke to me about his belief that corruption was endemic in the industry, and so deeply embedded that many dubious practices were accepted both by participants and sections of the Jockey Club."

Scott's argument clearly made an impression on Justice Morland, who threw out the Chandler application, ruling the content of the letters raised three important areas for *Panorama* to explore:

- "...the integrity and fairness of bookmaking to the betting public..."
- "...the relationship of bookmakers to trainers and racing stables..."
- "...the effectiveness of the Jockey Club's regulatory role over the sport and industry of horseracing..."

He said: "I am satisfied that those questions are of proper and serious concern to the public and, in particular, to the very many hundreds of thousands of people interested in horseracing, very many of whom will place bets from time to time.

"Although the two letters were written many years ago, I am satisfied they remain relevant to the serious question of the integrity of racing, which is of current and topical interest now that the series of criminal trials with a racing slant have ended. Now is an appropriate time for a *Panorama* programme."

Describing the relationship between bookmakers and trainers as "still currently a matter of controversy", Justice Morland highlighted evidence during the hearing of Tony Stafford, a racing journalist who had recently retired from the *Daily Telegraph*.

Stafford said: "Trainers will indicate their thoughts on their own horses whether they bet with their own money or in an arrangement whereby they are offered a free bet of modest proportions. My experience is that if the trainers were able to have a small free bet he would be just as likely to supplement it with a much bigger one paid by himself if the horse in question were strongly fancied to win."

Stafford also suggested that special arrangements had been "common among major bookmakers and some trainers" prior to the Jockey Club's code of conduct.

"The reason for these special arrangements could be in part one of wanting to find out where the likely money would be coming into the betting market, or otherwise just as a favour to trainers who might be handling horses for those bookmakers. Such intelligence would encourage bookmakers to shorten the odds of those horses and compensate by lengthening those of some others," he added.

The favours didn't end there. Stafford raised "another not generally known issue . . . the convention that certain insider racing journalists expect, and get, preferential odds on certain ante-post events in exchange for positive publicity for the major bookmakers which provide these opportunities."

Stafford isn't wrong here. It does go on. It's a PR exercise. It's worthwhile for bookmakers, through their representatives, to keep journalists 'sweet' in an attempt to receive free publicity in the newspapers. It would be wrong to imply it is endemic and that journalists continually feast themselves on preferential odds. But yes, it does go on.

It's just one illustration of racing's incestuous ways.

Perhaps Justice Morland could help out and provided an expert, considered view? It often takes an outsider to identify when the public should be concerned about horseracing and when it need not.

12

A THANKLESS TASK

It's not easy writing this, you know. In fact, right now it feels like trying to keep up with a runaway train.

Here's why. No sooner had the dust settled on the dispute with Victor Chandler, than *Panorama*, through the BBC, and Roger Buffham found themselves back in the High Court – this time with the Jockey Club as their adversaries.

The powers of Portman Square were seeking to prevent *Panorama* broadcasting information that it regarded as confidential and was said to "reveal the existence or apparent existence of widespread corruption within racing".

By now, that possibility may not surprise you.

At the centre of this legal dispute was whether the makers of *Panorama* were bound by the injunction, issued in May 2002, which prevented Buffham from breaking a confidentiality agreement he had signed the previous September.

Panorama wanted to use information from 20 documents, or parts of documents, that Buffham had supplied to them. You can see why. The documents, according to the judge in charge of the case, Mr Justice Gray, included:

- "... a catalogue of information, apparently received by the police, about an individual who is alleged to be responsible for a large measure of corruption in racing." Any guesses?
- "... another police document, evidently provided to the Jockey Club, consisting (of) an interview with an Irish jockey." That jockey is Dermot Browne.
- "... intelligence about numerous jockeys and others suspected by the Jockey Club of involvement in corruption."

- "... a Jockey Club Security Department intelligence/information report about a particular jockey and a summary, marked 'Secret', prepared about him in order to decide whether he should be charged." Graham Bradley.
- "... a collection of documents about another individual, employed by a firm of bookmakers, who is also the subject of investigation by the Security Department". This is Ladbrokes' PR chief Mike Dillon, a man with the best contacts book in racing. Dillon is credited with igniting Manchester United boss Sir Alex Ferguson's interest in horseracing, which has provided the sport with an enormous amount of favourable publicity. Dillon was the subject of a three-year, Buffham-led, surveillance operation by the Jockey Club. The the enquiries focused on his friendship with Mick Kinane, the stable jockey to Aidan O'Brien's immensely successful Ballydoyle yard, with which Dillon also has close contacts. "People who have known me for a long time know the way I operate and they know I conduct myself professionally and with integrity," said Dillon. There is no evidence against Dillon and the Jockey Club have confirmed that there are no ongoing enquiries.
- "... documents provided to the Jockey Club relating to a particular race which was suspected to have been fixed." This is the Man Mood race at Warwick.
- "... a memorandum prepared by Mr Buffham headed 'Confidential (NFD)', recording information received from the Hong Kong Jockey Club about the refusal of a licence to ride in the case of two jockeys."
- "... a Jockey Club memorandum (headed 'Secret') about a police operation investigating the connections between jockeys and members of Chinese gangs or 'triads' operating in the UK."
- "... A memorandum (also headed 'Secret') on the related topic of contacts between British jockeys and triad members in Hong Kong."
- "... a police memorandum dated 5 September 2000 which deals with infiltration of racing by Chinese triads and the police operation established to deal with it." Greater Manchester Police made its own submission to this hearing, expressing concerns that "certain passages in the Jockey Club documents upon which the BBC wish to rely on might risk revealing the identity of Police informants."

The Flat jockeys mentioned in connection with the Hong Kong reports included John Egan and champion jockey Kieren Fallon. Both are top riders. Both deny any wrongdoing and Fallon has an ongoing claim for libel against the *News of the World* who suggested otherwise.

At the time of Mr Justice Gray's ruling, Egan was the subject of an arrest warrant in Hong Kong after failure to return there to answer bail. He was accused of accepting HK $20,000 (£1,633) from an owner as an inducement to, or reward for, passing on tips for a race in Hong Kong in January 2002.

The former colony's powerful Independent Commission Against Corruption even wanted Egan banned from riding in Britain, which the Jockey Club, despite expressing "great concern", refused to do. That was on the grounds that it felt the charges facing Egan did not "warrant the immediate withdrawal or suspension of his licence."

With such a box of tricks in its grasp, you can see why the *Panorama* team was so keen to use it, and why the Jockey Club would rather it had been confiscated for good.

The court heard executive director Christopher Foster argue that making the documents public would prevent the Jockey Club from "operating as an effective regulator of racing", according to Mr Justice Gray.

"Mr Foster maintains that the documents include much secret and confidential intelligence information gathered by the Jockey Club from a variety of confidential sources.

"The trust built up over the years with those sources would be destroyed by their being made public. Disclosure of the intelligence and other information might also prejudice the ability of the Jockey Club to pursue leads and obtain evidence."

Foster also expressed concern that *Panorama* had contacted Jockey Club informers, even though "disclosure of their identity would place them at serious risk".

A witness statement from Buffham's successor as head of security, Jeremy Phipps, argued, in the words of Mr Justice Gray, that use of the documents would "undermine the trust that the Jockey Club has with all individuals connected with the sport", would "severely damage ongoing security department operations", and "severely damage the relationships between the Jockey Club and outside agencies in gathering intelligence and investigating possible breaches of the Rules of Racing or any other criminal offence affecting horseracing."

Panorama, of course, was having none of that. In his own witness statement, Steven Scott told the court that the programme intended to focus on four areas:

- "... relationships between all or any of the following: bookmakers, trainers, racing stables, jockeys and known criminals in the light of evidence given in a number of recent trials."
- "... action taken or not taken by the Jockey Club in relation to corruption and the integrity of racing and the way in which the Jockey Club has exercised or not exercised its powers as the regulator of horseracing in the UK."

- "... the integrity and fairness of racing and bookmaking in the UK."
- "... the effectiveness of the Jockey Club's role as regulator of the sport and industry of horseracing."

No wonder the Jockey Club was worried. Scott said *Panorama*'s investigations had established, "interwoven but identifiable strands containing examples of corruption and an account of what the Jockey Club has done or failed to do." The fact that the programme was able to do so highlighted again the malpractice that had so quietly and effectively eaten its way into the sport.

Those strands were surely too serious to be suppressed, even if Mr Justice Gray recognised: "It is a material factor that the information sought to be protected here has come into the possession of the BBC by reason of a breach of contract on the part of a former employee of the Jockey Club, honourable though he asserts his motives to have been for making the disclosure."

The Jockey Club lost its case. "The public interest in disclosure outweighs the right of confidence of the Jockey Club," Mr Justice Gray ruled. "It appears to me that information revealing the existence, or apparent existence, of widescale corruption within racing is of legitimate concern to a large section of the public who either participate in racing or follow it, or who bet on the results of races."

The argument that some of the information that *Panorama* intended to use "dates back some years" did not concern Mr Justice Gray, who pointed out that the programme had been hampered by the reporting restrictions surrounding the Woolwich and Southampton trials.

"In any case the information suggests that the problems are continuing ones," he said.

JOCKEY CLUB LEFT FRUSTRATED

Joy and justification for *Panorama*, whose editor Mike Robinson said: "*Panorama* has always believed its investigation into corruption in horseracing and whether the Jockey Club has the backbone to regulate the sport and the business of racing is in the public interest."

Despair and considerable frustration for the Jockey Club, for whom Christopher Foster said: "We are deeply disappointed that parts of a few highly classified intelligence documents stolen by an ex-employee and now a paid consultant to the BBC are able to enter the public domain through a side-door.

"The Jockey Club has never wished to stand in the way of the BBC making a programme about criminal activity in racing and the effectiveness of the Jockey Club as regulator. We believe that our role should be open to scrutiny provided that scrutiny is fair and balanced.

"However it is also our duty to preserve the confidence of secret intelligence documents, disclosure of which might have made us less effective in carrying out our regulatory role. The documents at the centre of our dispute with the BBC mostly contain no more than intelligence information which falls well short of being legally admissible hard evidence of wrongdoing."

That view was not shared in court. "The fact that hard evidence of criminality may be lacking does not negate the legitimacy of this concern," Mr Justice Gray said. "I have well in mind the inhibitions to which the Jockey Club feels itself to be subject in cases where the evidence goes no further than to establish, for example, an undesirable association between a jockey and a bookmaker.

"But it has been made clear on behalf of the BBC that its case is not solely that the Jockey Club failed to take more effective action but also that, if effective action cannot be taken, more effective means must be found to preserve the integrity of racing."

So there you have it. Another High Court judge insists that racing had integrity issues of genuine public interest, despite the Jockey Club's attempts to ensure otherwise.

The irony is that long before *Panorama*'s dramatic intervention, the organisation working hardest to highlight the sport's vulnerability to corruption was the Jockey Club itself.

And not many people were listening.

A QUESTION OF INTEGRITY

Considering the modern-day media deluge of prods and scrutiny to which they are subjected, it is hard to identify any sporting authority that isn't regarded as badly managed and ineffective.

Think of the Football Association and the accusations of bungling and procrastination that it seems to face on a daily basis; or read Simon Wilde's *Caught – the full story of cricket's match-fixing scandal* to realise how unprepared that sport's global and domestic leaders were to deal with such outrageous rule-breaking.

How does the Jockey Club, so often, and unfairly, dismissed as a self-elected bunch of self-congratulatory old duffers, compare?

It has come a long way since it was founded in 1752 by a group of well-heeled gents with an interest in horseracing and breeding. For nearly 250 years it controlled the racing calendar until the formation of the British Horseracing Board in 1992, which took over issues of finance, race-planning, politics, and the overall administration of racing, leaving the Jockey Club to regulate, or police, the sport.

Now it oversees medical and veterinary issues, the licensing of trainers and jockeys and the registration of owners and stable staff. It appoints the stewards in charge of each meeting, whose role it is to look out for misuse of the whip, careless riding, interference in races and horses who aren't being allowed to run on their merits.

And, of course, it is responsible for the integrity of horseracing. This is where the strain and struggles begin. None of the Jockey Club's other roles – even such emotive issues as use of the whip – provide anywhere near as stern a test of its capabilities. Let's face it, get the integrity issues wrong and you are fucked: give a sport a bad name – swimming and cycling spring to mind – and it sticks. Possibly for good.

So the Jockey Club's responsibilities were considerable. It was in the latter part of 1996 – up to a decade after Brian Wright emerged as a major player in the betting rings – that the Jockey Club was first told that he and his associates were fixing races through a small group of jockeys.

Via an informant, it was given the names of those jockeys, as well as some of the races they were supposed to have fixed. These are not necessarily the races that featured in the police investigation. We now know, though, that Wright is alleged to have been fixing races since the mid-1980s, when Dermot Browne was one of his 'men'.

Then there was the doping spree that took place in 1990. The Jockey Club simply can't say whether horses other than Bravefoot, Norwich and Flying Diva were doped. Neither can it be sure that horses were tested but somehow escaped detection. By the time Dermot Browne 'coughed' and the Jockey Club learned the full extent of his confessions, it no longer had the records of which horses had been post-race tested in 1990.

Browne, incidentally, says that in the early 1990s a meeting – through media contacts – had been arranged for him to talk with Christopher Spence's predecessor as Jockey Club senior, Lord Hartington. He was ready to tell all then, but the meeting never took place. You wonder if this was a period when the Jockey Club slept while others cheated.

But once the 1996 intelligence was received, the Jockey Club carried out its own surveillance of the jockeys named before handing over its evidence to the police in May 1997. Just as it was completing its investigations, the Jockey Club discovered that Avanti Express and Lively Knight had been doped that March.

The information handed to the police made no mention of Lord Rooble, another horse we have suggested was doped on the day Lively Knight was 'got at' at Plumpton. We'll never know if that was the case. Lord Rooble wasn't tested.

The police investigation was a catastrophe, almost from beginning to end. It badly damaged the Jockey Club's credibility within racing. Which may have been unfair.

This is probably as good a time as any to shatter a few myths.

The common conception is that the Jockey Club skipped gaily hand in hand with the police as both sides, jointly, blundered their way through the investigation. That's certainly what I had thought – until the Jockey Club told me otherwise.

"After we handed over our own evidence and the police decided to investigate, it became their investigation and their investigation alone," said Christopher Foster. "They are under no responsibility to keep other parties informed of the progress. The only contact we had to the police was, quite rightly, through Roger Buffham. As head of security he had been responsible for developing our relationships with external authorities such as Customs and Excise and the police.

"Because of the Jockey Club's limited powers and the apparent serious criminal activities of Brian Wright and his associates, we needed to involve the police for the investigation to progress further. Only the police had the necessary powers.

"The consequence of passing it to the police was to relinquish not only control, but also any input unless requested.

"People assumed that the Jockey Club were being kept fully informed on a daily basis and had a hand in selecting those individuals to be arrested. That was not the case.

"As I recall, the only advance notice we were given, through Roger Buffham, was of the first three jockeys arrested, Leighton Aspell, Dean Gallagher and Jamie Osborne, and that was the night before the dawn arrests.

"We were not given specific reasons as to why the arrests were made."

Another problem for the Jockey Club was the inevitable and one-sided clash with Customs and Excise, who were at the time investigating Brian Wright in connection with drug-smuggling allegations. "Our hands were severely but quite properly tied because of the on going Customs and police investigations into Brian Wright and his associates," Foster said.

Unconfirmed reports suggest that, for a short period and unbeknown to the other, Wright was under surveillance by both Customs and the police investigating the doping and race-fixing allegations.

Aided by hindsight, Foster admitted that the priority the police attached to the investigation – it was often put on the backburner while other inquiries were pursued, and overall responsibility for the inquiry continually changed – was "unsatisfactory". Ditto the police's lack of expertise in betting and racing.

Not that the Jockey Club was blameless throughout. The decision to take away the riding licences of Aspell, Gallagher, and Osborne, much to the outcry of a racing industry that felt the trio was being judged prematurely guilty, is now viewed as a mistake.

"The Jockey Club just did not know what the public response would be,"

Foster said. "We were concerned about the impact on the integrity of racing of doing nothing following the arrest of the three jockeys. The decision to suspend their licences was a protective measure.

"We knew there was a possibility of licensed individuals being arrested, so we had considered what options were available to us in the event of this happening.

"We took legal advice and looked at other professions and what action other racing authorities had taken when the police had got involved. For example, in Hong Kong jockeys were, and still are, suspended indefinitely following arrest.

"We were in unknown territory at the time and we learned lessons from dealing with the first set of arrests which were reflected in how we handled subsequent arrests.

"Subsequent to those first three arrests, the Jockey Club reacted in a different way whenever a licensed person was arrested, such as Graham Bradley and Ray Cochrane, and in a different way again when Graham Bradley was charged with a serious offence in connection with racing."

When Bradley and Cochrane were arrested they were allowed to continue riding; it was only after Bradley was charged that his licence was withdrawn. It was returned as soon as the race-fixing charges against him were dropped.

Even then, the decision to stop Bradley from riding was greeted with outrage. The Jockey Club should be used to that. Throughout its troubled times, the one thing it continually lacked was support from its own constituents. If there were trainers, jockeys or owners who espoused the Jockey Club's actions, they were habitually smothered by the cries of the indignant majority.

The more the Jockey Club tried to clean up the sport, the greater was the opprobrium that followed. This was not helped by the silence that had to surround the supposed activities of the Wright Organisation until the Woolwich and Southampton trials were completed.

Effectively, the Jockey Club had to introduce anti-corruption measures without being able to explain why. "The gulf in knowledge between what we knew and what was in the public domain made it difficult, and understandable that we did not get full support from racing because it was simply unaware of the details," said Christopher Spence.

As far back as November 1996, not long after the first warnings about Brian Wright's involvement were received, the Jockey Club introduced a Warnings Protocol in an attempt to clamp down on trainers and jockeys mixing with 'undesirables'.

Any licensed person – usually jockeys, occasionally trainers – thought to be doing so were summonsed to a disciplinary hearing to be warned in person about their future conduct. In this first six years of the Protocol being introduced, 20 warnings were handed out. It has been estimated that around one in 20 of Britain's jockeys have received one.

If the warning was ignored, a jockey or trainer faced the prospect of being warned off by the Jockey Club on the grounds he or she was not considered a "fit or proper person" to hold a licence.

The Jockey Club made it quite clear why the rule was introduced, citing at the time "reports implicating a small number of jockeys and trainers in situations which cause considerable concern for the integrity of racing.

"The most disturbing aspect of these reports is that the information shows licensed people regularly meeting or receiving favours from well-known criminals.

"The (Jockey Club) stewards believe that the Protocol is necessary to meet the threats posed to the integrity of racing by a small minority, who consistently become involved in unacceptable activity."

Could it have made things any clearer?

Seemingly not, because in May 1999, following further reports of jockeys mixing with Wright, a letter was sent to all National Hunt jockeys from Gurney Sheppard, the head of the Jockey Club's licensing committee. The much-publicised golf tournament in Spain, which featured a high level of top Jumps riders, is thought to have been the main catalyst for the letter.

It said: "I would like to remind you of the dangers of regularly meeting with people who might wish to corrupt horseracing.

"Additionally, you should avoid receiving favours from such people which could put you in a compromising position at a later date.

"It is obviously a matter for you to decide with whom you associate and how you spend your time, but I thought I would warn all jockeys that there have been instances where licensed persons have accepted favours or hospitality, such as holidays or nights on the town, and have subsequently found themselves compromised.

"Please be alert to these dangers and avoid putting yourself in a situation which is likely to cause my committee concern."

Fair enough. That warning was followed with even stronger words in December 1999, a time when the police investigation had been completed and five men were awaiting trial. That none of that quintet were directly involved in the sport may have heightened the belief that the race-fixing and doping investigation was one big mistake, and that racing folk could put the ordeal behind them and live happily ever after.

Christopher Spence told them otherwise in an unprecedented and stark warning of racing's vulnerability.

Spence chose a somewhat lofty occasion, the annual Gimcrack Dinner at York, to air his views but at least he knew that, somewhere amid the bonhomie and the cigar smoke, lurked the racing and bookmaking bigwigs he needed to induce.

Making clear the Jockey Club's frustration at a lack of support for its own investigations from the betting industry, Spence said: "Their business equally depends on the punters' trust in the integrity of our racing.

"And yet when 'foul' or 'fix' is cried, for whatever reason, and often by the larger firms, we, surprisingly, receive no information about the people who struck bets with them, on the grounds of client confidentiality, when the information that they have, may very well be the key to the perpetrator or perpetrators being brought to justice."

Spence added: "I do not believe the integrity of racing is under threats to which we cannot find answers and I have no wish to be accused of scaremongering, but its vulnerability to criminal activity and corrupting influences through the betting it attracts needs to be addressed.

"You should be aware that betting and thus racing are being used as a conduit for money laundering. You should be aware that illegal betting not only increases the potential for corruption, but reduces the income to both racing and Government through levy and duty.

"You should be aware of the growth in the number of undesirable characters who turn out to own horses and even trainers' yards, very often not in their own names. You should be aware, because of the very substantial amounts of money involved, of the temptations that are faced by those directly involved in the outcome of a race.

"This is evidence of the need for greater regulation of the betting industry and in particular for disclosure of information."

That speech was the harbinger of much that the Jockey Club tried to do over the following two years in its attempts to clean up racing. It also provided an early indication that the Jockey Club felt it lacked the clout to do the job on its own.

"We need Government to address the under-regulation of betting on horseracing in a similar way to the approach used when they established the Gaming Board to address the threats facing casinos from organised crime," Spence said in his speech.

"The criminal law also needs to be addressed so that there is a realistic prospect of those who corrupt racing being brought to justice and, if the Jockey Club is to keep undesirables out of racing, we must have access to criminal records." This is a continuing Jockey Club campaign that has found only limited support outside Portman Square.

You can't say that the Jockey Club was not trying

Away from the spotlight, it made a frank and confidential submission in July 2000 to the Gambling Review Group, a Government-appointed body that was told to examine in detail all betting and gaming issues.

It told of the dangers that its licence holders and the public wasn't allowed to hear. "Because our submissions were made in confidence we were able to talk to them more openly and frankly about our concerns than we were in public," Spence said.

And they did. "The Jockey Club, as racing's regulator, is concerned about the vulnerability of horseracing to criminal behaviour, and other undesirable activity as a consequence of betting," the submission said.

"Criminal intelligence and other information obtained from the police during the course of various police inquiries over the last three years have identified potentially serious problems for the future of the sport.

"Whilst horseracing has always attracted the unwelcome attention of individuals seeking a dishonest or unfair advantage, the modern criminal is constantly exploring new and fertile areas in which to conceal and invest significant sums obtained by criminal means.

"The infiltration of such individuals within horseracing has led to associations with licensed persons (trainers and jockeys) resulting in the potential for corrupt influences entering the sport.

"Both the police and the Jockey Club security department have assessed intelligence concerning collusion between a small number of jockeys and trainers and persons known to be involved in organised crime.

"Regrettably, much of that material falls short of the required standard of evidence for proof either before the Jockey Club's disciplinary committee or the courts."

Nonetheless, "it has been apparent for many years that criminals and illegal layers (bookmakers) actively attempt to cultivate trainers and stable employees with a view to obtain information about horses, particularly those that are unlikely to win, whether for valid reasons or malpractice.

"At its worst it may lead to race-fixing by one means or another."

Even though Brian Wright had been arrested and then cleared from the police's doping and race-fixing investigations, the Jockey Club's submission to the Gambling Review Group laid much blame at his door.

"Relationships (between criminals and licence holders) are often cemented by offers of hospitality in clubs, casinos, and massage parlours, as well as by means of cash payments," it said. "In one case a person with connections to organised crime, both in the UK and abroad, is strongly suspected to have corrupted jockeys and trainers during the last 10 years. The person concerned has recently been indicted for serious drug offences and is currently the subject of an international arrest warrant.

"There is evidence that racing and betting are being used for money laundering purposes. There are also allegations of corruption by criminals of those directly involved in the outcome of races, and that illegal betting, to the detriment of Government revenues, is being carried out on a large scale. One leading bookmaker has estimated that up to £1 billion a year is bet illegally."

The Jockey Club also claimed, not for the first time, that the betting industry

– over which it has very little control – was under-regulated "in so much as it is devoid of effective measures to deter corruption and thus renders racing vulnerable to malpractice."

Bleating alone gets you nowhere. What action was the Jockey Club looking for in its fight against corruption?

Above all else it wanted the creation of a powerful organisation that could control all gambling matters in Britain, including the licensing of bookmakers.

It would also be a 'one-stop shop' to which the Jockey Club could hand over evidence of alleged corruption in racing, in the expectation that the new body would have a bespoke understanding of racing and betting – something that Britain's police forces traditionally lack. The Jockey Club also called for a specialised police unit to deal with gambling matters, but that was rejected.

Overall, the Jockey Club's submission brought largely successful results when the Gambling Review Group published its findings in July 2001. The highlight was the recommendation that the Government should indeed introduce a Gambling Commission along the lines of that sought by the Jockey Club

It also said bookmakers should be obliged to hand over details of betting on any races that come under investigation by the Commission. The Jockey Club believes that some previous investigations – such as that concerning Man Mood – were hampered by bookmakers' refusal to co-operate.

There was a boost in attempts to crack down on money laundering through betting with the recommendation that the strict regulations that apply to potential money laundering in casinos should be extended to betting.

"Submissions from the Jockey Club, the Metropolitan Police and the National Criminal Intelligence Service (NCIS) expressed concerns that bookmaking is an unregulated sector and offers money laundering opportunities," the review group said.

But the Jockey Club's calls for doping of racehorses to be made a criminal offence, as well as a law to tackle "corruption in connection with horseracing and other sports", were both rejected, as were attempts to get access to criminal records.

"Although we are not unsympathetic to the case that has been put to us – for example that there should be a specific offence for doping a horse – we do not consider it is properly within our remit to make recommendations relating to such an issue," the review group said.

"Secondly, we consider that sports bodies could do more to regulate the participants in their sports and they should not always look to the criminal law to enforce their regulations."

FOX IN A CHICKEN SHED

In fairness to the Jockey Club, it has worked hard at introducing a series of 'self-help' measures. They were as well received as a fox in a chicken shed.

Take the ruling, in December 2000, that the Jockey Club could seek sensitive information such as telephone bills, betting accounts and details of horse purchases, from trainers, owners, jockeys and even their valets.

Anyone who refused faced the prospect of being fined or even warned off, unless they had a good reason . . .

And that's not all. The 'show us your records' threat was one in a series of new measures that included: stringent guidelines on who jockeys and trainers should mix with; strict limits on associations between jockeys and bookmakers; and rules to deter "licensed persons passing on information for reward about horses which is not publicly available." By now it all sounds rather familiar.

At the same time, concern was growing that a few jockeys were using mobile phones in weighing rooms to pass on the latest information, prompting the Jockey Club to consider a ban on these devices.

Among the new measures, however, was the code of conduct for trainers referred to in the High Court case between Victor Chandler and *Panorama*.

A separate code was introduced for jockeys, which said they were to "avoid the company of persons whose conduct, character, or reputation indicate that they may pose a threat to the integrity of racing", and "report to the stewards of the Jockey Club any instances of actual or attempted malpractice which may compromise the integrity of horseracing."

All in all, these rules – which came under the remit of the Security and Investigations Committee – were guaranteed to send blood pressures soaring around the weighing rooms and training centres of Britain.

Spence said at the time: "It is vital that the public has confidence in the integrity of the sport, and equally important that the industry has confidence in our ability to regulate it.

"I would like to make it clear that we do not believe that malpractice and corruption within racing is widespread. However, the Jockey Club has made no secret of its concern about racing's current vulnerability in this area and of the need to ensure the sport is better protected in the future."

Since he made his Gimcrack speech in 1999, Spence's stance had barely shifted. Neither had those from other sections of the racing industry. Still outraged, still disgusted, still unable to accept what they were hearing from the Jockey Club.

The National Trainers' Federation said it was "deplorable" that new measures should be introduced which "further damage the image of racing by implying the problems of corruption were more widespread than they actually are."

Whoops. That sounded better at the time than it does now.

The NTF was critical of the presence of Christopher Foster on the committee, following what it saw as his close involvement in the race-fixing and doping investigations.

The Jockeys' Association's executive manager Michael Caulfield, was similarly critical, saying: "We still cannot believe that the head of security, Roger Buffham, retains his position and that Christopher Foster is part of a new security committee to whom he is answerable. This only highlights the Jockey Club's inability to see its own failings."

Rather than failing to see its own failings, Spence believes the Jockey Club has been prepared to confront the inevitable. "So long as betting and racing are so closely connected, there will be those who will seek to gain an unfair advantage," he said. "That is the case wherever there is betting.

"I hope people can understand more fully why, in 1996, when we became aware of a potential problem, we introduced a protocol to warn licensed individuals from associating with undesirables. Likewise, why on a number of occasions in recent years I have publicly expressed concern about racing's vulnerability to criminal activity through its connections with betting.

"This key issue cannot be the responsibility of the regulator alone. All participants in the racing industry are able to play a part through their own conduct in maintaining public confidence which is so vital for the prosperity of the sport.

"Consequently, we will always need to be vigilant but the measures we have introduced in the last five years or so mean that racing is considerably better protected now than it was in the early 1990s or before."

However you look at it, trying to do that has been a pretty thankless task. Especially when *Panorama* was about to tap on Britain's TV screens and claim to the nation that the Jockey Club is not up to the job of protecting racing.

We're about to find out what the programme said. But first, a word or two from Dermot Browne.

13

MEETING DERMOT BROWNE

You didn't think he'd gone away did you?

He's standing before me, instantly recognisable. The thick black hair is cut short, he looks fit and well. Neither a wreck of a man nor a monster.

Dermot Browne is friendly, not awkward. Relaxed and ready to talk.

All I can do is tell it as I found it, and listening to him talk in detail about the dopings, it's as if he's reading straight from the police transcripts we already know about. But he isn't. He's tucking into a warm chicken salad and looking me straight in the eye.

We met shortly before Browne featured on *Panorama*. As if in anticipation of that, Brian Wright had let it be known that he regarded his former ally as a "serial fantasist".

If that's the case, he is a convincing fantasist, consistent in his claims. It is often said that Browne has hawked his story around for many years, to any mug with a notepad that's prepared to listen, and that his only motive for doing so was money. So it's worth pointing out that in this case, while he may have been talking to a mug, no financial transactions were involved.

As he has all along, Browne said he was spurred into spilling a supermarket shelf full of the beans after Jamie Osborne named him, in court, as the go-between in that £20,000 offer from Brian Wright for Osborne to stop two horses.

In his evidence at the Old Bailey, during the trial of Bob Harrington, Osborne twice told how he had rejected the offer; once after Dermot Browne had contacted Harrington's QC Richard Ferguson to claim that he had, in fact, accepted it.

This is why Harrington's trial proved so astonishing. Without it, we might never have heard the incredible detail of Browne's allegations. "I'd been out of racing for quite some time, living my own life, doing my own thing, then

Osborne saying what he did appeared on the front page of the papers," Browne said.

"Fine. If he wanted to open a can of worms then let's open the whole can."

Which is just what Browne has done, fuelled also by his belief that he was left short-changed from his involvement with the dopings. Browne is angry with Brian Wright. "He owes me a lot of money," he said. "I kept my mouth shut for him the whole time I was in custody for a week [after the Doncaster dopings, for which Browne was never charged]."

'Dissing' Brian Wright hardly seems sensible. Browne is unconcerned. "I'm not scared of him," he said. "Why should I be? He's the one who's on the run. Of course, he's going to have contacts. Fine. But if I met him face to face, I know who'd be more scared of who."

Oh, okay. Browne, it becomes clear, has little regard for his former associates, even 'Alfred', who he has done no favours at all by incriminating him in the dopings. "So what? We were mates to a point," Browne said. "But when I found out that he (Alfred) was getting paid and I wasn't, it changed things. He knew more about what was going on than I did.

"At the time when Brian Wright told me only the three of us knew what was going on, I believed him. But I now know there were plenty of other people making money from it, there had to be. I know they were doing things they weren't telling me about."

Was he the patsy of the whole operation? "Yes, looking back I probably was."

But the most important issue is whether he is he a patsy telling porkies. On *Panorama*, Graham Bradley, someone else who would hardly be enamoured with Browne's revelations, refers to him as "an absolute lunatic and a liar".

And of all the elements of his police statement, the one that stays with you is the doping of Timeless Times at Ripon on 27 August. That was the day when one of Barry Hills' staff said Browne was at Chepstow asking about one of the stable's runners, Oriental Mystique.

Browne's answer is unflustered and firm. "No, no. I wasn't in the two places at the same time. That's not right. He's wrong. I did meet him at Chepstow, but it was a different day.

"I was in Ripon for a couple of days and I know for a fact that we stayed n Harrogate and went out that night with the cast of Emmerdale."

Browne pointed out that he and 'Alfred' were in the middle of a lengthy stay in Yorkshire, an area where they completed nine straight dopings before dropping south to Leicester.

"Brian Wright kept us up there," he said. "He knew that if we came home we'd want paying. But if we kept going for the week he'd have a chance probably to get the cash."

The way Browne tells it, Wright was not the satchel-smashing punter that others say. "His pals would paint that picture," Browne said. "He was obviously having problems, that's why he couldn't pay us. That's why he resorted to what he did (the alleged dopings) because it wasn't working out the other way (paying jockeys). In his own words, he said to me one day at his own house in Frimley, he said he woke up one morning and thought if he keeps going the way he is going he'll be skint."

FEW REGRETS

The lasting impression of Browne's alleged doping sprees from reading the police transcripts is that it was an operation running out of control. Desperately so.

"I *was* running out of control," Browne said. "I coped with it all by drinking too much. That was it really, I suppose, just living from day to day. I know that now. I was just trying to find a way through life. I had a lot of debts, people weren't paying their bills.

"It was a horrible time. I'd split up from my first wife and that sort of thing. A lot was going on."

He was still training, but "a lot of the time I wished I didn't have the yard. It's an expensive business and I was building up a lot of debts, so I needed the money. I'm glad it's all over.

"I was just exposing myself too much. I was going in and doing it myself the whole time and, had I got caught, I had a lot to lose.

"It all started off okay but then Brian Wright was asking me to do one or two horses in a race of like 15. What's the point? That's when I knew he was under pressure. Initially, the atmosphere was like if it can be done, fine, if it can't just leave it. Tomorrow's another day, six races a day. There's no panic. But then it was getting to days when he wanted to do this race and wanted to do that race.

"I tell you one thing though: if he'd sat down and thought about it properly and said, I want to stop and reassess it and get the thing right, it could have gone on for a year and no one would ever have known."

No one would ever have known. They are words that hardly reek of remorse for what he has done.

"I have got to the stage now where I don't really care. Cos anytime I meet new people they either like me or they don't. If they don't, too bad.

"People can picture me in whatever way they want, it doesn't bother me in the slightest. Absolutely doesn't bother me because they are not part of my life and they are not going to be."

If anything, Browne's regrets are on a personal level. The crimes of the son have been visited on the father. Dermot Browne may have walked away from racing, Liam is still picking up the pieces.

"It's had a massive effect on my father. In the 1980s, at one stage he had 150 horses. After 1990, it didn't take long until he was down to 40," Browne said.

"It was all hard graft with him. It was buying cheap horses, turning them into winners and selling them on. That's what he did, buying and selling. Everything is for sale, even my mother at the right price.

"But he wouldn't have had to sell *himself,* like I would. That wouldn't have been his strong point. He wouldn't have put up with the kerfuffle that a lot of owners bring.

"My father's my best friend, always has been, still is. My Ma, we get on great. I couldn't ask for better parents. They have always been there for me."

So what went wrong?

"I never had been a rebel. I didn't have my first drink 'til I was 21 or 22. I was very naïve at the time. I was just into my horses and my racing. At that time, I was basically doing what my father wanted me to do – what I wanted to do. Try and do it right. That's the way it was.

"I suppose when I went down to Lambourn really that's when things started to go wrong. I always say in Lambourn: everyone has a wife, but whose? That's the way Lambourn is.

"I'd get involved with the wrong kind of people and got myself in a situation whereby I made things more difficult for myself."

Browne now spends much of his time with his teenage son, who, he said, is unfazed about his dad being a doper.

"Whether he fully understands it, I don't know yet," Browne said. "He's old enough to read newspapers. That's not a problem. He knows me, he's my best friend. He loves me, I love him. We're buddies. I speak to him every day, see him at the weekends.

"He thinks it's kind of cool, you know what I mean?

"In actual fact, most of the people I have been associated with in the last few years when something crops up in the papers, say: 'bloody hell, that's great stuff'. It's cool for them. They have never been in the papers and there is a bit of celebrity status to it."

Browne is relieved his son is away from racing and not "growing up in Lambourn with a Lambourn accent and a Lambourn attitude."

He added: "He's a great kid, 100 per cent, he's sound. Whatever he wants to do that's fine by me, but racing no. He'd have no chance in racing, because of my name, because of the stigma that's attached to it. It wouldn't be fair to him. That's why I'm lucky that he didn't get the bug, and I reckon it is a bug because once you get out of it, it's very hard to get it out of your system."

I ask Browne what he is doing now, bearing in mind some reports have said he is "understood" to be working as a labourer or as a taxi driver in Dublin.

"I sell advertising," he said.

You can't help but think he'd be good at that. "All you need are two ears and a mouth."

And confidence? "Oh yeah, I'm not short of that."

Certainly not. Take his description of an early night out at Tramp, when Brian Wright had laid on women – "stunners" – for the jockeys he entertained. Surely Browne became involved? "I don't want to sound funny like, but I never needed to."

SQUEAKY CLEAN JODHPURS

Browne knows his name is soiled, but remains angry at the blithe way he is regarded as someone who can't be believed. Let's be quite clear: he has had his brushes with the law, he has had to live parts of his life under an assumed name. But if anyone's going to lift the lid on horseracing's wrongdoing, it is going to be someone like him, not someone with squeaky clean jodhpurs.

It had been widely anticipated that Browne was going to give evidence at the Southwark doping trial, until the prosecution decided he should not be used.

"Who are the people who have branded me an unreliable witness?" he asked. "All I have done is read about it in the papers, but I don't know who actually said it.

"I decided I wasn't going to be a witness. The police didn't decide. I decided I wasn't going to be one and I told them that. I said I would be a witness against Brian Wright but I wouldn't be against the others. So they thought there was no point in using me.

"I'm not doing all this for a laugh. Things were left alone. People can think what they like. Every race that I discussed; you can see the betting patterns for yourself, in most cases."

As you have already seen, the betting markets in which Browne said he doped horses often sent out some strange smoke signals.

And See You Then? That definitely looked strange. We need to know if we can add the 'strangling' of a leading Champion Hurdle candidate to Dermot Browne's extraordinary litany.

Apparently not. "That was really the starter's fault," Browne said, adding he had set himself up to stalk the front runners. He had shouted that he wasn't ready to go, was in the process of turning Browne's Gazette right round to bring him in again to face the tapes when . . . whoosh, the field set off while his mount was facing in practically the opposite direction.

That won't stop people wondering, though. "Of course people will think I stopped him. No way. It broke my heart. I was gutted. On the day I thought he was going to win that race. Definitely," Browne said.

"It's sod's law that people will think wrongly, but they can think what they like. It doesn't matter to me. It's not part of my life anymore.

"I had a good time, I was lucky, I've won things that a lot of jockeys never have, probably never will do. It was great and I have always got that to look back on."

And while Browne walks off into the racing sunset, he leaves behind him a lot of scratching heads.

Has anyone any idea of the scale or extent of the race-fixing and corruption he was involved in? "No. There will never be anything on the same scale again."

Let's hear from *Panorama*.

14

POSTSCRIPT

Panorama produced the kind of reaction that the programme makers wanted and horseracing badly needed.

An audience of 3.9 million suggested there was more interest in racing's problems than the threat posed by Saddam Hussein, who attracted an audience of 3 million when featured on *Panorama* two weeks earlier.

'The Corruption of Racing' was billed as "a story about one of the biggest scandals in the history of British sport".

"For the everyday punter having a bet on the race, they've no chance," said a by now, rather familiar figure – Dermot Browne, looking scrubbed up and sincere. We were told how the Jockey Club, "whose patron is the Queen", had run racing in Britain since 1752; how nearly half of its members were titled; how these "Grandees of the Turf" represented "one of the most powerful sporting institutions in the world – but today they are in trouble."

The hyperbole over, we got our first glimpse of "the man who's turned on them". Roger Buffham.

Buffham had waited over a year for the chance to have his say and he didn't hang about. "After almost ten years in horseracing I say with some sadness and great disappointment that racing is not as straight as the Jockey Club and others would ask the public to believe it is," he said.

"I believe that racing is institutionally corrupt in some respects and I believe that the Jockey Club falls short in regulation, in having the moral courage and resolve to deal with some of these problems."

Buffham's claim that racing was "institutionally corrupt" was not the only sweeping statement he made. According to him, "an entire generation of National Hunt jockeys had close links to organised crime."

Big, bold words like those need backing up. The overall impression was that both Buffham and *Panorama* had failed to do that.

Not that the man nor his media outlet could be summarily dismissed. *Panorama* told us what racing's participants had decided to ignore. That Buffham's credentials on taking the job were "impeccable. He'd come from military intelligence where he'd got an MBE for his work in counter-terrorism."

Then we are told that Buffham was sacked, without a clear explanation of why, although Jockey Club executive Christopher Foster does later refer to alleged "gross misconduct".

Cue trainer Jimmy Fitzgerald. He is shown being confronted over the letter addressed to him from Victor Chandler offering free bets, his face turning an extraordinary shade of purple. Gay Kelleway, the other trainer mentioned in connection with the Chandler letters, simply walked away.

The suggestion that Chandler had offered trainers 'no lose' accounts was highlighted by *Panorama* as a sign of Jockey Club inertia. Remember, the aim of the programme was as much to question the Jockey Club's efficacy in dealing with corruption issues as it was to make new allegations.

FOSTER TAKES GUARD

Christopher Foster was sent out to bat for the Jockey Club and displayed the sort of diligence – while lacking any dazzling stroke play whatsoever – that most cricket teams would cherish in their top order.

He told *Panorama* that the 'no lose' accounts were "quite unacceptable," adding, "there's no way we would approve of bookmakers effectively paying for privileged information."

"In that case, why is Victor Chandler's name all over your racecourses?" Foster was asked.

"I guess because one of the reasons would be that the Jockey Club has no jurisdiction over betting. We are the regulator of the sport of racing," he replied.

Back came the question: "If you consider someone's behaviour unacceptable and you have the power to warn him off why didn't you use that power with Victor Chandler?"

"Because I believe that would have been a disproportionate use of that power for the actions that Victor Chandler was taking," Foster said. "What he was doing was not an offence under the rules of racing. If it happened again, there is action we could take."

"But you're not going to do anything about Victor Chandler?"

"No"

After the programme had been broadcast, Chandler said *Panorama* "gave the erroneous impression that we had something to hide – nothing could be further from the truth" and that the letters "at the time contravened no guidelines.

He added: "We have long discontinued this practice and fully embrace the Jockey Club's decision to introduce a new Code of Conduct in 2001."

Having dealt with the Chandler letters, *Panorama* moved on to Brian Wright, "one story which will forever haunt the Jockey Club. It is a remarkable tale of their abject failure to deal with one man."

Dermot Browne, whose 10-year ban from racing was not mentioned, tells the programme that he doped "about 27 races" between August and October 1990 on Wright's behalf. That's a slight exaggeration on previous accounts.

More importantly, *Panorama* claimed that an initial attempt by Browne to tell the Jockey Club of his wrongdoing and the people he was involved with was ignored. The Jockey Club have countered that it was on Roger Buffham's advice that an approach from Browne in 1992 was declined. Buffham denied this, while the intermediary in this approach, journalist Mike Gallemore, caused further uncertainty by saying, later, that it was not made until 1993.

The plan had been that Browne would meet the then Senior Steward of the Jockey Club, Lord Hartington.

"I was willing to give him any information he wanted, confidentially," Browne said.

"And if he'd offered you a deal, you would have been prepared to admit that you'd been involved in doping around 20 horses in 1990?" reporter Andy Davies asked him.

"Yes."

"And the systems that were being used and the people behind it?

"Yes."

"You would have named Brian Wright?"

"Most certainly. Definitely."

"Would you have named the jockeys involved with Brian Wright?"

"Yes, if he asked me to, yes, definitely, and that wouldn't have bothered me in the slightest."

According to *Panorama*: "When the Jockey Club finally decided to talk to Browne they concluded that he was telling the truth.

"But they'd wasted eight years in obtaining this vital evidence."

It is certainly true that the Jockey Club, and particularly Foster, was inconsistent in its assessment of Browne.

Foster was asked on the programme if it was "a mistake" to have ignored Browne in 1992.

"Well with 20/20 hindsight it might be. At the time it seemed a reasonable decision to those who took those decisions," he replied.

Yet that answer did not tally with a remark he made on the day after *Panorama*, when Foster said: "The programme was based on flawed information and the evidence of a discredited witness."

Panorama was in no doubt that the initial spurning of Browne was "a huge misjudgement by the Jockey Club – it left Brian Wright free to bribe his way into the heart of racing."

Davies told Foster: "You should have warned him (Wright) off a lot earlier shouldn't you? You've got to admit that."

Foster said: "Well, if we had the evidence we would have warned him off earlier. We didn't have any evidence until 1996. And from 1996 until 2002 we were either compromised by the fact that there was serious criminal investigations going on, or we couldn't act because a judge had put down (an) order in court restricting reporting."

"The Jockey Club's insistence that its hands have been tied over Wright for years is not quite accurate," countered *Panorama*. "In 1998 they received intelligence that he'd been entertaining jockeys in the south of Spain. He has a villa here in the luxury resort of Sotogrande.

"The jockeys were on a golf trip organised by Wright's old friend Graham Bradley. The Jockey Club could have taken action then, but they didn't."

WRIGHT PLACE WRONG CAMERA

We got to see Brian Wright for ourselves. He'd just completed a spot on sunbathing in Lapta in northern Cyprus. *Panorama*'s search for the man they call 'Uncle' featured only briefly in its programme, but was rich in off-camera drama.

Through a tip-off, two members of the *Panorama* team traced Wright to The Celebrity Hotel in northern Cyprus. They were having lunch at a nearby restaurant when Wright walked straight past them on his way to a two-hour massage, sunbathe and swim session. It was Wright's daily routine, one that was interrupted only by England and Ireland's World Cup matches in June 2002.

With Wright located, Panorama producer Steven Scott and reporter Andy Davies flew to southern Cyprus, to where the flights were more frequent. But because of political tensions on the island, visitors from south to north were allowed only a limited stay, 8.00am to 5.00pm. Their cameras attracted the attention of police guards and they were followed.

According to the *Panorama* website, after a couple of days, the team was ready to collar Wright, aided by a plan from two BBC security advisers.

On signal, one of those advisers, as well as Davies, Scott and cameraman Andrew Mott would descend via a hotel service road and confront Wright – without Wright and his companions interpreting the approach as some kind of attack. That could have proved nasty.

Davies walked down the service road, Scott and Mott in tow, but Wright did not stroll directly back to the hotel as he had normally done – he hung around under the parasols talking.

This left the *Panorama* team in limbo and trying to act normally. The plan was about to be aborted when Wright moved towards the hotel. Davies pounced with the essential question.

"I want to talk to you about corruption in horseracing."

Wright didn't want to talk. "I've got nothing to say to you whatsoever."

There was only one problem, the camera had failed. The sound was crackly. The secured footage amounted to only eight seconds in close up of Brian Wright's back.

He remained a man of intrigue and mystery.

Panorama's attempts to pin down Graham Bradley led to them approaching him at Newbury after he had ridden in a charity race. Both on camera and later, Bradley denied being involved in race-fixing, pointing out he had been cleared of all charges in connection with Man Mood's race at Warwick.

Bradley responded well to *Panorama*'s presence. Others didn't.

Newbury's chief executive Mark Kershaw strolled over and started aggressively pushing the camera crew away from Bradley. It was a gormless response that enhanced the view that racing folk came across badly in the programme, a shifty bunch with collectively something to hide.

Willie Carson – a BBC employee, just like the *Panorama* team – added to that image by rushing over to Bradley, saying: "You handled that well. I couldn't save you – but you said the right thing."

Doh!

THE CASE OF MAN MOOD

Man Mood. This was unarguably a part of *Panorama* where we were supplied with something new, a letter to the Jockey Club from William Hill director Mick Norris. He had watched the Warwick race and said: "based on my experience of watching horseracing for 30 years, this bore all the hallmarks of being a fixed and crooked race".

On the insistence of the William Hill management, Norris had to withdraw the statement. We never had a proper explanation as to why.

Back to Foster. "What did you think of the lack of support from William Hill in the Man Mood investigation?" he was asked.

"Well, I think it's an example of the difficulty that the Jockey Club faces in examining potential corruption of races. Our inability to get hold of betting information and certainly the lack of betting information in a number of cases has prevented us from taking matters any further."

(Is it just me, or do all these answers come across as even less impressive in black and white than they did on TV?)

Foster wasn't off the hook. "You haven't answered my question. What did you think of William Hill's action in that particular investigation?" Davies asked him pointedly.

"Unhelpful. Definitely unhelpful."

"If their action was unhelpful, did you ever go back to William Hill and say to them that if they continued your investigations you'd consider taking legal action against them?"

"Well, there's very limited . . ."

"Yes or no? Did you ever go back and say anything to them?"

"There was very limited action that we could take."

"Yes or no?"

"I'm sorry, there was very limited action that we could take against a betting organisation."

"The important question is here. Mr Foster, why did you do nothing about William Hill in 1996 (when the Man Mood race was run)?"

"Because we don't have jurisdiction over betting organisations".

"You can warn bookies off racecourses. That is a jurisdiction."

"That would be an abuse of our power."

Too many times, there were too many reasons for a lack of action – abuse of power, lack of power, hands tied, no jurisdction, fear of the Jockey Club's actions being challenged. It wasn't reassuring.

Neither was the allegation from *Panorama* that a few British jockeys had been seen associating with people with criminal links in Hong Kong. Champion jockey Kieren Fallon was mentioned in connection with this. He objected so strongly to this link, which was also raised in a national newspaper, that he launched legal proceedings.

Nonetheless, Fallon was approached at York racecourse, wearing the Queen's colours, by the fearless Andy Davies. After pointing his whip towards Davies' nostrils, Fallon fixed him a terrifying look, a cross between Hannibal Lecter and The Incredible Hulk. For his refusal to flinch alone, Davies deserves some kind of bravery award.

Meanwhile, *Panorama* added that "the alleged links between British jockeys and suspected Chinese criminals are not confined to Hong Kong.

"In Britain the Manchester Police have been investigating the infiltration of racing by Chinese triad gangsters." The Jockey Club, it was said, "knew all about it".

Let's hope they were doing something about it, too.

THE PHIPPS SIDESHOW

And then there was Jeremy Phipps, the unexpected head on a plate of the programme. What a sideshow he provided – simultaneously hilarious and sad.

Phipps was put up by the Jockey Club to explain to *Panorama* the ways in which it had been addressing the security issues that racing faced. It did so unaware that Phipps had been secretly recorded during that meeting with Buffham at Tapster's wine bar.

At Tapsters', we first of all heard Phipps refer to the transcripts of Graham Bradley's Southampton Crown Court evidence as "dynamite".

"Brad's gone and shot his fucking mouth off," he added. "We wrote to Brad and we wrote to Brad's solicitors who didn't want to say anything. Total silence."

Buffham said: "It's pretty horrendous stuff isn't it."

"It is," Phipps replied . . . and all exactly what you said I'm afraid . . ."

Buffham: ". . . but no-one wants to do anything about it though. That's the problem I've got."

Phipps: "They fucking well are now."

Buffham: "Well I hope you make sure they do."

Phipps: " I had David Oldrey (a senior Jockey Club figure) in my office this afternoon. I said why the fuck have you not done anything about this before . . . apart from the odd warning."

Buffham: ". . . nothing's happened"

Phipps: "nothing's happened."

Buffham: ". . . don't you think that's reprehensible?"

Phipps: "it's not just... it is yes. It is actually the back bone that is not terribly strong."

This transcript was shown to Phipps during his official interview at Newmarket racecourse. His reaction was too painful to watch.

The interview was interrupted by the Jockey Club's public relations director John Maxse leading Phipps away by the arm, rather as if he was an old gentleman in a nursing home when it's past his bedtime.

Maxse is shown talking vigorously to Phipps. The interview resumes and Phipps "remembers" that he was talking in such derogatory terms about his employees in order to win Buffham's confidence in a bid to establish whether his predecessor had been breaking his injunction. Again, it was not convincing.

Phipps left his job three days after the programme was shown. The position of Jockey Club head of security is clearly cursed. One leaves after unfairly being portrayed as a lecherous despot, another goes after coming across on national TV as a loose-tongued decrepit.

And you are left thinking: who appoints these guys? Isn't it time for him to go, too?

In fitting with his billing as a heroic whistleblower, the last word on *Panorama* went to Buffham, who said: "The irony is not lost on me. I feel sad in many ways that over the last few years the Jockey Club has been aware of a number of people, a significant number of people including jockeys and trainers, who have been involved in corruption or corrupt activity.

"And at the end of the day, the only person they forced to go is the person who was trying to address these issues and these problems on behalf of horseracing and that is me."

PREDICTABLE DEFENCE

Amid the reaction to *Panorama* were the tediously predictable claims that the programme produced "nothing new", that its makers "didn't understand racing", that it used "discredited witnesses", and was based largely on "a man with a grievance".

On the latter point, what did people expect? Of course Roger Buffham had a grievance – the Jockey Club sacked him. There is, after all, probably no such thing as a contented whistleblower.

The High Court verdicts of two senior judges – that racing had corruption issues that should be aired as a matter of public interest – appeared to have been overlooked in the aftermath, even though one of those judges said the problems were "ongoing".

The response to *Panorama* tended to be more realistic outside racing's tight, cosy perimeter than inside it. Paul Hayward, the *Daily Telegraph*'s award-winning sports writer who started his career on the *Racing Post*, cut to the point: "Sorry, but anyone who dismisses *Panorama*'s revelations about corruption in racing as fabrications is either a coward or a fraud," he wrote.

"This is racing's chance to stop pretending; to abandon the nudge-nudge, wink-wink culture on which it rolls along."

Another man to see the broader picture was Jon Holmes, managing director of the SFX Sports company, whose clients include England footballers David Beckham, Michael Owen, Emile Heskey, and in racing, Walter Swinburn and Brough Scott.

Holmes knows a thing or two about image. "The most damaging aspect of the programme for the Jockey Club, in my opinion, was that the authority appeared to have done nothing when a hard-nosed stance was required in dealing with certain issues," he told the *Racing Post*.

"You have got to be seen to be tougher. Occasionally that means people have to be made examples of, and sometimes you have to dispense a little rough justice. It seems to me there was an attitude at Portman Square of turning a blind eye."

Perception is everything. And if that is an expert's perception of racing and the Jockey Club then there's clearly a problem.

At least the Jockey Club, while dissatisfied with many aspects of *Panorama*, which believes it has enough material for a second programme, said it would look at the programme to see what lessons could be learned. And overall you couldn't help but sense recognition of the need for change. *Panorama* was having a hugely purgative effect. It was astonishing the speed at which a sense of acceptance developed that changes were needed to the way racing was policed.

How much damage these corruption issues caused is hard to guage; although it is clear that the sport's standing *had* been adversely affected, and that the walk on the wild side had gone way past acceptable boundaries, even for an activity that has always had the smudged lines that racing has.

Optimists can look on all this as a wake up call. For indeed, what's the point of a scandal if you can't learn from it.

It would be nice to think that horseracing's time in the dock is over.

But could you bet on it?

Not with any great certainty. No.

Index

The index is arranged alphabetically except for subheadings, which appear in approximate chronological order.

PHOTOGRAPHIC ACKNOWLEDGEMENTS

Colour section: Central News: 9 bottom; Daily Mirror: 11 bottom; Daily Mirror / Ian Vogler: 4 top right & bottom left; Daily Mirror / P. Harris: 6 bottom; Dan Abraham: 4 bottom right, 6 top, 7 top, 16 top & bottom; David Hastings: 15 top; Enterprise Photos / Mark St George: 5 top centre, 5 top right & 5 bottom left; John Grossick: 13 top; National Pictures / Mottram Tasha: 4 top left; Photo News Service: 10 centre, 10 bottom; Photo News Service / Nick Razzell: 5 top left, 5 bottom right; Press Association: 1, 8, 9 top, 10 top; Racing Channel / Racetech: 2; Racing Post: 11 top; Racing Post / Edward Whitaker: 13 bottom, 15 bottom; Sporting Life: 3 top; Sporting Life / Pat Healy: 7 bottom; Sporting Life / Phil Smith: 3 bottom; Universal Pictorial Press: 12